STOP MA

CW00855225

Manchester City,
Mother Russia
& Me

Peter Brophy

The Parrs Wood Press
<u>MANCHESTER</u>

First Published 2002

THE PARRS WOOD PRESS
St Wilfrid's Enterprise Centre
Royce Road, Manchester, M15 5BJ
www.parrswoodpress.com

© Peter Brophy 2002

The right of Peter Brophy to be recognised as the author
of this work has been asserted

ISBN: 1 903158 33 8

Printed by:
MFP Design and Print
Longford Trading Estate
Thomas Street
Stretford
Manchester M32 0JT

To Marta, with love.
To Kevin, with sincere gratitude.

*"They are not long -
The days of wine and roses"*

CONTENTS

INTRODUCTION

A Genetic Flaw

LET ME EXPLAIN. It isn't that I look for problems. On the other hand, when everything is plain sailing, I somehow feel a lack of edge and excitement. When difficulties arise and make things more complicated, life just seems so much more interesting.

On the face of it, I've never been much of a rebel. I went to a private school, followed it up with a degree course at a traditional university and then made my career in the law. I had parents who both had degree-level qualifications, and who were both in professional jobs, though admittedly teaching wasn't especially well paid. Obviously, we weren't rich by any means, but nor did we have to go without. My parents were prepared to make sacrifices both for me and for my sister which went beyond what most parents would have been prepared to do for their kids. As a bloke, I'd never been on the sharp end of sex discrimination. Being white, I'd never been a target for racial prejudice. But that doesn't tell the whole story, not by a long way.

I came from a chaotically large Manchester-Irish family, and at a young age became aware of ancestors I'd never met who'd followed rather unusual paths. It probably wouldn't be appropriate to recite them all here, but most notable among these was my great-great-uncle on my mother's side. He was born in Leeds and grew up in Wigan, which, with all respect to Wiganers, isn't the most exotic of locations. However, at seventeen he emigrated to America. He became a gangster in New York, made millions from bootlegging in the Prohibition and had his life commemorated on celluloid in a big-budget film.

Then there was my great-grandfather on my father's side. He was a hard-drinking itinerant musician who divorced in the early part of the century and thereby became ostracised by friends, family and the Catholic church. The thing was, in most families people like this would be regarded as a lone black sheep, but in ours he was merely one of a crowd. I was delighted by such rich heritage, although I've never really felt that, whatever accomplishments I've had to my name, I'd done justice to my lineage.

My parents were the first in their respective families to break through the educational barrier, and even then, a century later, the odds were against them. My mum won a scholarship to Manchester High School for Girls, which in those days was a direct grant school. Had she not been a star performer in her year's entrance exam, she'd have had to turn the place down as her parents simply couldn't have paid the fees. She duly obtained good exam results and read French and English at St. Andrew's University. She completed the last two years of her degree in a sanatorium, having lost a lung through tuberculosis. She later became a Fleet Street journalist in a high-flying position she'd nailed down while still in her twenties.

My father left school at fourteen and worked as a paint technician until he had a severe bout of pneumonia. He pursued his musical education in the army, gaining a qualification equivalent to degree level and later attained a teacher training qualification and a master's. Neither had done things the easy way.

Those family members I did meet were also on rather idiosyncratic personal odysseys. One uncle ended up renting a bed-sit in a less than salubrious area of Manchester, in a dead-end job whose demands he could fulfil without difficulty while single-handedly subsidising the brewing industry in north-west England. Another uncle, on the other side of the family, ended up running a pub in Rochdale. My dad stood in for him one year when he was on holiday. My abiding memory is perching on the bar late at night as the local CID enjoyed an after-hours drinking session.

My maternal grandfather, widowed and exiled in London, remarried after his move back north, wedding a German woman who had tales of fleeing her home in the Polish corridor in the wake of World War I and arriving in England just after World War II. My paternal grandfather had dragged his wife and three kids round a variety of locations while attempting a string of business schemes. Some were rather hare-brained, some potentially brilliant, but the common factor in all was the lack of success. He later relocated to Yorkshire and also remarried.

I remember trips to see my dad's Auntie Dot, the half-sister of the erratic entrepreneur. She had a council flat in the Manchester district of Fallowfield, near Maine Road football ground, so my dad and I used to drop in on our way to the match. Apparently, in her youth, Auntie Dot had enjoyed nights on the town, behaviour that would now be considered innocuous having courted scandal in the less liberated climate of the wartime era. But those days were long gone by the time I used to visit her. Her flat was adorned with an eclectic collection of ornaments, of which she was immensely proud but which in truth were objects of neither value nor beauty. Her tea was quite comprehensively the worst I've tasted in three decades on the planet. She also had a dog, according to her an Alsatian. I was never able to verify this, as Bruno was always kept locked in the kitchen when we visited, and I have my suspicions that he might actually have been a wolf.

His constant howling was a permanent backdrop to the conversation and, from time to time, he could be heard literally hurling himself against the kitchen door in an effort to break it down. Auntie Dot would periodically come to his defence. "He's a good boy really," she'd contend, before adding the rather superfluous observation, "but he's a bit wild." A trip to see Auntie Dot was undoubtedly always an event.

Given the propensity of countless members of my family for the offbeat and the eccentric, and bearing in mind their attraction to the turbulent, there could only have been one English football team they could possibly have followed. I suppose I should regard as a genetic flaw the committed support for Manchester City that's passed down to me.

Manchester City, you see, is the only team to have been relegated as reigning league champions (managing the feat despite having one of England's all-time greats in goal and being the league's top scorers in the same season). It is the only team to score and concede 100 league goals in the same season. It is the kind of place where what would be jokes at other clubs actually come true. For instance, as City fan and writer Bill Borrows once related in an article in The Guardian newspaper, there was the time when a fan threw his season ticket on to the pitch in disgust at yet another inept display. He then received it back through the post three days later, with a short note that read, "I am returning your season ticket, because if we have to suffer this rubbish, so do you." And West Yorkshire magistrates once refused to follow anti-hooligan legislation by imposing an exclusion order banning City fans caught up in a fracas at Bradford from attending games. The reason? It was a greater punishment to make them be present.

Not surprisingly, the history of the club is littered with larger-than-life figures. In the 1890's, City introduced a certain Billy Meredith to professional football - a wing wizard who was arguably English football's first major star, scored the winner in the FA Cup final, was the scourge of the football authorities as he fought for player's rights, was banned in a bribery scandal, was forced to transfer to the club's hated rivals as a punishment, and later returned to play in a Cup semi-final at the age of fifty.

In the late 1940s, we signed a German paratrooper who'd spent the latter War years as a prisoner of war in Warrington. He became a sensational goalkeeper (the legendary Russian Lev Yashin once said, "There are only two great goalkeepers, Trautmann and myself") and earned everlasting fame by playing the last fifteen minutes of an FA Cup final win with a broken neck. He was the custodian in the year City scored and conceded 100 goals, but without his brilliance we'd probably have given away 300. What other team could he have played for?

In the mid-1960s, with the club in the most moribund of states, two contrasting characters arrived to form the managerial partnership which was to effect a spectacular turn-around. While the senior partner, Joe Mercer, was a dignified, genial elder statesman, his young lieutenant Malcolm Allison was brash and flamboyant, with a penchant for smoking cigars, drinking champagne and wearing fedoras. When Mercer left the club in 1972, Allison lasted less than a year in sole charge before leaving for Crystal Palace. There he presided over two successive relegations before a final swansong when he inspired an improbable run to the FA Cup semi-final. His subsequent career included glorious success at Portuguese club Sporting Lisbon and a sacking at Middlesbrough for refusing to comply with directors' demands to sell key members of his promising young side. Oh, and there was a bewildering period of almost two years as manager back at Maine Road when he replaced a host of internationals with a series of expensive misfits. By doing so he ensured that for any City fan under forty years of age he's associated with miserable and self-destructive failure rather than the successes of the great team he was so pivotal in inspiring.

With characters like these and countless others, it's not surprising life at the club has always been a soap opera. Not just a soap opera, though - there have been elements of farce, comedy (including liberal dashings of the blackest of humour), and, for the committed fan, tragedy. To someone like me, who's followed the story with fervent devotion over more than two decades, it's been a bewildering but compelling saga; compelling enough to hold my interest and the interest of thousands of others despite the fact that brutal disappointment has been a regular, almost constant companion - especially in the dark days of the late 1990s. It was after I went to work in Russia in 1996 that I started to write pieces about City for various fanzines and websites. And while that was a coincidence, it now strikes me as entirely appropriate, because what had drawn me to Russia was the same need for excitement that kept me tied to City.

It's hard to describe Russia to someone who's never been there. I once wrote that foreigners consider England an eccentric country, but Russia should be sectioned under the Mental Health Act. That was a throwaway line rather demeaning to a place for which I have tremendous affection, but it does convey the sense that Russia is another world. Different rules and assumptions apply, just as surely as they did to Dorothy in The Wizard of Oz when she was warned that she wasn't in Kansas any more. There's the famous Churchill quotation about the country being "a riddle inside a mystery inside an enigma", but, to paraphrase the legendary Bill Shankly's quote about football being more than a matter of life and death, he was wrong: it's much more complicated than that. My old Russian teacher once told me that the Russian language would always continue to hold a fascination for me because I'd never feel I'd mastered it, but the same could be true of any attempt to understand the place.

It's the contrasts that make the task so difficult. I spent most of my time there in St. Petersburg, a city of extraordinary beauty and at the same time wretched squalor. When I first went there, the Soviet Union's superpower status was undoubted yet it was apparent from the moment of my arrival that the country's infrastructure was creaking. I was surrounded by people who, when I got to know them, were incredibly warm and generous, yet who in public would invariably be surly and even downright rude. Many of my friends and colleagues would speak about the country's problems with real insight and humour, yet I used to look around me and wonder how, with such talented people representing a real resource for the country, it was in the mess it was. But if I couldn't actually understand why all these things were so, I did feel that Russia created an unpredictable and exciting environment, and interesting things always happened to me there.

That's why it felt appropriate to be observing some of the most turbulent days even in City's chequered history from a vantage point of a Russia that was struggling to adapt in the post-Communist era. I still saw several games each season, and thanks to the marvels of the Internet I could follow in depth what was happening. At a club where events had often over the years defied rational explanation, life took on an ever more surreal aspect, and it struck me that someone should write a book focusing not so much on the events themselves but on the drama associated with being a supporter living through them. Yet while there have been many fine books published recently on the subject of Manchester City, none has focused on this particular angle. Reviewing pieces I'd written in the late 1990s persuaded me that I had material with which I could start the task, and since then I haven't looked back.

Thanks go to the fanzine editors Dave and Sue Wallace of King of the Kippax, Noel Bayley of Bert Trautmann's Helmet and Ashley Birch of the e-mail-based MCIVTA for printing my material in the first place, and four or five of the chapters here are reworked versions of articles which originally featured elsewhere. Bob Young of the www.mancity.net and Steh and Paul Stevenson of www.talkincity.com have also provided a platform for some of my musings over the years. As the project developed, Colin Shindler, Gary James and Mike Barnett offered advice and assistance that was invaluable given my lack of knowledge of publishing. Several friends encouraged and assisted me throughout the long writing process, and I'm especially grateful to Greg White, Richard Sigee, Peter Hamblett, Tania Northorpe and Irina Maurits. Enormous gratitude goes to Andy Searle of The Parrs Wood Press both for believing in the book and for his hard work in bringing it to market. And finally, I should acknowledge David Byrne and Talking Heads for having thought up an album title that seemed to sum up the contents of my own manuscript admirably.

There's always a suspicion of autobiographical works by authors who aren't famous, and maybe rightly so; after all, why should people be interested in reading about a person whose life hasn't brought them to public attention? In this case, I believe that Manchester City fans will appreciate a humorous but affectionate look at their club and its foibles over the years. I hope that fans from other teams will enjoy reading about the background behind the often incomprehensible events at Maine Road. And I consider that readers without any real football interest might be attracted by an account of how a thirty-something professional male tried to inject into his life the colour and drama missing in his experiences in a very traditional educational and career background. But most of all, I'd like to think that readers will be entertained by a story that hasn't so much stopped making sense as barely ever started.

1

Infant Thuggery

I WAS BORN at an auspicious time. When I came into the world, in August 1969, Manchester City were in the middle of their most successful period. The astute, experienced manager Joe Mercer and his flamboyant young assistant Malcolm Allison had fashioned an exciting team that was making a determined assault on English football's major prizes. Fifteen months previously, the league Championship had been won in some style. A year after that success, the FA Cup was won while I was in my mother's womb. I later took personal pride in that victory over Leicester; my dad was on the pitch that April afternoon, although as a bassoonist in the Welsh Guards' band playing at that final rather than a member of the great Mercer-Allison side. And in the first season of my lifetime, 1969-70, the team became the first to win both a European and domestic major trophy in the same season.

Needless to say, it hasn't lasted, and instead of experiencing rousing success after rousing success, my support has frequently seemed like a huge impediment, a source of constant frustration and bitter disappointment. Of course, in my infancy in South East London, where I spent the first three years of my life, none of the reason for this was clear, but I certainly know now - Manchester City's effect on my life mirrors the influence I had on the lives of my parents.

When I was born, my mum had progressed from editing the Marks and Spencer in-house magazine and the Police Review to become Readers' Editor on a newspaper called Reveille. I have no real recollection of it myself since it folded in 1978, but from what I can gather it was a kind of weekly equivalent of The Sun and apparently was the publication with the biggest circulation per issue in the country at the time. My mum edited the letters page (apparently one week, she lost them all so she and my dad sat at the kitchen table making them up). She also produced a column called "Answers", where she replied to all kinds of bizarre queries sent in by readers. However, although she spent much of her time finding out whether there were any working windmills left in Britain, or how seahorses reproduce, it was an excellent job.

My father was a musician. He obviously had an outstanding natural aptitude for it, because he hadn't touched an instrument at the age of twenty but was managing to obtain professional engagements five or six years later. He originally started out as a paint technician, but never went back to it after a serious bout of double pneumonia (if you have any sympathy, forget it - he sustained it through a soaking suffered watching Manchester United). He joined the army, in part because he was due to do national service in a year or two anyway and in part because he fancied a crack at learning music. By the time I was born, he'd progressed via stints with the King's Regiment in Nairobi and Berlin and with the Royal Engineers back in this country to the Guards band he was with that day at Wembley. Both of them were achieving great things and they could have looked forward to fulfilling, and, especially in my mum's case, lucrative futures.

From what I'm told, it seems that from an early age I set out to make my parents' lives as difficult as possible. For example, my mum has refused to wear earrings for nigh on thirty years because I shredded her earlobes by constantly pulling on the dangly ones she favoured in those days. My dad evaded malicious physical assault - I simply took to spitting milk all over the bearskin hat that was part of his Guards uniform. It caused him a devilish cleaning job. I also refused steadfastly to sleep, so had to be dragged round the streets of SE26 at 10 p.m. every evening to induce fatigue.

Having said this, I'm not sure I believe all the stories they now relate. I have the feeling that they're rather embellished to humiliate me at family gatherings or whenever I've wanted to bring a girlfriend home. The combination of anecdotes of my eccentricities as a baby and countless embarrassing photographs from the same period is a particularly devastating one. For the record, I refuse to countenance the possibility that, when we were on holiday just before my second birthday, I knelt down aiming to share a meal with the hotel cat (though admittedly this early enthusiasm for consuming pretty much anything edible could be seen as having prefigured adult weight problems). I'm dubious, too, when stories are related of me running into a full-length mirror at my parents' friends and knocking myself unconscious, having failed to realise that the rotund, smiling figure moving towards me at equal speed was in fact my own reflection.

Whatever did or didn't happen (and I'm aware that my total lack of memory of this period probably doesn't exactly enhance the credibility of my denials), my outbreaks of infant thuggery were the least of their worries. I managed to put a stop to all the laudable strides they'd made in their chosen fields of endeavour.

I didn't achieve this straight away. After her initial maternity leave, my mum worked for four days a week. My dad continued in the Welsh Guards, and, as this wasn't a nine-to-five undertaking, he could also look after me sometimes during the week. When they were both working, my maternal grandparents looked after me. They owned a sweet shop in Bromley, a little further out of London to the South East than where we lived in Forest Hill. The arrangement worked well for eighteen months or so, but then the untimely death of my grandmother, who was only in her early sixties, put a stop to it. My grandfather sold the sweet shop and headed back to Manchester, leaving my parents to reconsider their childcare plans.

Basically, there were two options - career sacrifice or a childminder. They chose the former. My mum gave up work completely and my dad packed in playing music to become an instrumental music teacher instead. This was followed by a move back to Manchester, the city which had been the original home to both my parents. I presume that a major part of the reasoning was to compensate for the big drop in income with reduced mortgage payments. Less than a year after our return, and about three weeks after my fourth birthday, my sister was born.

My mum never went back to journalism, which always seems a waste to me. Her degree at the time conferred a teaching qualification, so she chose to pursue this avenue instead, seeing the job's hours and holidays as fitting better with the demands of two school-aged kids. My dad didn't totally sacrifice playing music for teaching it straight away - for a time he did both. He played in occasional concerts with Manchester's Hallé Orchestra when an extra bassoonist was needed. When they decided to make the post permanent, he was asked to audition, but he also ultimately decided that an itinerant and not particularly well-paid job was incompatible with his family obligations. I'd finally done for him too - I was impeccably even-handed.

I don't really think it can have been much fun for him. He wasn't a qualified teacher, but would receive a decent pay hike if he became one. He therefore spent the 1973-74 academic year at teacher training college, my sister having been born at the very beginning of his studies. He still continued to teach for a forty-hour week, though, and still had his playing engagements. He also had an infant daughter, who in terms of recalcitrance and an unwillingness to sleep outstripped even me (though she was given less opportunity to wreak havoc, my mother's ear-ring phobia still persisting and the Hallé orchestra not insisting on the wearing of a bearskin). It probably wasn't surprising that he suffered tangibly from stress during this period.

Looking back, I have to confess that I feel a little guilty about all this. However, I also feel it's a salutary lesson for me. Earlier, I used to think I wanted children of my own. Now I am set against the idea. This is because I'm old enough to understand the consequences.

It isn't just the career sacrifices. I know now that I don't have the patience or inclination to subjugate my own interests to the degree necessary to be an effective parent. My solution to the problem of a toddler who wouldn't sleep, for example, wouldn't involve tramping the streets round my house in all weathers. It would incorporate strong alcoholic liquor or powerful narcotic sedatives. I have subsequently become a solicitor, and I fear that in the wake of the prosecution by Social Services, the Law Society would revoke my practising certificate on the basis that I wasn't a "fit and proper person" to be pursuing my chosen profession.

Thankfully for me, my parents eschewed such unconventional parenting methods. But although I didn't know it at the time, they did have the last laugh - they exacted a cruel and terrible revenge for the havoc I'd wrought in their lives. We moved north in 1972 and they had to wait until just three short years had passed, and I'd reached the age of six, to put their dastardly plan into action. Of course, at the time I had no idea of the impact it would have on my life but it's definitely had a colossal effect on everything that's followed. They introduced me to Manchester City.

In truth, it was something I'd been longing for in the preceding months, possibly years. I seem to recall already being aware that it was a part of the family heritage, something I should aspire to, a natural and vital part of my identity. I desperately wanted to join in, and I whinged and pestered at length to be allowed to do so. On Boxing Day 1975, my dad relented.

I recall little of that first afternoon apart from it being a bright but cold winter's afternoon, and the crowd being big and noisy. The record books show the team on view featured several players who still remain among my personal City favourites, but despite this fact, the day did set the tone for much of what was to follow. I'm again indebted to the record books for the knowledge that my debut saw an 18-game City unbeaten run shudder to a halt thanks to a 1-0 defeat by Leeds. Others who saw the match have told me that it was marked by comprehensive but slightly toothless City domination only for defeat to ensue thanks to a breakaway goal. But even if not, it seems wholly appropriate for me to think in these terms given the frequency with which I've since witnessed games following a similar pattern.

I have to question my father's role in this. He must have known how vulnerable I'd be to the highly dubious charms of Manchester City FC, but went ahead and exposed me to them anyway. It was a desperately vindictive act with far-reaching consequences, albeit, I suppose, a just payback for what I'd done to him and my mum. But

City were in on the conspiracy, too. For over the next few years, they hid their true nature from me until it was too late; by the time they'd revealed to me what they were really like, I was hooked.

2

The Days of Wine And Roses

IN MANY WAYS, I regret that I couldn't have started watching City ten years earlier. I missed out on many of the great figures in our history. I attended my first match in December 1975, so I never saw outstanding players like Francis Lee or Mike Summerbee inspiring the club to a raft of trophies around the turn of the decade. Six weeks prior to my Maine Road debut, that team's midfield inspiration Colin Bell, still at his peak at only 29 years old, had suffered a horrific knee injury. The player who returned on a memorable Boxing Day afternoon in 1977 after a two-year absence was blessed with superb positional sense and exceptional passing ability but was manifestly not the same player I have since watched on videos from the late sixties and early seventies. The gifted ex-England international Rodney Marsh was still on the staff, but had already played his last game for the club after irrevocably falling from grace; he would be transferred across the Atlantic within a month. The manager of the great late 1960s side, Joe Mercer, had by this point retired from football altogether. His lieutenant, Malcolm Allison, is to me the cigar-puffing clown who returned to all but bankrupt the club by signing a series of expensive flops like the ludicrously overpriced Steve Daley rather than the brash young coach of a brilliantly successful and entertaining Manchester City side.

However, at the start of my City supporting career, the club managed to hide its penchant for eccentricity and underachievement from me. Over the next three years or so following my initiation, the team enjoyed success to degree never even remotely approached since. More or less two months to the day after my first game, we were parading round Wembley with the League Cup. We played in

Europe for three successive seasons, in which time we managed to beat Italian giants Juventus and thrash AC Milan. We twice finished in the top four in the league, attracting an average home gate of over 40,000 each time, a feat way beyond all but two other clubs in that era. In the days before large numbers of foreigners plied their trade in the English top flight, I saw seven City players selected for the full England team. We also had the England Under-21 captain and two regulars in the Scotland side that went to Argentina for the 1978 World Cup finals. And, just to show how long ago we're talking here, pundits and fans of both teams saw the Manchester derby between City and United as a game which genuinely could go either way.

There's a poem called Vita Suma Brevis by a Victorian poet, Ernest Dowson. My mum often quotes the opening lines to me: "They are not long/The days of wine and roses". Actually, Dowson's days were not long altogether, as he died at thirty-three. But what the poem's about is a brief, idyllic period that's gone, never to return. For my mum, this evokes memories of her days in London in the sixties, when she was still in her high-flying career as a Fleet Street journalist and jetted out to spend weekends in Italy or the south of France. For me, it sums up my first few years of following Manchester City (we've never played in Europe since) and the carefree life I enjoyed at the time. For this period, the first three or four years after I discovered the club and as I was making my way through primary school, also represented my own personal time of wine and roses. In many ways this is slightly ironic - I've spent so much since then moving from city to city, country to country even, trying to build the kind of life I want, but I sometimes wonder if the answer wasn't right in my own back yard. I don't spend too much time wondering, though. I know that it's not the particular location or specific people I miss, though I look back with great fondness on both; what I've really been lamenting is the passing of those happy, untroubled days, and of a decent Manchester City side.

I do have some vague, almost dreamlike memories of life before the age of three, when we still lived in London. I can recall that my mum used to drag me along when shopping in Forest Hill

Sainsbury's, and that we always used to stop for a coffee in a café next door. I'd insist on a window seat so I could look out on the bustling activity in the world beyond. I still recollect my third birthday, when my parents had planned a fairly small party for me with three or four kids from the same street who were around the same age. To their consternation, I tramped round the district inviting everyone I could find with the result that a host of older kids showed up. But those fragments pretty much represent the sum total of what I can remember.

When we went to Manchester, I was taken to a playgroup for a couple of afternoons each week, and this is where I met a couple of the children who lived round the block from me. I have very little in the way of memories of the playgroup itself. However, a cutting we still have from our local free newspaper fills in some of the gaps. I'd always thought of myself as a pretty affable child, but the reporter obviously found me somewhat different. Apparently, he approached me when I was rooting in a box of toys, evidently finding the task of busying myself for the afternoon a far from simple one and rejecting every possible source of amusement which came to hand. When asked why I wanted nothing to do with a particular item, I apparently spat, "Because I don't!" with a vehemence precluding all further discussion. I was obviously highly awkward and self-willed even then.

However, it was as I progressed through primary school that I increasingly came into my own, and by the age of eight or so, my school reports were standing out compared to most of my fellow pupils. Later, I'd progress to establishments where there was nothing remarkable about my record at all, but junior school was my time when I had a little bit of star status and I enjoyed it while it lasted. Yet it wasn't just that I was positively enjoying school in a way I haven't enjoyed attending any of my places of education or work since then.

But if what I've said about having a good academic reputation at this time gives a perception that I was a serious, bookish or one-dimensional kid, though, this would be a mistaken impression. I wouldn't look back on this period as some kind of golden age just because I had a reputation for being quite clever. It was the time when I had the widest range of outside interests and the best social life too. Precociously, I liked to regard myself as something of an all-rounder.

Though I didn't have much in the way of football skills (had my formative years as an ardent football enthusiast been spent watching Manchester City between 1995 and 1998 rather than following the good side they had in the mid to late 1970s, this probably wouldn't have seemed like such a barrier!), I wasn't entirely lacking in sporting prowess. My particular arena was the swimming pool. I represented Old Trafford Swimming Club, which, bizarrely, was located right in the middle of Stretford while the home pool of our rivals, Stretford Swimming Club, was in the Old Trafford district, near the football and cricket grounds. I wasn't the new Duncan Goodhew or anything, but I wasn't bad either. I managed to gain the gold and honours personal survival awards at the age of eight and won prizes in local swimming events.

However, the main focus of my outside activity was music. In addition to singing in the choir at St. Matthew's Church, I played piano and trombone. The church choir was a little bit of an unlikely destination for me, really. I'd not been christened, and my parents showed no inclination to give Sarah or me a religious upbringing. However, I had a decent voice and my friend Andrew Thewsey was in the choir, so I joined up too. Still, I always regarded the piano and trombone as my main pursuits, and, receiving tuition from colleagues of my father, who by now was a peripatetic music teacher with Manchester City Council.

The late 1970s may not be many people's idea of days of wine and roses. The country was beset by economic problems and political uncertainty; the industrial unrest in the 1978-79 'Winter of Discontent' saw rubbish uncollected on the streets and the dead not being buried; and the Yorkshire Ripper was terrifying the whole of the North of England. All in all, though, things looked pretty good to me. I was doing well at school, I had several outside interests in which I was achieving reasonable success and I had several good friends both at school and in my neighbourhood. And, of course, things weren't just good for me but for City as well.

I didn't go to every home game in those early years, but I was attending often thanks to my persistence in mithering my dad, and after the slightly disappointing circumstances of that Leeds game, everything was fairly plain sailing. In my first three seasons, the records now show, we lost only six times at home in 63 league games and a further fifteen cup ties, including some in European competition. I turned up for every home game I attended expecting a resounding win, and my expectations were usually fulfilled.

My idol was Dave Watson, the imperious England centre-half, and I regarded him as mine in a way I haven't done with any other player since then. This was partly because I was tall for my age and dark-haired, and as these were his traits also, I could claim a tenuous physical resemblance. But it was also because he'd put himself out on my behalf - a family friend was his local GP, and he allowed himself to be talked into obtaining all his team-mates' autographs for me. I was immensely proud of the two pages in my autograph book where their signatures lay. But if Watson was my undisputed favourite, there were others who weren't far behind: the imposing goalkeeper Joe Corrigan; elegant full-back Willie Donachie; midfield dynamos Gary Owen and Asa Hartford ("If Hartford plays well, City play well," I remember manager Tony Book writing in his programme notes); the wingers Barnes and Tueart, who provided the team's attacking flair; and the chief goal scorer Brian Kidd.

As I became captivated by that team, I had little idea that homework and exams and career considerations and stress and responsibility and financial worries and relationship problems would intervene - some of them imminently - to annihilate my serene, carefree existence. And I had little idea that my Manchester City fantasy world would soon come crashing down around my ears. For me, the two were linked - City and I had been successful together so far, and we were fated to go from strength to strength in tandem. Needless to say, I'd never ever heard of Ernest Dowson.

3

Coming of Age

I WAS JUST beginning to experience my first doubts when, at Easter 1979, four months before my tenth birthday, my parents took my younger sister and me to London. We stayed in Ealing with my mum's Auntie Alice and her cousin Robert. Like so many events whose significance magnifies in retrospect, and just like the first defining episode, it all seemed so innocuous at the time.

The trip was a cause of big excitement for me. I'd been born in London, but we'd moved north at the age of three, so I was excited to be returning to the city where I first saw the light of day. And I have several memories of our visit. I remember having a picnic on a sunny day in Kew Gardens. I remember having a meal at a Greek restaurant near Ealing Broadway tube, which is probably the first time I recall eating out. I remember boarding the wrong tube train and, to the sniggering amusement of the other passengers in the carriage, helplessly watching the rest of my family recede from view on the platform as the train drew out of the station. And I also remember our journey south - perhaps not surprisingly, given that it involved a long drive in a bright orange Citroen 2CV nicknamed the "Flying Jaffa" by my dad's work colleagues.

Yet the real reason the London visit had such significance for me is only clear in hindsight. Coupled with an event two months before, it was a highly resonant time in both my life and in my City-supporting career, one that punctured my previously unshakeable faith in our destiny.

The first pivotal moment came in February 1979, a month after City had sacked their first-team coach Bill Taylor, a man rated highly enough to have been invited to occupy the same role with the England squad. We reappointed Malcolm Allison, who as Mercer's right-hand man had been instrumental in the great successes of a decade previously. Allison's tenure didn't begin in the brightest of fashions, and though I wasn't too concerned, my dad wasn't so sanguine. He cautioned darkly from the outset that, if Allison was allowed a free rein, no good could come of it. He had some theory, which I didn't really bother with, that the guy needed the moderating influence of his former mentor Joe Mercer if he was ever going to prosper. It wasn't to be the last time I ignored warnings from my dad that I should have listened to.

I remember him being particularly agitated when we saw City scrape a goalless draw at home to lower-division Rotherham in the FA Cup. He was muttering about this being the same man whose profligacy had cost City the league Championship in 1972 when, with the team holding a comfortable lead in the title race, Allison had spent a near-record fee on the extravagantly skilled crowd-pleaser Rodney Marsh. In typical City fashion, the new boy was plunged straight into the side, disrupting the team's pattern of play, and the prize slipped from grasp.

In truth, 1978-79 had been a strange season, one in which our fine home form of the past few years had suddenly become a thing of the past. For a couple of months, this troubled me, but then I'd understood. In the previous couple of seasons, we'd been a top English side but hadn't made an impression on Europe. Naively, I was sure that this new bloke had arrived to supervise the final push towards putting that right. I ascribed that season's disappointing form in the league and domestic cup competitions to the fact that we must be saving ourselves for the greater challenges to come in the UEFA Cup.

I wasn't even swayed when the same players who'd thumped the mighty Italian league leaders AC Milan in a European tie in December crashed out of the FA Cup to minnows Shrewsbury Town (at that time, it was simply inconceivable we'd be playing the Shrews in the league just over four years later). We were just continuing a self-imposed winter break, albeit one in which we had to suffer the minor inconvenience of fulfilling fixtures. When I saw on TV the absolute delirium with which Shrewsbury celebrated their victory, I was impressed by our magnanimity. After all, we'd never move in the same circles as a team like that, so we'd graciously allowed them their moment of glory. We had bigger fish to fry and the defeat was a small price to pay for the much more glamorous triumphs to follow.

However, I knew that we needed to be on a roll by the time the crucial European game against crack German outfit Borussia Mönchengladbach came round in March, so I was looking for us to improve during February, moving up smoothly through the gears and being in overdrive when it mattered. A comprehensive 3-0 win at Spurs was the result I seized on to tell me I'd been right all along and that the mouthy bloke with the big cigars was going to produce exactly the effect I was expecting. However, that the return to form should happen at Spurs was particularly opportune given the following Saturday's fixture - Manchester United were visiting Maine Road. Even if we weren't especially interested in the league, we simply had to win that one.

Obviously, the derby was a vitally important game for every City fan, but I always felt that it was a bigger match for me than for any of my fellow supporters. Living in Stretford, I could see the Old Trafford floodlights from my bedroom window, and sometimes the cheers when they scored were audible from our garden. My impeccable Blue credentials on both sides of my family had saved me from the lure of the dark side, but the same wasn't true of most of those surrounding me. All our neighbours were Reds and so were most of the kids in my primary school class. I took a lot of stick, but, incredible as it seems today, I had plenty of ammunition of my own. We'd finished above United in the league for the previous two seasons, and in derby matches they had at least as much reason to fear us as we did them. So whatever bragging rights my classmates felt they had, I was normally ready with some kind of answer. However, I had suffered greatly after Joe Jordan's last minute winner at Old Trafford in the first derby of the season the previous September, so I'd been eagerly awaiting the return. It was payback time.

Though heavily outnumbered at school, I wasn't on my own. Including me, there were actually four City fans in my class. Two were fairly dispassionate, but there was one kid whose enthusiasm matched my own - his real name was Stephen Hornsey, but he was nicknamed Stan for reasons I've now forgotten, if I ever knew them in the first place. Stan and I gave each other support when we came under attack from the United fans and we certainly weren't averse to the odd pre-emptive strike of our own.

Both of us were absolutely certain that there'd be only one winner at Maine Road the following week and we took every opportunity to inform anyone who'd listen. City's convincing display at White Hart Lane, which we'd watched on the old regional ITV Sunday highlights programme, had reaffirmed the team's quality. I can't remember what United did the same day, but I'd guess from our sublime confidence that they lost. I definitely recall that they had something of an injury crisis which had dramatically reduced their options up front, and we guffawed all week to the United fans that they wouldn't score if the match lasted until the start of the first derby of the following season. They in fact managed the feat early in the game, and eventually ran out 3-0 winners. And even to someone who viewed proceedings with the unremitting bias I did at that age, United's superiority on the day was beyond dispute.

It was a deeply troubling development. If the players were capable of ensuring my humiliation by being thrashed at Maine Road in the derby - in my view about as serious a breach of trust as they could have committed - how could I rely on them to do anything at all? I certainly couldn't have faith in their future ability to match my confident words with the appropriate on-field action, and resolved that I'd be much, much more careful with what I said in future. I understood, too, that even when I had high expectations, there was always the risk they'd be dashed - I've never been blithely expectant of victory in the same way since. And no subsequent defeat, not even ones which were objectively much less likely, has been quite as much of a shock to me. It seemed appropriate that the season meandered to a close, Mönchengladbach seeing us off fairly comfortably, 4-2 on aggregate.

When I went to London a few short weeks after the derby disaster, my eyes had been opened for the first time. It was my first glimpse of the misery Manchester City could provide, the way they could let me down in the most important of circumstances. Having hitherto regarded my fate as inextricably linked with the club's, I decided that they no longer deserved my trust, and resolved not to tie my fortunes to theirs as I previously had.

Robert provided me with an example. His lifestyle involved a well-paid job and had the advantage of no responsibility. He had no children or family considerations to hold him back and the way in which he was able to enjoy the considerable fruits of his labours immediately enticed me, as did his apparent opulence.

He was probably around forty then, and he was a partner in a small firm of solicitors. My parents were both teachers and obviously regarded his lifestyle as highly desirable. I was aware of this even at the time - indeed, they made no bones about it - and I could see why. Their joint income paid for a three-bedroomed semi-detached house in a reasonable but not prestigious suburb. Robert had a big, old and opulently decorated abode in a good area of a city where property prices were considerably higher. Whereas we'd go out for meals only rarely, he was obviously a regular in the Greek restaurant and, by the sound of it, a fair few others. Whereas in my early childhood, our family holidays had been in the Lake District, Robert spoke of trips to glamorous-sounding foreign locations. I don't mean to knock one of my own country's areas of outstanding natural beauty - it just had less allure by virtue of its location an hour and a half up the M6 (or about three hours if we were in the Flying Jaffa).

I decided I wanted some of what Robert had and I reckoned that in the route he'd chosen; if those benefits came from life as a solicitor, then that would be what I'd do too. The thought never left me and I was more or less committed even at that point to a life of orthodoxy and rationality.

For someone captivated by another world - ancestors of ill repute, late-night drinking dens and sipping undrinkable tea with Auntie Dot to a backdrop of canine lunacy - it was never going to be enough. Shortly after I left Robert's imbued with resolve and ambition to carve out an eventual career in the law, I started a period of hard study which was to last for fourteen years. The discipline needed to complete this successfully was totally at odds with my background and ideals, meaning that I needed to look for another source for the irrational and inexplicable to brighten those days.

In later years, I was to show a remarkable flair for seeking out these qualities outside a footballing context, but at the age of ten, only Manchester City appeared to offer me such possibilities. I soon became yet more absorbed by this beguiling institution, and I know now that, in addition to my career choice, my obsession was the second far-reaching consequence of the trip to cousin Robert's. I'm not always sure that it's something I should thank him for.

4

The End of Innocence

THERE'S A PARTICULAR incident I can recall that shows how resolutely I had started to march down the path I'd chosen once I returned from Robert's. I remember the sunlight streaming in through the classroom windows. I can visualise Mr. Eaves, the head of my junior school, standing in front of 4K asking us in turn what we all wanted to be when we grew up. I've forgotten what anyone else said, though I seem to think (quite possibly erroneously) that Andrew Thewsey had ambitions of becoming a policeman. I do, however, recollect my own response with absolute clarity. With unwavering certainty, I declared that I wanted to become a lawyer.

Andrew Thewsey never went into law enforcement; we lost touch, but I ran into his mother, by chance, years later and I think she said he was working for a bank. Whether any of my other contemporaries in the class of 1979-80 at Victoria Park Junior School, Stretford, ever fulfilled their nascent hopes of those long-gone days I have no idea. I did, though.

It was an aspiration that never left me. I seriously considered a law degree both when I was choosing which subject to study at university and at the end of my first year, when I had the possibility of changing to another course. Eventually, I rejected the option on both occasions, but after graduation, I elected to continue my academic career for two years so I could enter the legal profession. For the last ten years, I've been first studying law and then practising it. In fact, I never really contemplated another career. The only job I ever really thought I'd prefer would have been a professional footballer. However, even by the time I reached 4K, I was fully aware that this wasn't an option.

Coincidentally, things at Maine Road were to start going downhill at this very point, and, in retrospect, despite my absolute lack of aptitude for playing the game, if Steve Daley was a million pound footballer, then I perhaps shouldn't have been so downcast about my prospects. Daley played for Wolves in the old First Division and was a competent enough player for them, but certainly no more; there certainly wasn't a clamour for him to be included in the England squad as far as I can remember. In September 1979, City paid a staggering £1.4 million, a British transfer record, to bring him to Maine Road.

It wasn't an isolated occurrence, either. Michael Robinson, a young striker with only a handful of games behind him at Preston, was signed for a fee of £750,000. It was a supreme irony that, when opting to buy a young striker from a north-west club and a combative midfielder from the Black Country, we plumped for Robinson and Daley. Had we taken what may well have proved at that time the cheaper options of Ian Rush and Bryan Robson, we'd have had two of the English game's biggest stars of the 1980s. And later in the season, Allison shelled out £1.25 million for Kevin Reeves of Norwich - although he, at least, was on the fringes of the England team and had just made his debut for the national side. Even some of the lesser buys were wildly extravagant. The fee for Steve MacKenzie, a Crystal Palace teenager who hadn't even made an appearance for their senior side, was £250,000 - though he proved just about the only incoming signing to be a success - while Wrexham's Bobby Shinton, an uninspiring lower division forward, cost £100,000 more. In the meantime, many of the best players left (internationals like Hartford, Barnes and Watson were all shown the door) - at fees substantially lower than those we squandered on their inept replacements.

In the summer of 1979, I went with my mum and sister to stay with family friends in Italy. They were followers of Milan and remembered their team's two UEFA Cup ties against City the previous campaign. They'd been enormously impressed, and spoke about our team in the kind of revered tones I'd have reserved for Brazil's legendary 1970 World Cup winners. But it was obvious that after the summer transfer madness, we wouldn't see that kind of display again for some considerable time.

I knew that the Milan games weren't entirely representative, of course. If we'd played like that consistently, we'd not have finished in fifteenth place in the league table, and nor would we have been knocked out of the FA Cup by Shrewsbury. The team that had underachieved the previous season undoubtedly needed surgery, but judicious pruning coupled with two or three astute acquisitions would have been sufficient. In fact, the old team was completely dismantled. I'd already lost my unshakeable sense of destiny where City were concerned, but this was something else entirely. It was madness, the decisions having no logical basis whatsoever. Even I, as a ten-year-old, could see that, although a total absence of logic at Maine Road was something I was to get used to.

There was a new departure in my own life, too. Exams made an appearance in my life for the first time. That morning when I mapped out my future to Mr. Eaves, he'd warned me that to become a lawyer, I'd have to sit many exams, and the first step along the way was to end up at the right secondary school. I still lived in an eleven-plus area even though comprehensive education had become widespread throughout the country by this stage, so I was obliged to take two papers to determine whether I'd go to the local grammar school. But it wasn't just on this educational institution that my parents and teachers had their eye.

In February 1980, I sat the entrance exam for Manchester Grammar School, a private school which had an outstanding academic reputation. The exam was in two stages, with maths and English tested each time. However, as I had begun learning a couple of musical instruments, I was asked back for an audition with the senior music teacher (this skill was supposed to bring kudos to a candidate's application). And I also had to take an exam set by my local authority, who provided twelve scholarships to a private school. For all the kids in a borough with a population of 300,000, twelve places wasn't many, in statistical terms at least. But there was a degree of pressure too, because I'd been given to understand that if I didn't win the scholarship, I wouldn't go to the school even if I won a paying place. And while that would have had certain compensations, like staying with my friends, the importance others were attaching to it meant it also assumed great significance for me.

I think, looking back, that what happened in 1979-80 was that the fun went. It certainly wasn't enjoyable watching City. Even if the league position was only a couple of places lower than the previous season, there was a world of difference. A year before, we might have underachieved for much of the campaign, but, with a team of international players, there was always the possibility that they might gel. And, as the warm reminiscences of our Italian friends testified, when they did, they could be a match for even the best. The team of the following season was simply a desperate, directionless outfit whose quality, if anything, was overstated by a finishing position just above the relegation zone.

There were three or four decent young players who were trying to make their way, but the struggle certainly wasn't their fault. It owed more to the ineffectiveness of the men brought in to replace the stars we'd sold. How were the youngsters supposed to prosper if there was no leadership from the men around them? Allison's baffling answer to this conundrum was to make his Yugoslav signing, Dragoslav Stepanovic, his new captain. Aside from failing to adjust lamentably to English football (even time didn't help - he reached his nadir a year later in a particularly horrible 4-0 home defeat by Sunderland), he spoke no English.

Of course, I didn't understand at this stage just how gloriously Manchester City all this was. Selling all the best players at a great loss and replacing them with overpriced dross, putting the club in colossal financial strife as a result, was the kind of inexplicable and baffling behaviour which I later grew to expect. But when I was ten years old, I didn't like it. We were supposed to be good - this was my fifth season, and in each of the first three we'd qualified for Europe, while even in the fourth there was the odd, isolated high point. Now there was nothing.

I confess that at some point, and I can no longer remember when it was, I felt so betrayed that my faith wavered. One day, I decided to try my hand at supporting Liverpool; after all, City had been pretty much as good as them just a couple of years previously, and while they'd continued to sweep all before them, we'd simply thrown it all away. City had let me down, and I believed that only a switch of allegiance could punish them sufficiently. I remember listening to Radio Two the first Saturday afternoon after I'd reached this momentous decision. Liverpool were playing away to relegation-threatened Coventry in a First Division fixture, and there was live second-half commentary on the game. I listened in utter disgust as my new favourites slid to a 1-0 defeat against their lowly opponents, and decided that if that was all the thanks I'd get for pledging my loyalty to them, it would be unpledged without further ado.

I'd been taught my lesson. I understood that I was in for the long haul with City, that my contract had no get-out clause; someone was watching over me and had made sure of the appropriate result in the Liverpool game: I'd been taught my lesson. I can only apologise to those fans who'd travelled that day from Merseyside to the West Midlands only to see their team produce what must have seemed an inexplicably wretched performance. I'm afraid it's inexplicable no more, though as they won the league easily again that season, I'm sure I'll be forgiven.

I'm glad, now, that Liverpool lost that game. I like, of course, to think I'd have come to my senses. But I live with the dark fear that had they won handsomely that afternoon, I might have been seduced into a shallow and essentially phoney support for a club which I have often admired but with which I have no tangible connection. And had that happened, I would have been deprived of the uniquely surreal, often frustrating but always beguiling input City have had into my life.

I say this with the benefit of hindsight. As the team struggled desperately, I felt that I was watching football in black-and-white rather than in the Technicolor I'd been used to previously. And it felt that way in the rest of my life, too. I had to prepare for all those exams, and that meant homework, and plenty of it, too - something which hitherto had been outside my experience and which I didn't embrace with any fondness. I was under pressure to perform and had to wait for my results, knowing whether I could go forward in the way expected of me was in the balance. And the resultant tension was, I suppose, my first brush with stress in any genuine sense of the word.

In the years to come, what had seemed like two sudden and unexpected developments were to become regular fixtures in my life. However, I responded to them in different ways. I grew to enjoy the bizarre and frankly incomprehensible behaviour of Manchester City, taking a perverse pleasure even when things got far worse than they had in my eleventh year. The abject greyness of my school life was to persist, too, but I could never make myself love that. Eventually I did manage to find additional outlets, but, for the time being, City offered the only route to escapism that I knew. The seeds of my obsession had been sown.

5

The Cracks Start to Show

MALCOLM ALLISON'S TENURE came to an end in October 1980, some 21 months after he'd returned to the club amid the glare of a frenzied media spotlight. Even by our standards, it had been an astonishing time - never had a football club spent more money less wisely, and I think most football supporters were incredulous, not just us. His spell in charge had seen the club regularly in the headlines, but in all honesty, the publicity was of dubious value. The column inches and the TV and radio coverage focused on a football club that was shooting itself in the foot repeatedly and which as a result was to walk with a limp pretty much ever since. The 1980-81 season began even more pitifully than the previous campaign had ended, and with City adrift at the bottom of the table without a win in eleven league games, Allison was unceremoniously fired.

He was replaced by another flamboyant character, John Bond, who was poached from Norwich City amid some acrimony (the East Anglian club didn't appreciate the way we went about snaring their manager). And the new man at the helm inspired a remarkable improvement. His first game was a pitiful 1-0 defeat at home to a desperately ordinary Birmingham side who nonetheless fully deserved the win, even if their goal did come from a last-minute penalty. But thereafter, things suddenly improved, and Bond was to win the Manager of the Month award in November and December as City stormed into a secure mid-table position.

The new boss had obviously identified failings which had remained mystifyingly ignored by the previous regime for well over a year. He immediately recruited left-back Bobby MacDonald (Allison saw no need for a specialist in this position), while midfielder Gerry Gow and veteran winger Tommy Hutchison added respectively the steel and flair missing from his predecessor's hapless side. Results improved, and with them came the crucial ingredient of confidence - the fresh faces were ineligible to play in the League Cup, in which City reached the semi-final only to lose narrowly to reigning champions Liverpool 2-1 on aggregate. And we were left with a sense of righteous injustice after a highly contentious refereeing performance helped Liverpool win 1-0 at Maine Road in the first of the two legs.

I liked to think that my approach to the new stage in my education mirrored Bond's at Maine Road - fearless and refreshingly positive. I'd passed the Manchester Grammar School entrance exam and earned warm praise from the music teacher for my proficiency on the piano and trombone. Then I won the scholarship I was in for, saving my parents the choice of whether to compromise themselves financially to give me a chance of what was perceived to be a better education. And, at first, I flourished in my new environment.

If I'd thought that 1979-80 represented a sea-change, I discovered it had merely been an hors d'oeuvres for the main meal ahead. There was a fairly ferocious homework regime that, as I recall, demanded hours of study each evening. I was showing commendable aptitude, especially in the arts subjects, and so I enjoyed the feeling of achievement. It demanded a considerable sacrifice, though. No longer did I have a social life to speak of, at least during term time. My whole life revolved around school and trying to make myself a success there.

I'm not sure how healthy this was. There's little doubt in my mind that the educational rigour at Manchester Grammar School helped me to obtain better 'O' and 'A' level results and that this, in turn, helped me in later years to achieve more in career terms than I might otherwise have done. On the other hand, I have to say that sometimes it felt rather like a conveyor belt.

The school was proud of its academic record, and one of the key indicators of success in this sphere was how many pupils won places at either Oxford or Cambridge Universities. In my first year, my mum and dad went to a parents' evening where it was predicted that in six or seven years, I'd be studying an arts subject at Oxbridge. That this did actually happen leaves me slightly unsettled. On the one hand, even at the age of eleven, for this prospect to be held out before me was slightly intoxicating. I knew that, certainly in the circles I'd started to move in, Oxbridge was regarded as a marker of success. Of course, I wanted to be successful, and as I hadn't developed any ideas of my own as to what success might be, I decided to aspire to what others wanted for me.

If the school was ideally placed to help me to where it thought I should go in educational terms, I'm less convinced as to the assistance it gave me in terms of learning about the non-academic side of life. I've always been dubious about the value of single-sex schooling anyway; the only places in later life where one could encounter a similar environment would be a prison or a monastery, and I never had any intention of ending up in either (I eventually did, but that comes later in the story). But the most serious drawback at this stage was the lack of a social life for forty weeks of the year. I still saw my primary school friends in school holidays, but barely at all during term time so preoccupied was I with the demands of schoolwork. And this kind of part-time camaraderie hardly facilitated the relationships I'd previously enjoyed.

John Bond seemed to have sensed what was up, and he certainly did his best to teach me a little about life. Unfortunately, the main lessons were that things are not always what they seem to be and that disappointment may always be lurking round the corner even when you least expect it.

City may have fallen at the penultimate hurdle in the league Cup early in 1981, but the FA Cup was a different story and we marched all the way to the final, the drama intensified by a couple of remarkably ironic pairings in the early stages. In the third round, we faced Malcolm Allison's new club Crystal Palace. The Londoners were bottom of the First Division, and we were expected to beat them, but we made heavy weather of it until we were awarded a somewhat dubious penalty halfway through the second half. We scored, Palace collapsed and we went on to win 4-0. Next up were

Bond's old side, Norwich, for whom his son still played. They were hit for six.

The coincidence of facing these two clubs certainly took on the appearance of an omen, and we duly went all the way to the final, defeating Fourth Division Peterborough (scrappily), Everton (in a Maine Road replay in front of an emotional full house) and title-chasing Ipswich (memorably and unexpectedly at Villa Park). But in the final, we came up against opponents with an omen of their own - and it was too strong for ours. Until 2001, Spurs had seemingly won a trophy in every year ending in a one since some date back in the Middle Ages so when they reached the FA Cup final, the press found it hard to talk of little else.

There's no doubt that, were there any justice in the world, City would have won the FA Cup in 1981. Spurs should have been disqualified from the competition for their simply shocking Cup final song by Chas and Dave, which featured the team's gifted Argentine midfielder Ossie Ardiles periodically boasting in his broken, Hispanic-accented English, "I going to win de Cap for Totting-ham." But such musical crimes against humanity notwithstanding, "Totting-ham" were allowed to compete - and win.

As ever, City raised our hopes. We went 1-0 up through Hutchison but the same player deflected a Glenn Hoddle free kick, which was going wide anyway, into his own net with around ten minutes remaining. City had hit the post before Spurs drew level (a second would surely have killed the game) and were clearly the physically stronger side in extra time without being able to force a winner. So a replay was necessary, but that it turned out to be one of the classic Cup final games proved scant consolation.

Again, it looked for a while that glory may be ours. Their less celebrated Argentinian, Ricky Villa, had given Spurs an early lead, but after a searing volley from MacKenzie levelled matters within sixty seconds, City went in front just after half-time when Reeves converted a penalty. It couldn't last. Spurs turned the screw, putting together a series of fluent attacking moves, and despite the heroics of our goalkeeper Corrigan, who won the Man of the Match award for his efforts, the dam eventually burst. First Steve Archibald equalised, and then Villa embarked on a mazy dribble through our defence to score a memorable winner. It's a goal City fans are never allowed to forget, much though I for one would love to; I must have seen it repeated hundreds of times on TV over the years. On every single occasion, as he starts his run yards outside the penalty area I inwardly (or outwardly if no-one else is in the room) scream to Ranson, Caton and the other defenders who try to tackle him and miss the ball, "Take the bastard's legs". What, with Villa's goals and Ardiles's singing, had I been in 10 Downing Street, we'd have been at war with Argentina almost a year before they invaded the Falklands.

Those two Cup final games took place just a few weeks before my first taste of Manchester Grammar School first year exams. All through the year, we were encouraged to be relentlessly competitive in academic terms. We were awarded grades in each subject every term (a letter from A to E to denote achievement, and a number from 1 to 5 to denote effort). These had to be filled in on a card, and there was a kind of points system to allow for easy calculation of overall attainment. I have memories of nauseating little swots eyeing each others' cards and coming out with comments like, "Ah, you got a B2 in Maths; look, I got an A1." And the other precocious prat would probably counter, "Ah, but I got an A2 in history." I never had any time for this, personally, even though my grades were invariably good and I acquitted myself very well in the end-of-year exams; indeed, there were several of my classmates I'd have happily shipped off to Buenos Aires before the first missile strike.

Not much changed for the next year. City still flattered to deceive, while I still did well at school despite feeling an overwhelming sense of frustration at the whole ethos of the place and the fact I didn't have a life outside of it. For the first, and not the last, time, I was left looking to City to provide some solace; I wasn't happy with my lot, and though I knew City couldn't cure the problem, I thought that a little success would provide a little welcome cheer. For a while, it looked like they might oblige, but the truth was merely that John Bond was in teaching mode again.

He seemed to have made a decent fist of turning around Allison's no-hopers, and the next step was to improve further so that the team could challenge near the top of the league. England international striker Trevor Francis arrived to spearhead the drive for honours, and made an immediate impact with a two-goal salvo at Stoke on his debut. Francis was frequently injured, but when available for selection, regularly showed his quality, and he quickly came as close to being my real City idol as anyone has since Dave Watson; I even spent my school dinner money one day opening an account at a building society I passed on the way home just so I could get to meet him.

On 28 December, a spectacular late winner against struggling Wolves sent us to the top of the league, and it was no surprise to anyone that the moment of inspiration came from Francis. We'd played more games than other teams around the summit, and few thought us strong enough to hold on and win the title, but as New Year started, the return of European football to Maine Road the following season looked a distinct possibility.

It wasn't to be. Francis's fitness problems continued, and the team looked woefully short of attacking spark when he didn't play. Meanwhile, we'd signed him on at a wage we couldn't afford, and had also paid over the odds for some of Bond's other new boys. In an undignified scramble, we cut costs by offloading several senior players who were unable to command a regular first-team place - leaving ourselves desperately short-handed when the inevitable injury crisis occurred. The end to the season was shambolic, typified by the wretched Easter weekend when we conceded nine goals in the space of three days as Liverpool and Wolves filled their boots against a dispirited and injury-hit side.

Nor were things much better for me; much to their chagrin, I told my parents I wanted to leave for the local grammar school, where my friends were. In retrospect, it's clear to me now that both for me and for the team, some kind of collapse was in store. It didn't take long to arrive for either of us.

6

The Wheels Come Off

IN ONE OF THE FINAL games of 1981-82, as the season limped to its dispiriting close, Trevor Francis had played a blinder and scored against Coventry. He was the only City player to have produced even a remotely decent performance that day, and we were beaten 3-1. After the game, John Bond promised that new buys would be brought in to complement the quality of the star man, and season tickets sold well as fans looked forward to seeing him play again in the new season. We never got the chance. He went off to play for England in the World Cup finals, and when he came back in July, was sold to Italian club Sampdoria for about two thirds of what we'd paid for him. By this point, we'd sold most of the season tickets we were going to sell, a fact that might be viewed by those of a cynical disposition as not entirely coincidental.

It can't have been much of an eventful summer for me, since the departure of Trevor Francis is the only event I can actually remember. There were school exams again in June, but after that I must have waited aimlessly for six or seven weeks for the football season to start. It duly did begin, and City won their first three games. But even so, there wasn't much excitement around Maine Road. Crowds for the early games were around 7,000 down on the previous season's average, and those who were there didn't seem overly enthused with proceedings. I couldn't really blame those who opted to stay away, though; with Francis departed, there really wasn't much else worth watching.

So I hardly felt reinvigorated when I went back to school. I'd moved into a new class, and if anything the workload was greater. I certainly felt under more pressure, anyway. I was to take my 'O' levels a year early, in the fourth form, at which stage I still wouldn't have reached my fifteenth birthday. I regarded this as a problem. It wasn't that I thought I couldn't cope, I just didn't see why I should have to. I had less aptitude in the science subjects than in the arts, and I didn't respond to the way I was expected to study physics and chemistry. Understanding, it seemed, wasn't required; rote learning, with a view to an impressive 'O' level grade, was in order. I couldn't learn in that way and became bitterly disillusioned.

This wasn't the only difficulty. My parents moved into a much bigger house in Sale, the next suburb out on the railway line heading south west from the city centre to Altrincham. It was regarded as a better area, but despite the fact that it was only a few miles from where we'd lived previously, I was no longer a short walk away from friends I'd lived close to previously. And though for a few months I did make a few visits back to Stretford during the school holidays, I quickly lost touch with them. At school, I also found things hard on the social side. I'd moved into a different class from my best friends in the first couple of years, and again we rather drifted apart (I know this doesn't sound an insurmountable barrier to continued contact, but obviously the friendships weren't strong enough to survive even this most basic of tests).

Something else happened that year, too. My uncle died. He'd divorced and was living alone in Accrington, where he worked in the Hollands Pies factory. A diabetic for as long as I remember, he'd started to suffer more and more, and I recall him spending time in hospital in the winter of 1982-83. At the end of February, he lapsed into a coma after failing to take the correct dose of insulin, and he never came out of it. I can still visualise the police calling because they'd found our address in his house, and I can see to this day my mum weeping uncontrollably (she'd lost both her parents by this stage as well now as her only sibling).

My own grief was delayed somewhat, I suppose because I didn't really come to terms with the finality of his death. My maternal grandfather had died five years previously, but he'd been in his mid-seventies so was old (I knew other people who'd lost grandparents) and in any case, I'd been much younger at that time and thus less capable of understanding. Now, I couldn't quite believe it, and when the realisation did dawn, I regret to say that my overriding emotion was one of self-pity. I felt I was growing apart from my parents at this stage, since I couldn't see that they had any sympathy with the way I was feeling at all. I remember one particular incident, and though it occurred a year or two before this, it nevertheless summed up the way they and I failed to see eye to eye.

I'd walked into our classroom at break where a fight was taking place between two members of the form. There was quite a commotion, and in the chaos, a teacher entered. I had my back to him and failed to see him, and as everyone else scattered, I remained blissfully unaware of his presence until he yanked me round by the hair, and, to make an example of me, imposed a punishment of several nights' detention in a row. I was outraged, and asked my parents to write to the school on my behalf. They didn't, and, even worse from my point of view, nor did they even appear to comprehend why I was so bothered about it.

In contrast, when Uncle Frank came to stay (in the preceding few months, he'd been to stay with us on two or three occasions), I had someone I could open up to and who would listen to my side of things. With him gone, I saw myself as being totally alone. Not only was he a big loss to me, he was also a major influence, and he always encouraged my sporting passions. After my dad, he had been the person most responsible for inducting me into the Manchester City religion, always showing a willingness to take me to matches whenever he could. This undoubtedly had a positive effect on our relationship, though it would be wrong to say it was solely responsible for the warmth between us. He'd taken me to games on several occasions when my dad was working and he was always willing to talk about it, or to kick a ball round with me. He also took me to see Sale play rugby union, which was never more than a passing interest, and to see Lancashire play cricket at the 'other' Old Trafford, which certainly was, but it was the bond with City that was the closest.

In 1982-83, however, I spent most of the time wishing that the link with the club had been emphatically severed. Despite three wins from the first three games that catapulted City to the top of the league table, the season had never really caught the imagination. In my past experience, even when City had been an unequivocally bad team, mainly under Malcolm Allison's stewardship, we were certainly high profile. There was colour and drama, we seemed to have plenty of money and we hogged the headlines. Now, even though we didn't seem half as bad as Allison's misfits, we were simply dull. Of the four pre-season signings, two were free transfers - Chris Jones of Spurs and Newcastle's Ian Davies, while we paid money for West Ham's David Cross and Southampton's Graham Baker. With all due respect to them, they weren't exactly a quartet to set the pulse racing.

Still, there certainly wasn't any hint of what was to come when we briefly occupied a flattering second place in the First Division in November, or when a 4-1 win over a poor-looking Norwich side in January sent us up to eighth and left them looking relegation probables. The week after that Norwich game, we earned a creditable point from a 1-1 draw at Aston Villa, but then came a defining moment in the season. A win over Sunderland in a third round replay had encouraged hopes of a run in the FA Cup, and even though we faced First Division opposition again at the next stage, the fact it was lowly Brighton only added to the optimism. We couldn't have been more wrong.

City were battered 4-0 on the south coast, a scoreline which could easily have been even more embarrassing, and within a week manager John Bond had walked out. Bond claimed later that his decision was prompted by an incident which happened as he travelled back from the south coast following the Cup defeat; City supporters allegedly spat at him. His departure was followed by lurid stories in the tabloid press claiming that the departed manager had been having an affair with a 35-year-old brunette who worked in the club's offices. John Benson, Bond's less flamboyant lieutenant, assumed charge.

His first game saw a comeback from two down against Spurs to draw, and not too much seemed wrong. But that was the last time the team showed any real fight. There soon followed a dismal 4-0 defeat at Coventry, while the 1-0 reverse at home to Notts County a week later was also desperately poor. The Saturday after Uncle Frank died, which was the Saturday before his funeral, we took on Manchester United at Maine Road. Kevin Reeves gave us the lead. I remember looking at the league table before the United game and realising that we could do with a win just to take the pressure off. But though we took the lead, Frank Stapleton's double strike meant another derby defeat, and we then managed just two victories and seven defeats in the following nine games. We also, bizarrely, sold top scorer David Cross after the transfer deadline, when it was too late to replace him, even though he'd scored twice as many goals that season as the next most prolific marksman. So even though we were out of the bottom three, with two matches remaining, relegation was a strong possibility.

Spice was added by the fact that the last two fixtures were also against teams struggling at the foot of the table. And when we extracted revenge for Brighton's Cup win with a 1-0 away victory which consigned them to relegation, our escape looked a formality. A draw at home to Luton the following week would see us safe - at the visitors' expense. It was a desperately nervy game, but as the second half wore on with neither side able to break the deadlock, it looked like all would end well. Then, with around three minutes remaining, Luton's Yugoslav substitute Radomir Antic scored, to send us down and save his team.

Following Manchester City is an occupation punctuated with moments where things are worse than devotees can ever imagine, and at that point, I'd never before contemplated Maine Road hosting football outside the highest division in English football. We'd been in the top flight since before I was born, and our resources should have been greater than those of other strugglers (it's slightly simplistic, but the equation should roughly be that more fans - we always had decent crowds - should bring in more money, and more money for player salaries and transfer fees should lead to a better team). I was learning that it all counted for nothing.

As things turned out, I was to emulate City's crash. Unhappy at school and with no-one to confide in or to console me, I simply stopped putting in any effort at all. We were subjected to a rigorous homework regime and I ignored it totally. I had enough aptitude in the arts subjects to get by anyway, but my abject efforts in the end of year science exams fully reflected the lack of effort I'd put in. I was at such a low ebb that I knew I couldn't go on this way. It wasn't just City who had some rebuilding work ahead.

7

Watershed

THE SUMMER WHEN a boy reaches fourteen, observes Humbert Humbert in Nabokov's Lolita, marks him for the rest of his life. And in August 1983, three months after Luton sent us down, I reached my fourteenth birthday. I wasn't affected in quite the way Humbert Humbert was - for those unfamiliar with the story, he retains a fascination for very young girls, inspired by the memory of his own first love affair. In fact, teenage love affairs were in depressingly short supply for me at this stage, but nonetheless, it was a tellingly influential period in my life.

In the few weeks immediately following my birthday, the pattern was set for much of what has followed. I'd spent the early part of the summer catching up on the schoolwork I'd neglected the previous academic year. But the big event for me came just three days after I'd reached the age of fourteen. As part of a school group, I made my first trip ever to Russia. We travelled on a package tour that took us to Moscow and Leningrad together with a brief jaunt to Suzdal, a small town about 200 miles east of Moscow notable for having eleven Orthodox monasteries. But while I was later to get to know the country much more intimately, that first trip definitely sowed seeds of fascination. And when I returned to Manchester, I saw City playing outside the top division of English football for the first time. And although I didn't appreciate it at the time, both of these elements would be part of a recurring pattern.

The Russia I visited that year was, of course, markedly different from the same country today. Until November 1982, Leonid Brezhnev was still alive, and even after his death, things continued along very much the same conservative track under his successor Yuri Andropov, formerly the head of the feared KGB. And I think part of the fascination, at that early stage when my acquaintance with Russian life was barely scratching the surface, lay in the fact that the Soviet Union, as a closed society, was a mystery not just to me but to more or less everyone else in the West. There was also an element of fear, too, which lent an edge of danger and thus excitement.

This was brought home to me on my first trip, and looking back, the incident undoubtedly contributed to the mystique and allure of the mighty monolith on the other side of the Iron Curtain. And ironically, I knew nothing about it until I was back on home shores. We discovered that all our parents had been frantically worried for us, because in the first week of our two-week stay, the Soviets had shot down a Korean passenger airliner killing all 269 people on board. It transpired that the plane had gone off course, and the Americans admitted that they did sometimes use such aircraft for spying purposes. Nevertheless, the West was livid at the ruthless way the Soviets had responded in a situation where innocent civilians were involved, and this was the time when President Reagan came out with his famous dismissal of the rival superpower as an "evil empire".

To me, though, it was no such thing, and it took on an entirely different aspect, that of a place where everyone, working feverishly to circumvent authority, has their own little scams. For this was when I had my first taste of a pervasive aspect of Russian life - the black market. The first time I visited, jeans and Western pop music were in demand, and good money in roubles was on offer. Later, as Gorbachev's reforms ensured the wider availability of these items, they simply wanted foreign currency and exchange transactions became all the rage. But deals which resulted in us receiving roubles were of limited practical value because we were hardly likely to queue for ages for the limited wares on sale in Russian state shops. The special foreign currency shops, known as beriozki, were a much better bet to stock the goods we wanted. I think it was more the excitement that we were looking for when we concluded these transactions.

At the time, doing deals on the black market seemed an incredibly risky, daring and exciting thing to be doing. It wasn't, of course, but the illusion was there - such was our impression of Soviet authoritarianism, it almost seemed as if we were risking a lengthy stretch in the daunting Lyubyanka prison for the sake of changing a few quid illicitly into roubles; we knew that in theory customs officers could check our customs declarations forms on arrival and departure and could request receipts from the beriozki to assess any discrepancy. As a result, dealing with the fartsovshchiki, as black marketers hanging round the hotels used to be called, always involved subterfuge. I remember on one occasion covering with towels any object in my hotel room I thought might be concealing a bug, and then turning on a cassette player to maximum volume before discussing a potential transaction. Another time, to change some foreign currency at the more advantageous illicit rate, I had to pick up the roubles that my co-conspirator had hidden in a plant pot in a hotel restaurant, and carefully place the sterling in the same place. And though all this was very low level indeed (quite why I imagined that the KGB would be remotely interested in me I'm not sure), it all seemed impossibly exotic to a sheltered fourteen-year-old.

What was indisputably not exotic was City's transfer policy. Over the summer, we'd appointed a new manager, Billy McNeill, who'd come from Celtic after the hapless Benson was axed in the wake of relegation. And given that he'd come to a club with no money to spend on players, the Scot had to resort to some creative dealing of his own as he sought to build a side capable of an instant top-flight return. As far as I know, no plant pots were involved, the new occupant of the Maine Road hot-seat instead opting to bring in players familiar to him from north of the border. Derek Parlane, a free-transfer striker, arrived from Leeds but before his career took a turn for the worse, he'd previously starred for Glasgow Rangers and Scotland. His new front partner, Jim Tolmie, was another Scot who had been signed from an obscure Belgian club for a cut-price fee. And a third Caledonian acquisition was Neil McNab, a midfielder whose fiery temperament was cited as the reason Brighton were prepared virtually to give him away.

When I returned to England from my eye-opening fortnight in the Soviet Union, the season was four games old. City's start was reasonably satisfactory, with two wins, a draw and a defeat from those games but it hardly indicated we'd sweep all before us. Nevertheless, as City had been in the old First Division for the eight years I'd been a fan, I felt that we didn't quite belong at the lower level, and I looked forward to our processional return to the top flight within a year.

My first viewing of McNeill's re-shaped team came in the third home game against Blackburn, and it seemed to indicate that my optimism was fully justified. This was Blackburn in their previous incarnation of homely Lancashire mill-town club rather than the 1990s outfit bankrolled by the colossal investment of the hugely wealthy industrialist Jack Walker. Nevertheless, they were one of the section's better teams, and they were, quite simply, demolished. That day, City ran out 6-0 winners with Parlane grabbing a hat-trick. Tolmie's early performances drew comparisons in certain newspaper reports with Kevin Keegan (though in part this assessment owed to a spectacularly unwise bubble perm). But the two hit it off marvellously in the early months of the 1983-84 season, and with more than 25 goals between them by Christmas, they threatened to fire City back to the big time. The Blues were some distance behind runaway leaders Sheffield Wednesday, but since we occupied second place, there was every reason to be optimistic about prospects for the New Year.

Everything wasn't as it seemed. The Soviet Union wasn't the impregnable edifice of military power everyone had thought. Its might in world terms had always depended on the perception of the threat its mighty armed forces could pose. But as the 1980s wore on, it became clear that the edifice was crumbling. Brezhnev had functioned almost as a living corpse for years. And when Andropov took over as the main man, he lasted only a few months before sustaining an illness that forced his removal, if not from his post, then from public life. When he died, the equally elderly and soporific Konstantin Chernenko assumed the position, though he, too, could stay alive for just barely a year. And all the while, necessary economic reforms were neglected, enormous problems for the future storing themselves up.

I next visited Russia two years later, in 1985. It was another four years before I was back, and then a further two after that. And these three visits spanned Mikhail Gorbachev's era. He had attempted to reform the old system, but what he really succeeded in doing was letting the Genie out of the bottle. Things would move on rapidly from hereon in.

On each subsequent trip, I would become more acquainted with Russian life. And on every occasion, its allure grew. Russia was to become the scene for great drama - both in terms of what I was observing and what I was living through. I witnessed military coups and financial and political crises, while I experienced several chaotic and turbulent personal attachments. But in 1983, all that was to come.

When I look back now, the best part of two decades later, I can see that with Manchester City, too, 1983 marked a watershed. Of course, up until that point we'd also had our dramas. But I'd been convinced that these would be nothing more than diverting interludes back to a more fitting level - if not the top of English football, where the club had been when I discovered it, then to somewhere close. In the early 1980s, we'd recovered from Malcolm Allison's surreal second coming to surge to the FA Cup final. Then we'd signed Trevor Francis and looked set for great things only to suffer a disappointing end to the season. Even when we sold him and were relegated, I assumed it was a temporary setback. By this stage I was used to the fact that life at Maine Road was something of a rollercoaster (ever since that derby disaster four years previously, I knew the team, whatever its individual components, wasn't to be trusted with any degree of confidence), but I was convinced there'd be plenty of highs to compensate for the lows.

In particular, I foresaw a triumphant march back to the First Division compensating for our dismal slide into the Second, and City had indulged the illusion. It clearly wasn't to be, however. An FA Cup defeat at Fourth Division Blackpool at the start of January presaged a miserable second half of the campaign. City did cling, if a little desperately, to a promotion place until mid-February. But then a home defeat against rivals Newcastle, who included McDermott, Waddle, Beardsley and Keegan, dropped them out of the promotion places for the first time in months. And, basically, that was that.

Tolmie and Parlane stopped scoring (they managed seven between them in the whole of the second half of the season) and there was a string of depressing defeats. When Charlton and then Huddersfield triumphed at Maine Road, the game was up. City limped home to a finish in fourth position - immediately outside the promotion places, but an immensely significant ten points behind Keegan's Newcastle. In truth, we hadn't even been close. So much for the Second Division being a blip that we'd put behind us with effortless ease.

When I write about this period in my life, I'm conscious of it being a watershed: it's now that elements that feature prominently in the story from this point make their first appearance. City are not just inconsistent and behaving in a bizarre fashion, but are starting to yo-yo between the divisions. I've discovered a location where my sense of the unusual can flourish. And, even in the academic arena, my attitude has been formed.

At first in secondary school, I'd worked hard to achieve. Then, after deciding I wasn't enjoying myself, I decided not to try at all, to reject any idea of educational progress, to live as I wished to. Now I found a compromise. I elected to work enough, to do just what was necessary to allow myself to progress to the next stage, to live a balanced life rather than one predicated either on scholarly achievement alone or one rejecting that aim totally. The conclusion then, as now, I saw as absolutely the right one.

I wouldn't say I was a different person in the summer of 1983. The essential features of my character were formed long before then. But I have no disagreement whatsoever with Humbert Humbert - it was an incredibly significant time for me.

When I look back, I can see how everything might have been otherwise. All it would have taken would have been for City to have failed to have conceded that late, late goal against Luton the previous May; for some of the things that went against me in the year 1982-83 to have turned out differently, and for my parents to have failed to find the cash for that school trip to Russia. But all those things did happen, and nothing was the same again.

8

Changes

IT'S UNREALISTIC to expect football to stand still. Life has changed immeasurably since the mid-1970s, when I first had even a slight awareness of a world outside my own little cocoon, so it's hardly surprising that the game has evolved too. Although that had happened to some extent in the decade since I'd watched my first game, by far the most striking changes came in the 1990s. Some of that was due to changing technology, but much derived from the way that problems plaguing the English game were tackled, and it was in the 1984-85 season that many of these problems came to a head.

English football had for years been suffering from declining crowds, poor spectator facilities and the phenomenon known as football hooliganism. The latter was, and still is, the subject of much discussion and writing, but it's something I knew little about. I rarely travelled to watch away games at this point, and witnessed very few incidents as I followed my usual match-day routine of parking about twenty minutes' walk from the ground with my dad, and then making our way through Alexandra Park, across Princess Parkway through to Lloyd Street South and then over to Maine Road. But the spectre of violence was always there, and television news bulletins always seemed to be full of the latest outbreak from somewhere or other. Crowds had been declining slowly but steadily for years, in part because of the off-field problems, but also because the product on the pitch wasn't especially thrilling. And with most clubs not exactly having a surfeit of cash, improving facilities for those fans who could be bothered to turn up wasn't exactly viewed as a priority.

It just seemed like business as usual, though, in the summer of 1984, as City prepared for the attempt to go at least one better than the previous campaign's fourth-placed finish. With Chelsea,

Sheffield Wednesday and Newcastle, three of the Second Division's biggest and best-supported clubs, having been promoted the previous year, there was a feeling that the competition would be a little less fearsome this time round. Billy McNeill had reinforced his squad by bringing in a promising young Welsh midfielder from Plymouth called David Phillips, and target man Tony Cunningham from Sheffield Wednesday, and we started off as bookies' favourites for promotion.

The first couple of games seemed to represent a satisfactory start. First we recovered to draw 2-2 at newly promoted Wimbledon having conceded two early goals to the kind of aerial bombardment that was to become their trademark. Then we strolled to an easy 3-0 win against a Grimsby side that had finished only a place below us the previous season. But those encouraging initial performances weren't maintained, and a series of poor results saw us anchored in mid-table at the end of October.

Thankfully, I felt that my own life was a little more on track. Having completed my 'O' levels, I had to choose the subjects that I was to study thereafter. At first, the choice hadn't been so irrevocable. The school had decided that I had to spend an extra year in the sixth form, because all of a sudden Oxford and Cambridge had changed their selection procedures and now wanted to make decisions on aspirant students before rather than after 'A' level. It was felt that I, and several colleagues, would be too young at that stage so we were held back for an additional year before beginning the 'A' level syllabus.

In fact, though I didn't formalise my 'A' level choices for a year, the die was cast. Having managed respectable performances in Maths, Physics and Chemistry, I was able, with some relief, to ditch these subjects and concentrate on the Arts side. I took 'O' levels in History and English Literature, having been constrained from doing so before because of my crammed two-year 'O' level syllabus. I studied politics, and took up Spanish, completing an 'O' level in the space of a year. And to reinforce my modern languages specialism, I also continued with French and Russian

Being able to drop the subjects I was worst at was a great source of relief, and I felt much happier as a result. And though City took a while to catch on, the team also soon hit their stride. The central defensive pair of Nicky Reid and future Republic of Ireland manager Mick McCarthy looked solid. The midfield of Wilson, Baker, Phillips and Gordon Smith had a good mix of industry and creativity, while the latter two especially chipped in with plenty of goals. And up front, new signing Jim Melrose hit a rich vein of scoring form no sooner had he been brought in to replace the disappointing Cunningham, who was offloaded to Newcastle. As a result of all this, there was a run of only two defeats in 21 games.

Towards the end of that run, on the first Saturday of March 1985, we went to the top of the table thanks to a win away to promotion rivals Blackburn, and the press reports of the game reflected my view that we now looked like promotion certainties. We also appeared to represent a good bet for the divisional title, though second-placed Oxford United could overtake us if they won games in hand. To end the fine sequence with a 3-0 defeat at Oxford's Manor Ground was disappointing, but at the time, it simply appeared that it would cause us to go up in second place rather than as champions. However, it heralded a six-match spell without a win in which we picked up three points. When an Easter Monday defeat by Leeds United at Maine Road was followed by what was unanimously rated as a dismal 4-1 thrashing at Grimsby (in truth, it's hard to imagine being caned by Grimsby as anything other than dismal), we looked set to miss out. Oxford and Birmingham were virtually up by this point. Portsmouth, managed by Alan Ball, a man later to become arguably City's most unpopular manager ever, had come up on the rails and were favourites for third place.

As it happened, there was a historical score to be settled here. In 1927, Portsmouth had edged out City in the closest ever promotion race. In those days, the old goal average system applied, and the south coast club took the last promotion spot available by a margin of one two hundredth (in decimal terms, 0.005) of a goal. We'd won our last game 8-0, but Portsmouth, whose own fixture was due to end fifteen minutes after ours, realised that one more goal would be sufficient for their purposes and duly scored it.

We stopped the rot in our 58-year bid for revenge with a 2-0 win over Sheffield United in a match of incredible tension. The goals came in quick succession in the final quarter of the game, both almost identical in construction, with defender Kenny Clements (of all people) and Jim Tolmie latching onto through-balls to slot home at the North Stand end. With Portsmouth losing on the same day, we were back in the hunt.

When we snatched a victory at Portsmouth's Fratton Park in the next game (I take particular pleasure now in recalling their manager's whinging about being robbed), that should have been that. We only needed four points from the last three games, of which two were at home against mid-table sides and the other was against a relegation certainty. Any normal side would have taken the points from the next two games and had done with it. Manchester City, however, are far from a normal side.

First of all, it was Oldham at home. Our ten men battled well in the second half after Andy May's sending off, and in the circumstances a goalless draw wasn't too bad a result. It meant we could have a nice Bank Holiday trip to Nottingham for the promotion clincher at Notts County's Meadow Lane. Going three goals down by half-time wasn't part of the plan. The eventual defeat allowed Pompey to make up five points on us in three days - we were now ahead of them only on goal difference. With Blackburn, Leeds and Brighton also still in with a chance of the last promotion place, it was obvious that we'd have to beat Charlton.

There was massive pressure for that last game, and City were badly hit by injuries and suspensions. With such a thin squad, a couple of injured players were forced to play when they probably shouldn't have. I, no doubt like most other Blues, was hoping for the best but secretly feared the worst. I was just praying that we could scrape a victory (and that Portsmouth wouldn't knock in seven or eight at Huddersfield to better our goal difference). In typical fashion, City delivered the unexpected again - a 5-1 win on a beautiful, sunny afternoon in front of a full house. For the enjoyment of the moment, it's still one of my top five City-watching experiences.

The day, however, was soured. At the same time as we were dismantling Charlton at Maine Road, a fire had started under the wooden Main Stand at Valley Parade. The stadium was packed as Bradford City, having already clinched promotion, celebrated their return to the Second Division in their home game against Lincoln. The match was abandoned, with the goalless result allowed to stand, but over 50 died. The same day, one fan was killed by a collapsing wall as fans rioted at the Birmingham v Leeds game. That outbreak of hooliganism followed a riot where Millwall 'fans' attacked the police on the pitch during a Cup tie at Luton, the television pictures of which seemed to indicate a new ferocity in this type of violence. And a couple of weeks later, 39 Juventus supporters died at the European Cup final between their team and Liverpool at Brussels' Heysel Stadium when a wall collapsed on them as they sought refuge from English fans running at them. UEFA reacted by banning all English teams from European club competitions.

The next few seasons post-Heysel were some of the most low-key in English football - to some extent, it felt as if everyone was going through the motions. But it was obvious that things couldn't go on in this way, and genuine fans made a real attempt to reclaim the game. One tangible manifestation of this was the appearance of fanzines, produced by fans themselves and a million miles removed from the anodyne complacency of official club publications. It was to take several years, and another major tragedy, before the powers that be really turned their attention to the way the game was headed but I think this was the point when it became clear that a change was needed.

I headed off for Russia again in the summer of 1985, having already opted to study languages in the sixth form. My path for at least the next couple of years had been chosen, English football's problems had been brought sharply into focus, and the likelihood that City would yo-yo between the divisions was also evident. We'd been promoted with a team that was not of top division quality and we had no money to put things right. It was clear we were in for an interesting couple of years.

9

Mancunian Bloke

MY 1985 TRIP to Russia, again with a school group, is one I remember as particularly enjoyable. We travelled overland, going by coach through Belgium, Germany, Austria and Hungary, before taking a train to Moscow. We also visited Volgograd (the renamed Stalingrad), and then moved down into the Ukraine, taking in Kiev and the border city of Lvov. We finally returned home by a different route that took in both the Czech and Slovak parts of what was then Czechoslovakia, before a marathon drive home in one single session from a stop-off in southern Germany. Few anecdotes leap out from my memories, but I remember we had more freedom to meet ordinary Russians, which we hadn't at all on the first trip. We were taken to meet members of the Komsomol (the Young Communist league) in Moscow and again in Volgograd, where a friend and I continued to meet a couple of them on each subsequent evening during the rest of our stay. It probably helped that they were the delectable Oksana and Irina, but whatever the reason, when I returned home I knew I wasn't done with the place.

Rather than plotting my return, however, my priority when I got back from Russia to find City nestled comfortably and satisfactorily in mid-table after their opening five matches was to begin the 'A' level syllabus. I'd already begun to develop a sense of the way language reveals much about those who speak it, and that would only be reinforced by my academic choices. The fact that the French for sportsmanship is "le fair-play" makes clear that they've had to import the phrase, which in turn tends to indicate that it's a slightly foreign concept to start off with. And not much commentary is needed on what the etymological relation between the word for 'work' (rabota) and the word for 'slavery' (rabstvo) says about the Russian psyche.

Football, incidentally, tends to have a language of its own. Everyone knows the clichés like "over the moon" and "sick as a parrot". And it doesn't take too sophisticated an analysis to pick up a few other key phrases; the manager is usually referred to as "the gaffer", while the "gaffer" will invariably talk about his "lads", even when they're in their late thirties, balding and with several kids. Indeed, one expert summariser has almost created a language of his own, which is explained further on the web page located at http://www.dangerhere.com/ronglish.htm. Ron Atkinson can come up with sentences which sound like gibberish even to football fans - who, for instance, could understand, "The winger's given the full-back a lollipop there and spotters badge for picking out the big man at the front stick. Little eyebrows and it's past the keeper." It actually describes a winger beating his man and then crossing to the near post, where the centre forward glances a header across the goalkeeper and into the far corner. Incidentally, if we're going to get all psycholinguistic with Big Ron, then the inference I draw from his use of language is that he doesn't give a toss whether or not anyone understands him.

In 1985, there weren't many, if any, Ron Atkinson commentaries as he was still in football management, but I was conscious that the manner in which I had to assimilate foreign languages was enabling me to understand consciously the skills and processes I had absorbed naturally in my own mother tongue. And I understood that it should be a cause of particular relief that I'd grown up in the north. This, I consider, has given me a much more versatile speech capacity than I'd have had as a southerner. Of course, I know that not everyone from south of Watford calls a spade an excavation implement, but I do think that in the north, there's more bluntness and, correspondingly, less bullshit. For instance, my mum, when cooking, always used to repeat a phrase her grandmother had used. "When it's brown," she'd reflect, "it's done. When it's black, it's buggered." It's hard to argue.

However, even in the summer of 1985, I'd already progressed far enough in education to be aware that such direct commentary would not be welcomed in my chosen fields of endeavour. This seemed a great pity to me, since I regarded this unpretentious observational voice gifted to me by my hometown as having great value. I was aware that when speaking at home, rather than in a classroom or in an essay, the language I used was quite different, and I really didn't think the analysis suffered from it at all. Later, a friend and I created a character that embodied the traits I admired but had to eschew. We called him "Mancunian Bloke", and through him, we expressed what we really thought and felt.

I was actually living in Russia when he and I made this connection, and I remember that I was explaining the aftermath of the 1998 financial crisis to him. There was much concern over the impact of the withdrawal of capital from overseas. "All the foreign investors have cleared off," I explained, though I suspect I may have used one of Mancunian Bloke's more earthy Anglo-Saxonisms, "so there's no money here any more." I was amazed at the number of 1,500-word articles I read which essentially said nothing of any more significance.

Mancunian Bloke isn't particularly warm-hearted. He'd have had no sympathy at all with Portsmouth when they found out in May 1985 that their last-day win at Huddersfield had been in vain. It's not that he has particular scorn for those from the great naval city - indeed, he recognises that they are as likely as any to treat their pets well and help old ladies across the road. But he's witnessed enough Manchester City disasters to have little time for fans of other clubs when they bemoan their lot. So he would have chanted, "Staying down, staying down, staying down," derisively at the crestfallen Pompey support that day. He's not among those who lament the passing in the modern-day game of Corinthian values of sportsmanship.

Around this time, it wasn't just Portsmouth Football Club who were in Mancunian Bloke's radar. And one object of his disdain was much closer to home - Peter Swales. The Manchester City chairman cut an odd figure. He had a peculiar fondness for cowboy boots, and also had a ludicrous comb over hairstyle which drew attention to his baldness rather than providing the intended camouflage. Best-selling author and City fan Colin Shindler took a leaf out of Mancunian Bloke's book when he wrote that Swales "made City look like shit." He did, but Mancunian Bloke would add that appearances were the least of Swales's problems; he made Manchester City shit, full stop.

It didn't take much linguistic awareness to be able to describe the progress of Manchester City in 1985-86. A knowledge of the word 'boring' would have been enough. McNeill had prepared for life back in the top flight by making three signings. Mark Lillis, a striker from Huddersfield, was a wholehearted trier and a lifelong City fan, though he was hardly a man to give the country's best defenders sleepless nights before they played against him. He was, however, by some distance the best of the new arrivals. Ex-Manchester United midfielder Sammy McIlroy was so far past his best that even Stoke City were prepared to boot him out on a free transfer. And the cut-price Rotherham centre half Nigel Johnson was so injury prone that he managed only four appearances in his entire Maine Road career. His occasional displays didn't hint that he'd have made much of an impact had his fitness been better.

The eight points won from five games while I'd been on my summer European jaunts didn't stop City from being in the bottom three at the start of November, but then a surprising run into February of just a couple of defeats left us pretty much safe from relegation. The highlight was a Boxing Day win over the eventual champions Liverpool, although in truth it was the kind of game for which the phrase "daylight robbery" might have been invented. Battered for nearly all of the ninety minutes, we scored with our only attack of note, and then hung on for dear life. No matter, by the end of February we were more or less assured of avoiding relegation - which was a good job, because in an awful last thirteen games, we didn't win once, a run that appeared to hint at things to come.

Such struggles were disappointing. City had the fourth-highest average attendance in England in 1985-6. Only Liverpool (the champions and FA Cup winners that season), Everton (runners-up in both competitions) and Manchester United (perennially the best-supported club in the land) drew bigger crowds. Arsenal and Spurs, the other self-appointed members of the 'Big Five' group of clubs who regarded themselves as an elite, couldn't compete with us in terms of gates. I draw attention to this statistic not to boast of the quality of Manchester City's support, but merely seek to illustrate the gap in resources between ourselves and clubs with whom, in theory, our fan base ought to have generated the funds to compete.

City's financial position had never really recovered from the profligacy of the days of Allison and Bond. But it was Swales who had signed the cheques - so even if the judgement of those in the managerial hot-seat was often dubious, the chairman had to take his share of the blame (in any case, it was he who'd appointed the managers). Moreover, Allison has since alleged (although as Swales has now died, we're never likely to know the absolute truth) that it was Swales who negotiated many of the more outlandish transfer fees, such as those for Steve Daley and Kevin Reeves.

Swales had a track record of talking big but failing to deliver. He frequently promised funds for team strengthening - yet after the sale of Trevor Francis, the club remained well and truly in austerity mode. And he announced, also in the 1981-2 season, plans to make Maine Road into one of the most impressive grounds in the whole of Europe. The work was supposed to be performed over a five-year period. Stage one was completed, providing a new Main Stand with an incongruous corrugated roof, but then the money ran out and no more was ever said on the matter. The man's attitude and public pronouncements made clear that he viewed himself as the best, indeed the only, man for the job of restoring City's former glories.

There were always various rumours of potential investors waiting in the wings. Of course, they'd have wanted a commensurate say in how things were run, and Swales, given that he viewed the club as his own personal fiefdom, would never countenance such a move. His incompetence and intransigence were to mark the City story over a long period, but if he'd have stepped down in 1986, he'd have denied me my only opportunity to make the headlines through football. Needless to say, Mancunian Bloke was there to lend a hand.

10

Keeping Gordon Hobson
Out of the Headlines

IT WAS OBVIOUS from the outset that 1986-87 would be a season of struggle. The improbable winning run in the middle of the previous campaign did nothing to disguise the fact; the wretched form that preceded and followed certainly offered a better indication of the team's quality. The club's perilous financial position meant that McNeill was obliged to wheel and deal over the summer, and instead of adding players of quality who might make a difference, we ended up with Perry Suckling, Trevor Christie and Robert Hopkins. And while David Phillips and Mark Lillis, traded for Suckling and Christie respectively, weren't exactly top-notch stars, worse players certainly stayed at the club. It didn't bode well.

The main hope for the future came in the form of the youth side, who won the FA Youth Cup in particularly satisfying fashion by beating Manchester United in the final and who were an unusually fine group of young players. A club will normally regard itself as lucky if even a couple of its juniors make the breakthrough at any one time but our 'class of 86' crop was far more fertile. Two of them went on to play for England, three more showed their mettle in the top flight and another couple made their mark lower down the leagues. The total transfer fees they generated came to about £4 million - chicken feed in contemporary football, but very big money in those days.

Chairman Peter Swales seemed to believe that these players would take the First Division by storm, but despite their undoubted ability, this was never realistic. They needed to be nurtured carefully, not thrown into a struggling team of highly dubious quality in the guise of potential saviours. Frustrated once more by the paucity of his transfer budget, McNeill quit to take over at Aston Villa. Even though he was greeted with derision on his return to Maine Road, a match that produced a rare City win, I could fully understand his decision. (It wasn't to be a happy move, though - his new team was relegated that season and, as unpopular with the Villa Park faithful as his abandonment of City made him at Maine Road, he was sacked).

Meanwhile, McNeill's assistant Jimmy Frizzell took over the club his former boss had left, but even though some of the youngsters were showing definite signs of promise, the team was in desperate straits. City had struggled all season and a couple of weeks previously had crashed 4-0 away to fellow relegation candidates Leicester (an abject performance, though we'd probably ploughed even greater depths in the 5-0 defeat at Charlton over Christmas). I decided it was time to take action.

The 1986-87 season had marked the beginning of a new Saturday afternoon sports show on Piccadilly Radio, as the local Manchester commercial station was then called. The programme was presented by DJ and City fan James H. Reeve, with ex-United manager Tommy Docherty as the expert pundit, and I enjoyed it tremendously. Reeve also presented a late-night phone-in on weekdays and I was an avowed fan. His dry but mordant wit was perfect for dealing with the post-pub callers, and it made for compelling listening. I was especially proud to hear that the brother of a school-mate working as an English teacher in Germany thought the same, so much so that he used tapes of the show in his classes. I found it a delightful thought that the English language role models for the kids in some small German town were pissed up Mancunians debating in slurred tones, and not always rationally, the existence of UFOs or the treatment of the working class in Thatcher's Britain.

On the Saturday show, Docherty was an ideal foil, forthright in his opinions and equipped with a string of one-liners. It was he who was once told after a run of poor results in the 1960s at Aston Villa that notorious chairman Doug Ellis was right behind him, and replied with the observation that, "I'd rather have you in front of me where I can see you."

As winter drew on, there was plenty of scope for Reeve to reflect on his own team's failings and for Docherty to poke fun at them. After taking over, Frizzell ditched McNeill's summer buys, Hopkins and Christie, and made several cut-price signings of his own, but still the team remained anchored in or around the relegation zone. That 5-0 defeat at Charlton over Christmas showed things were bad. And when the young striker Paul Moulden, who'd bagged four or five important goals in the first half of the season, sustained a serious back injury on the first Saturday of the New Year, our hopes took a serious dive.

It was obvious that a new front man was needed, and equally plain that the cash just wouldn't be forthcoming from Swales. At the time, there was much talk of interested parties willing to invest in the club, and though we'll never know how genuine they were, the chairman evidently didn't care. He was staying, whether or not someone more suitable or with cash to invest stepped forward.

Thus it was that when the spring of 1987 arrived, plenty of fans had come round to Mancunian Bloke's view that Swales was a "clueless tosser". By this point, we were staring relegation in the face. One thing about being a City fan is that if you want to protest or complain, they normally give you plenty of scope. I felt that Swales' position should come under close scrutiny, and I decided to take the debate to a wider public.

When I was looking for a vehicle to air my views, Reeve and Docherty's show seemed the natural choice. There were only a couple of problems - I wasn't sure if I had the bottle to go on a radio phone-in and I couldn't guarantee being at home at the right time even if I did, since I was usually on my way to or from a City match when the phone-in was on air.

I decided that I'd write a letter and structured my comments carefully. After a cursory introduction, I moved on to detailed arguments - I knew this section wouldn't be read out, but I wanted to show that some thought had actually gone into shaping my views, demonstrating that mine wasn't just a knee-jerk reaction to a poor league placing. Finally came a short closing paragraph, with my bones of contention recited in concise and, I hoped, listener-friendly bullet-point form. I felt pleased with my efforts.

In truth, I was only partially successful. What I had felt was a powerful conclusion had been ignored, and I considered that some of my most telling comments were overlooked in the ensuing debate. Nevertheless, when I listened later to my mum's recording of the programme's opening hour I wasn't entirely dissatisfied. The letter had been read out early on, and had ensured that Alex Ferguson's early troubles at Old Trafford were scarcely mentioned as discussion on the programme centred round City's plight.

My belief in my potential as an opinion former thus fortified, I considered what other outlet might allow for an effective further expression of my views. Mancunian Bloke helped me to decide that a more direct form of protest was in order, and the home match against Southampton in early April was nominated as the appropriate occasion. Before this fixture, we'd gone ten league games without a win, and had just suffered that shameful 4-0 battering away to relegation rivals Leicester. The purse strings had been loosened to sign the promising forward Paul Stewart from Blackpool, but it looked like a clear case of too little, too late. In these circumstances, I was confident that the planned protest would catch the popular mood.

At this time, I used to attend matches with a group of friends and all sympathised with my views, so a couple of them readily pitched in with assistance. One was responsible for producing all the plays put on at our school. He therefore had access to the props and to an assortment of other materials for the construction of scenery. Most crucially for our purposes, in the eclectic hoard of items under his custody were some pots of paint. Another friend brought in a large white sheet, and this gave us everything we needed.

The design of our banner was the subject of much careful thought. We especially wanted to emphasise that our complaints arose from a sense of concern over the club's long-term well-being rather than from poor results in the short term. We were anxious, too, to reiterate that our dismay over Swales's stewardship wouldn't detract from our enduring and resolute support of the team. In the centre, we painted Mancunian Bloke's simple, bold, black legend "Up or down - Swales must go" - in other words, even if the team avoided relegation, we felt the issue needed to be addressed. We painted "MCFC" in sky blue down each side of our sheet to affirm our loyalty to the club itself. The banner was completed on the Thursday before the Southampton match. On the Friday, I took it home and awaited the weekend, always keenly anticipated, with more excitement than normal.

I met my friends just after two o'clock, outside the Kippax terrace from where we would watch the game. This was earlier than usual, but we wanted our declaration on view for the greatest possible length of time. We normally stood roughly two thirds of the way back and two thirds of the way along towards the Platt Lane end. On this occasion, we held our customary line, but headed right to the front, determined to affix our handiwork to the perimeter fencing to ensure maximum exposure. This we did, under the watchful eye of a policeman who satisfied himself that we posed no security risk. For the next ten or fifteen minutes, our opinion of Peter Swales was on show to all early entrants into the stadium.

At this point a second policeman appeared. I heard a voice tell him over his walkie-talkie that the banner had to be removed. Needless to say, we were aggrieved, and I attempted to argue, putting forward a vigorous treatise on the importance of civil liberties in a democratic society. It was to no avail, and Mancunian Bloke risked ejection from the stadium by stating, justifiably but recklessly, that any law enforcement officer wishing to restrict this basic and fundamental right was a "Fascist". On reflection, I concede that the extrapolation of the incident from its original context to a symptom of the wider decay of the British democratic tradition may have been marginally exaggerated and melodramatic.

Accepting defeat, albeit with little grace, we removed the banner, and retreated back up the terracing. We resigned ourselves to the fact that our efforts had been in vain, and the three of us were muttering darkly about the injustice of it all. What we didn't appreciate was that Gordon Hobson would intervene on our behalf.

This was a Southampton side packed with star names, with players like Peter Shilton, Mark Wright and Danny Wallace in the line-up. But the damage was done by the little-known Hobson, a journeyman striker who spent most of his career in the lower reaches of the Football League with Lincoln and who also played for Grimsby. His one shot at the big time came after being bought by Southampton, and that day at Maine Road was his finest hour.

After an attack-minded City side went ahead early on, some slack defending gifted the balding and unassuming Hobson an equaliser just before half time. The unlikely assassin completed a hat-trick in the second period as Southampton raced into a 4-1 lead - City's defence had collapsed in a manner which would make the England cricket team's middle order batting appear a bastion of determination and resolve in comparison. A late goal reduced the arrears but didn't disguise the fact that City were now clearly destined for the Second Division; regrettably, no team that could make Gordon Hobson look like a cross between Pele, Cruyff and Maradona could entertain serious hopes of top-flight survival.

Of course, I desperately wanted City to win - this did feel like a make-or-break game for our receding prospects of survival - so his actions were most unwelcome. However, I have little doubt that if Hobson hadn't enjoyed his finest hour that day, our moment wouldn't have come either. As the final whistle drew near, word spread that fans were already gathering on the forecourt outside the Main Stand to express their fury. We were as upset with everything as anyone, so it was an easy decision to head round to the front of the ground.

Absolutely justifiably in view of the way the club has been run, such manifestations of anger have long since become de rigueur at Manchester City. For example, I have an abiding memory of the last home game I attended before leaving England to work abroad, as a managerless and directionless team slipped to a dismal home defeat by Oxford on a miserable November night in

1996. At the end of the match, I raced off to Lloyd Street South with my long-time City-watching companion Greg (the provider of the sheet) to catch a bus into central Manchester for a farewell drink with some old friends. As I turned to take one last look at the old stadium, I was confronted by the reassuringly familiar sight of a large crowd forming outside the main entrance to give vent to utter disgust.

Just under a decade previously, this type of occasion was much more of a rarity, and the one at that Southampton match is certainly the first I remember participating in. Regrettably, on occasions I've seen the protests turn violent. However, the peace was never breached on the afternoon we unfurled our banner and marched through the bottleneck behind the ground at the North Stand end towards the forecourt. By this point, Gordon Hobson was no doubt relaxing in a nice warm bath, imagining the future glories to which he'd progress after years of spadework in the game's lower reaches and contemplating all the "Hobson's choice" headlines which would dominate the next morning's newspapers.

As we turned the corner towards the front of the stadium, a few hundred fans were already gathered, but many more were coming from all directions. The press estimated that the eventual number swelled to more than two thousand and fans seeing our banner immediately identified with it. We quickly found ourselves at the head of a column which swept to the front of the ever-growing mass around the crush barriers surrounding the main entrance. The protest had more staying power than most I've attended, and half an hour after the final whistle, the crowd scarcely seemed to have thinned. The chanting was heart-felt and vociferous, though there were interjections of humour too, as anyone who's followed City for any length of time would probably expect. By half past five, people were starting to drift away, and as six o'clock neared, we too elected to give up the ghost. However, there was a hard core determined to remain defiant, and many of them expressed disappointment at the impending departure of the proclamation which had been a focus for the assembled multitude's feelings. Greg turned back with the banner and, to a hero's reception, he took his place at the head of the remaining protesters.

The irony was that the catalyst for the furore had been Gordon Hobson's performance, and yet the spontaneous show of supporter discontent had the effect of limiting recognition for his feats. The papers on Sunday and Monday were not emblazoned with weak puns based on the name Hobson, as the match became almost a footnote in most reports. Media interest centred round the demonstration, with the newspapers featuring photographs and detailed accounts. Regrettably, our banner wasn't visible in any of the pictures, but its existence was reported in both The Sun and the Daily Mirror, the two daily papers with the widest circulation. The Sun even went as far as to reproduce our slogan word for word. I believe Greg still has the cutting.

Obviously, as a child I'd dreamed of featuring in City match reports for my heroic on-field exploits, but I knew from an early age that it would never happen. The day after Gordon Hobson's finest hour was as close as I'll ever get, and that's why I can still recollect a desperate home defeat by Southampton which is no doubt long-forgotten by almost everyone.

11

Expectations Unfulfilled

EVEN THOUGH OUR protest at the Southampton match had received extensive publicity, our efforts were in vain. Peter Swales was to remain a divisive and controversial figure at the club for some years to come - though the off-field state of the club when he eventually gave way showed that Mancunian Bloke's withering assessment was right all along. But in August 1987, he was still in charge, and I held him responsible for the fact that, less than forty-eight hours after I'd discovered that my 'A' level grades were sufficient to meet the terms of a conditional offer I'd received from Cambridge University eight months earlier, City kicked off the new season back in the Second Division at home to Plymouth. The failure of our campaign to unseat Swales led me to feel that, as I prepared to begin my first university term, I was branching out and moving on, but City weren't.

In fact, I didn't make the most of Cambridge. I enjoyed myself, certainly, but hadn't had the kind of wild time experienced by friends who went to other universities. And while there's no doubt that Oxbridge is a dream for anyone with the desire to throw themselves into the study, for its own sake, of an academic subject in which they have a passionate interest, I hadn't been such a person. In my case, course work had been nothing more than a diversion when I got bored with Radio One's 'Steve Wright in the Afternoon' or between an evening meal and a trip to the pub.

I began my university career in October 1987, having had the most enjoyable summer I'd had in my life to that point. First, I went with five friends on an InterRail holiday around Europe. I recall dining out on the stories from that trip when I finally went to university, though regrettably I have relatively few memories now. I do remember arriving in Paris on the eve of Bastille Day hopeful of finding a bed for the night but eventually having to sleep on the street outside the Gare du Nord. It proved a futile task given the noise from what seemed like Europe's biggest party in one of the flats opposite, and the rather unsporting tendency of passing motorists to hurl fireworks in the direction of the hapless row of backpackers in which we'd taken our place. I remember several overnight train journeys when we tried in vain to fall asleep in an upright position. I remember the unholy row in Rome when the original five were reduced in number by two and how thereafter the remaining three of us sheltered from the sweltering midday sun in the shadow of the Coliseum, taking it in turns to dash across the manic highway to buy bottled water and takeaway pizzas from a stall in the metro station opposite. There was a 6 a.m. crossing over the Baltic as we headed from Cologne to Copenhagen, and a memorable, eye-opening couple of days in Amsterdam. And back in Paris on our last night, having managed this time to be organised enough to have booked a room before leaving Holland, we sat and drank beer in the shadow of the Eiffel Tower, anticipating picking up our 'A' level results less than 36 hours later.

Next was a family holiday in France, followed by a tour of the US and Canada with a brass band in which I played trombone. I stayed in a small town in Michigan with an elderly couple, Karl and Stella, who'd arrived in the States after the War. Karl, who died recently, insisted on greeting me and the two colleagues also staying with him with a glass of cold beer every time we arrived back from a trip out. We may not have seen the Grand Canyon, Disneyland and the Statue of Liberty, but I felt we'd been given a good insight into real-life small-town America. So the single word that would spell out what I felt about the summer was "adventure", and I was looking for more of the same at Cambridge. I'd come to the wrong place, and ended up feeling I'd traded in my chance to do a course that interested me in a place that suited me for the benefit of an impressive name on my CV.

At Maine Road, meanwhile, after a slow start (we were in seventeenth place when beaten at Ipswich in mid-October), events were gathering pace. There was yet another new manager, Mel Machin, a young coach eager to break into management who had arrived from Norwich after his predecessor Frizzell had been moved into a more administrative role. Unlike many in whose footsteps he was following, the new man wasn't comfortable in the media spotlight, but his team did his talking for him. After a patchy start, they simply caught fire. He had based the side almost entirely around the youngsters and they repaid him with an incredible twelve-game unbeaten run, which yielded the spectacular tally of 44 goals.

For almost three months, we just couldn't stop scoring. We put four past the early Division Two pacesetters Bradford on their own ground, three against each of the First Division teams - Forest and Watford - we beat in the League Cup, six against Plymouth in the admittedly meaningless Full Members' Cup and, most spectacularly of all, reached double figures when Huddersfield visited Maine Road, three players notching hat-tricks in the 10-1 win. It was breathtaking stuff, and it even prompted several articles in the southern editions of the national press on which I was now obliged to rely for information.

This didn't exactly mirror my experience at Cambridge. I was expecting moving away from home for the first time to be thrilling. As it was, I found it OK - nothing more or less. So though I don't really have any bad memories, and I'm happy enough to go back, the anticipated "best days of my life" never materialised. I suppose that, having travelled all summer, and met a whole range of new, interesting and different people, I wasn't much taken by almost all of my contemporaries being young, white middle-class Brits. Of course, I made some very good friends, several of whom I'm still in contact with today, but I never felt at home there.

Some people have a problem with Oxbridge traditions, but I wasn't one of them. I actually quite enjoyed the dressing up in gowns and dining in the oak-panelled halls. I think I was just a little disappointed with the fact that there wasn't much diversity in terms of where people came from. Another symptom was that everything seemed to be taken so seriously; I was keen to pursue my trombone playing, but never really found an outlet where fun rather than achievement was prized above all. And having wanted to escape from a male-only environment for years, it was a disappointment that the male-female ratio at my college was still so skewed (70% of my intake were men). I found I learned much more about life from the voluntary work I was doing, which had nothing to do with the university. Every Monday evening I used to help out at a social club for the mentally handicapped, and I also attended various summer camps. This was like coming into another world, one with more colour and lacking the constraints of the one I inhabited for the other 165 hours of the week.

I also wasn't helped by a complete lack of interest in my studies. I was interested in French and Russian, of course, but not in the way they were taught at Cambridge. The first year's course was more language-based, which suited my interests, but I didn't really appreciate having to translate the turgid nineteenth-century passages we were usually given - or the inaccessibly highbrow essay titles we were asked to write on. It was as if someone was trying to strangle from the subject all possible life and any potential relevance to anything in the outside world. As if to prove the point, the later years of my degree course coincided with a turbulent and fascinating period in Russian history. I don't remember those events even being discussed on my degree course.

The way we had to study literature was also a source of contention from my point of view. I wouldn't seek to belittle people who devote their energies to the pursuit of literary criticism but it certainly isn't for me. I remember at one point having to write an essay on how Tolstoy uses the structure of "Anna Karenina" to reinforce the themes of the novel. To me, this was like trying to work out how the magician performs his tricks and it diminished my enjoyment of the work; I find response, not analysis, the key to a satisfying consumption of a literary work. So being forced to research and write reams on a subject which held no attraction didn't make me a happy bunny. I wished I could have taken Mancunian Bloke's approach. "I'm sorry," he'd have written if instructed to produce that Tolstoy essay, "I just couldn't give a fuck."

To be honest, I found it all rather pretentious. I remember writing about Flaubert's character Emma Bovary, and noting that she was a reckless, irresponsible woman driven to frankly unwise financial and marital indiscretions by the crushing tedium of her life with her staid but decent husband. This is true, but Mancunian Bloke could make exactly the same point in a much more telling fashion. She is, he'd observe, a bored housewife who's absolutely gagging for it. If I couldn't have pursued my own subject I'd actually have been much more interested in an academic subject like politics or sociology, both of which I'd have preferred to be studying. I didn't turn to the Cambridge equivalent - a course called Social and Political Sciences - because I felt it was looked down on there, which I suppose is just another example of how out of step I was with the ethos of the academic authorities.

Fortunately, City managed to make my Cambridge years a little more interesting. Needless to say, in addition to the ups of the first autumn of my university career, there were plenty of downs. The spectacular winning run of the autumn of 1987 came to a halt in dramatic style; after the team had taken the lead against a physical Crystal Palace side, goalkeeper Eric Nixon conceded a penalty and was sent off, and an inevitable defeat followed. There ensued a six-game losing sequence over Christmas, and form continued to be erratic for the rest of the season. The main excitement came in knockout football as we reached the quarter-final stages of both Cup competitions, losing to Everton and Liverpool respectively. The next campaign, though, was much more successful in terms of the principal objective.

Over the summer, City sold striker Paul Stewart for big money. They used some of the proceeds to bring four new players to add strength to all areas of the team. The youngsters had another season's experience under their belts, and so optimism was high ahead of the new campaign. After an unlucky defeat at Hull on the opening day, they managed to puncture my faith by producing a stupendously awful display to lose 4-1 at home to Oldham in the first home game. They recovered and by mid-March were, along with Chelsea, absolute certainties to be promoted avoiding the play-offs. Then the youngsters showed that they understood this was not the Manchester City way. They didn't disintegrate completely, but the championship form of the past few months was certainly a thing of the past as Crystal Palace started to win every game and look as though they would consign City to the play-offs.

There were some quite remarkable games towards the end of that season. There was a win at Oxford in which we took a 3-2 lead eight minutes after half-time having been two down at the break. We then did our best to gift the home team a goal before getting bored and deciding that if they weren't prepared to take advantage of our kamikaze defending, we may as well march up the other end and score ourselves. Then we ground out a draw against Palace despite the handicap of playing half the game with an outfield player in goal. We threw away a golden chance to clinch promotion against Bournemouth by incredibly allowing them to snatch a draw after we'd enjoyed a three-goal half-time lead; the equaliser came from a penalty eight minutes into injury time. It meant we needed a draw away to Bradford in our final game to clinch promotion.

As we came out for the second half against Palace a goal up with emergency 'keeper Nigel Gleghorn between the sticks instead of the injured Andy Dibble, I decided that staying in my room and listening to the radio would be simply too tense. For the whole of the second half I was to be found tramping round the streets of Cambridge to avoid having to listen. It was the same as the second period wore on against Bradford. We'd gone behind on 23 minutes and seemed to be making a Herculean effort to find an equaliser. But as missed chance followed near miss, I decided I couldn't take any more. I was due to interrupt my friend Andy's revision so we could listen to the scores coming in together (his team Wrexham needed a win to clinch a play-off position the same day). After half an hour's nervous pacing around Christ's Pieces and Midsummer Common, I summoned up the courage, and he was waiting with a piece of important news.

When I think back, that's the most dramatic I can ever remember the place being. I didn't dislike it, or anything. I just wasn't really enthused by it. And that's why my favourite memory of Cambridge is walking up Jesus Lane where Andy had a room in a college-owned house on the last day of the season to see him hanging out of the window yelling as soon as I came into hearing range that Trevor Morley had clinched promotion by sliding in to divert the ball past the Bradford goalkeeper three minutes from the end of the season.

12

Five-One

GIVEN THAT I WAS studying Modern Languages, I had to spend the third year of my degree course abroad. So as Machin's promising young side were sweeping and then stuttering towards promotion, I had to give some attention to organising what I was going to do for the next year of my life. As with City the previous year, it didn't always look as though the outcome to my search would be satisfactory, but everything came together pleasingly in the end. First, though, it was time for another few weeks in Russia.

It was my most adventurous visit yet. At the time, independent travel over there was a real rarity, but I'd decided that travelling outside an organised group would both be interesting and would help me towards the objectives of my degree. My friend Andy, the guy who imparted the good news the previous May, was a medic so didn't have the same academic reason to make the trip but was keen to see at first hand the place I kept talking about. We travelled by train from London Victoria direct to Moscow, disembarking only for the crossing between Dover and Ostende. We'd then made straight for Leningrad where we'd spent a few days before returning to Moscow. On our way back home, we stopped off in Berlin, Cologne, Brussels and Bruges. However, the main part of the trip was a journey on the trans-Siberian railway to Khabarovsk in the Russian Far East.

We spent six days non-stop on the train (not surprisingly, we later returned to Moscow by plane), but it was an experience I wouldn't swap for the world, even though conditions were not exactly luxurious. The toilet facilities were basic to say the least, and the adjacent washbasin was the only place we could wash. Moreover, the restaurant car was scarcely plentifully stocked. The waiter, who used to calculate the prices on an abacus he'd refer to as his "russkiy kompiutr" (a joke that was funny the first time but not after hearing it three times a day for nearly a week), made us go through the same ritual every day. He'd show us the menu and we'd ask for the dish that took our fancy. On being told it wasn't available, we'd express our second preference, only to be met again with a polite shake of the head. Finally, we'd ask him to indicate what was actually available from the many options on offer, and would habitually have to make our selection from a short-list of one.

The encounter with him also summed up something that always happens to Manchester City fans when they travel overseas. When he heard where I came from, he greeted me warmly. "Bobby Charlton, George Best!" he exclaimed. Even if it's inevitable, it's profoundly irritating to be reminded of our neighbours so regularly. I tried to explain that the City of Bell, Lee and Summerbee had a run of only two league defeats out of fifteen against United in the late 1960s and early 1970s, but it didn't seem to sink in. But given what he could have done to my food, discretion was the better part of valour, and I refrained from administering a friendly warning in the style of Mancunian Bloke: "You mention Bobby fucking Charlton once more and I'll shove that fucking abacus right up your … "

The steward in the restaurant car wasn't the only reason the journey was memorable. We shared a four-berth compartment with two Red Army soldiers, who willingly shared with us the copious home-made provisions their mothers had packed up for them. Their remarkable spontaneous hospitality was coupled with a natural curiosity - at the time, they, like most provincial Russians, had never encountered foreigners. They were fascinated not just by the fact that we were from another culture and had been raised under a different political system, but also by the personal stereos and instamatic cameras we had with us. I have countless photos from that trip of the interminably wide Siberian rivers we crossed - our new friends delighted in activating the automatic wind-on facility on my camera, having never seen anything comparable before.

It helped that in our carriage were the only other foreigners in the train - a group of twelve Swiss. The presence of a block of foreigners encouraged many Russians from other parts of the train to make their way through to carriage twelve. Fortuitously, the Swiss had with them the biggest store of alcohol I'd ever seen in my life, so we effectively hosted a week-long party. It had a lubricious effect on my Russian, since I was the only one of the foreigners with even a basic knowledge of the language, and I became unofficial translator. This, coupled with a chance meeting in Khabarovsk with Yury, a Muscovite and one of the first wave of Russian businessmen (he sold timber from the Far East in his home city), who invited us to his home after our return to the capital, provided a much more fascinating insight into life in Russia than any afforded by my previous visits.

We headed home taking the time to stop off at points in Western Europe. First of all we took a train to Berlin, and then stopped off in Cologne, where we arrived on the morning of Saturday, 23rd September 1989. Our first stop at the station was to leaf through that morning's English papers for football news. By this point, I'd already discovered that City had won just one of their seven games of the season so far, and news of the League Cup defeat at Brentford on the night we arrived in Germany didn't seem to bode well. Now I learnt that for the game that afternoon, City would be missing goalkeeper Andy Dibble, midfielder Neil McNab and striker Clive Allen. I was most concerned by the latter's absence. "We've no chance," I told Andy, sagely. "I just can't see where the goals will come from." It was particularly painful to reach such a verdict given that our opponents were Manchester United.

We had no access to a radio, so to take our minds off things we decided to have a walk round the centre of the city. Unfortunately, that day Cologne seemed to be labouring under the misapprehension that it wasn't located in northern Germany at all, but rather in Punjab in the monsoon season, and we copped for a real soaking. We decided to take refuge in a cinema, and it turned out that The Blues Brothers was about to be screened. We bought tickets in the hope that the rain would have stopped by the time the film was over. The dialogue was dubbed into German but the songs weren't, so we'd already got lucky. A second piece of good fortune was that beer was on sale in the cinema, so we stocked up before the film began. Thirdly, we seemed to have the whole place to ourselves. Unfortunately, the final one didn't last. Just after the film began, we were joined by a German couple who obviously both lived at home with their respective sets of parents and who evidently couldn't afford a hotel room. All the time, my thoughts kept drifting away across the North Sea.

If I'd been at Maine Road instead of sitting in a cinema in Cologne wondering whether a pair of German teenagers were going to move on from very heavy petting and actually start shagging right in front of us, what I'd have witnessed would have surprised me. No sooner had play begun than there was a crowd disturbance in the North Stand, United fans having gained access to a City section of the crowd. Referee Neil Midgley took the teams from the field of play for a few minutes, and after the resumption, it was clear that City had been less affected by the unnatural break.

With eleven minutes on the clock, Oldfield scored for City, Pallister having failed to cut out a cross from White. Almost immediately it was two, Morley prodding a rebound home from close range after a Paul Lake shot had been saved by goalkeeper Leighton. The third came before half-time, midfielder Bishop's header rounding off a flowing move, but early in the second period Mark Hughes reduced the arrears with a spectacular volley. Given that the game in which we'd let slip a three-goal lead against Bournemouth was still fresh in the memory, the nerves must have been jangling at this point. But then the game was made safe by a tap-in from Oldfield and a bullet header from full-back Hinchcliffe to round off some terrific football.

I was strongly tempted to avoid writing about this game, because City fans have made too much of it over the years. Sure, handing your local rivals a thrashing is always immensely satisfying, but all the game represents now is a wonderful day many years ago (and the fact that I wasn't there doesn't mean it wasn't a wonderful day for me too

- when I phoned home for the score, I was as thrilled as anyone, and I certainly celebrated that evening with appropriate gusto). Because of what's happened at the club since, though, there's always been a temptation to latch onto "the five-one", as it became known, as meaning much more, presumably as throughout our disasters it was a reminder of better times. But when it's the only time you've beaten them, at any rate in a proper match, in a couple of decades, then to bring it up incessantly is just a little bit … well, sad, really.

Just as United moved on - and I don't think they'd have traded their parade of trophies throughout the nineties for avoiding this humiliation - so we needed to. For a while, I suppose that citing the memory of the match served as some kind of defence to United jibes; we could always remind them that, even if they had just won the double, they'd never in living memory inflicted on us the kind of hammering we gave them that day. Then, one November evening in 1994, they beat us 5-0 at Old Trafford. So for me the "five-one" wasn't about gloating, and my reluctance to discuss it in these pages stems from a fear that any reference to it might be seen as revelling in it. Like the 3-0 defeat against United ten-and-a-half years earlier, it was simply a game with a great personal resonance for me.

From Cologne, Andy and I moved on to Brussels, and from Brussels to Bruges. From there, we headed back to northern England, arriving the following Thursday, and in the last few days I began to feel a little perturbed. I've never before or since seen myself as a clairvoyant or having the gift of a sixth sense, but I did feel that something might be wrong with my grandad. And when I arrived home from the long trip, my parents confirmed it. He had emphysema and was having severe difficulty breathing.

I phoned him that Thursday evening, and we talked. He was a lifelong Blue, and he used to tell me stories about how he'd been in the crowd at City's FA Cup tie against Stoke in 1934, a day on which we recorded an attendance of over 84,000, a record for a British game outside London or Glasgow. He insisted that the gate was actually many more, as thousands had gained entry when a wall collapsed. We'd been to a few games together; the last one I remember was an eventful one against Watford in 1982, when City had played for all but three minutes of the game with full-back Bobby McDonald in goal in place of the injured Corrigan, and had won. So we naturally enthused over the win against United; his voice was a rasp, but it was obvious how thrilled he was. He died in mid-afternoon the next day, sitting in his favourite armchair, and it was a source of comfort that we'd had that conversation and that City had given him that moment of joy before he died.

I think through this I can see here the seeds of why I've retained a passion for football throughout the years, even when I've gone to live abroad and should have been able to forget my Maine Road misery for good. Manchester City are a part of my identity; wherever I've been and gone, whatever new ground I've broken, they provide a link to where I came from.

This isn't as muddle-headed a notion as it seems. My maternal grandfather was a lifelong City fan with whom I remember having long conversations about the day's football every Saturday evening until he died when I was eight years old. We used to do the pools and then compare notes on how I'd got on; in those days I used to study the form for hours, and was never able to understand why my reasoned selections for eight score draws failed every week to snare me a big money win. My mum still talks of Uncle Frank listening forlornly to the radio in the 1950s, abject at the dismal news of City's latest disaster (it sounds a familiar tale). I remember going to games with him, too - making our way home after a 5-0 win that relegated Spurs in 1977 and him telling me he was sorry that a club as big as them was going down, or debating whether Joe Corrigan was at fault for a Sunderland goal in the last game we went to together in October 1982. And of course there's my dad, born in 1939, who first went to Maine Road during the War, sneaking in after the gates were opened at three quarter time to let the rest of the crowd out. I've lost count of the number of games we've been to together.

And City have permeated other close family relationships, too. For a while, a visit to Auntie Dot's was a part of the pre-match routine, so memories of visiting her are bound up with memories of watching City. My sister, four years younger than me and to whom I've always been very close, has mostly been a fairly lukewarm fan, but went through an enthusiastic phase in the late 1980s when she regularly attended games and developed some strong opinions (she was dismayed at Trevor Morley's regular selection, I recall). When she burst an appendix during my student days, I came home to visit her in hospital, and I cheered her up by waiting outside Maine Road following a 3-0 win over Birmingham to get the players to sign the match programme as they left the ground. And my mum, though attending rarely and invariably being an unlucky influence when she has, for years throughout my travels has listened faithfully to local radio programmes and monitored the local press to provide letters and phone calls giving me comprehensive City updates.

Even the journey to the game when I was a kid seemed like a trip through my heritage, since it took in old family haunts. My dad would park up near the YMCA on Princess Parkway and we'd cut through Alexandra Park, always passing a large motionless metal post painted in sky blue and white that we'd named 'Kevin Bond' after the slightly statuesque City defender of the early 1980s (to be fair to him, after an uncertain start, he did go on and prove his worth). After crossing the Parkway and heading down Parkside Street, we'd cut through Burdith Avenue, the street where he'd lived in those early days just behind the Parkside pub. We'd cross Lloyd Street South, then progress down Lowthorpe Street, where his grandparents had lived and which adjoins Maine Road itself.

And so, as I travelled abroad and became more and more distanced from Manchester, and from my family, and as I lost both my grandfathers, Auntie Dot and Uncle Frank, supporting City was my main link with them, with Manchester and with my roots. It's City that have always made me feel I'm still in touch with where I'd come from.

13

Racing Uncertainty

THE VISIT TO RUSSIA had merely been the hors d'oeuvres. The main body of my year studying abroad was spent at Meudon, in the Parisian suburbs, as I'd elected to study Russian in France. This, I concede, was not an obvious move, but for various reasons which are not worth relating here, it was the best way I could develop both of my languages. What really made the year unique, though, was the institute where I ended up. I spent a year in a Jesuit monastery, although it was no ordinary monastery (if it had been, I suppose they'd never have let someone like me near the place).

The monks at the Saint-Georges monastery produced a magazine aimed at spreading the Christian word in the former Soviet Union, and so all of them spoke Russian. The monastery also became a magnet for émigré Russians, many of whom, through economic necessity, had obtained their diplomas in teaching Russian to foreigners. So to keep the place solvent, the monks had hit upon the rather neat idea of charging universities from all over Europe for Russian-language courses on which students could obtain intensive tuition from native speakers.

If this explanation has a semblance of logic in it, it nevertheless can't be denied that life at the Centre d'Etudes Russes in Meudon was frequently imbued with moments of pure surrealism. One of my most abiding memories is of the monks wandering round the gardens, deep in contemplation. All had a formidable academic pedigree, so I always assumed their thoughts were of weighty intellectual matters. Thus there would be the rotund, bespectacled Father René, a renowned expert on the works of Solzhenitsyn, weighing up his favoured author's theme of the dehumanisation of man and suppression of free thought under the authoritarian Soviet régime. The tall, bearded Father Alexei, who knew all there was to know about iconography, was no doubt reflecting on the Russian iconographic tradition and how it mirrored traditional Orthodox theological teachings. And Father Antoine, a dead-ringer for Flash Gordon's nemesis Ming the Merciless, was, I'm sure, formulating diabolical plans for world domination.

The setting quite clearly demanded the accompaniment of footballing drama, and, to be fair to City, they did their best to provide it from afar with a season of outrageous inconsistency. There were soaring highs, like the 5-1 win over Manchester United, which admittedly took place before I arrived in France. But there were also dismal lows, of which the worst was a catastrophic 6-0 reverse at Derby. There was a change of manager (Mel Machin was rather harshly sacked, but no-one could doubt the pedigree of his successor Howard Kendall, who'd recently won the title twice with Everton); a bewildering turnover of players; a mini-revival followed by a slump back into the relegation zone; and in the end a surprising escape sparked by a shock away win against championship-chasing Aston Villa.

For once, however, I wasn't just relying on Manchester City - for the first time, I also found footballing excitement closer to one of my temporary homes. This might not sound particularly surprising, but for a City fan, finding suitable replacement live football is not a simple task. I can safely say, with a substantial degree of understatement, that the experience of watching City is not an easy one to replicate. My own attempts prove the point.

At university, I watched Cambridge United, but never really developed a strong affection for them, despite witnessing successive promotions and two excellent cup runs. It didn't help, I suppose, that they were hardly a loveable team - they embraced sterile, physical, route-one football to an extent which made the brutal and basic Wimbledon of the same era look like the legendary Real Madrid side boasting the silky skills of Puskas and di Stefano. A number of years later, when my firm sent me on a placement to Brussels, I similarly failed to develop a passion for the local football. At Anderlecht, there was the glamour of Champions league games against Hajduk Split and Benfica. At RWD Molenbeek, it was the rather more mundane fare of Lommel and Aalst in the Belgian league. These contrasting experiences were interesting but ultimately unfulfilling. I actually had a greater affinity with the Belgian national team, whom I saw play Spain. They started well and took the lead, but, after a series of incomprehensible substitutions, finished a ragged outfit, with two central midfielders pushed up front and one of the centre backs stuck out forlornly on the left wing. In the end, they were lucky to avoid a more humiliating defeat than by the eventual 4-1 margin: this was more the type of thing I was used to.

After my arrival at Meudon, I became aware that my experience there would be somewhat more fortuitous - although I didn't appreciate it when I saw my first game in Paris. In my opening week at the Institute, I saw Paris Saint-Germain take on Juventus in a UEFA Cup tie. This was a memorable occasion, as after the match I was caught in a pitched battle between the Juve fans and the CRS (the fearsome French riot police). The threat to my safety didn't affect my view of PSG. They'd seemed to lack charm and I'd already felt instinctively that I'd never really take to them. With their rivals, Racing, whom I first saw against league leaders Bordeaux, it was another story.

Racing began the match attacking stylishly, their play full of flair and imagination, and their one goal half-time lead was scant reward for their superiority. This supremacy continued for the first twenty minutes of the second half but still another goal proved elusive. Then came the incident which turned the game. In one of their rare attacking forays, the Bordeaux right-back made an overlapping run and slung a high, hopeful cross into the Racing penalty area. It was an easy catch for Pascal Olmeta, Racing's extrovert, eccentric and intermittently brilliant goalkeeper but, under no pressure at all, he unaccountably dropped the ball at the feet of one of the Bordeaux forwards. The striker accepted the gift incredulously, and Racing simply fell apart. Bordeaux scored another two goals but in truth could have ended up with six or seven.

Any City fan will understand how reassuringly familiar it felt to see a team in sky blue and white perform like this. Needless to say, I was hooked and followed Racing for the rest of my stay. Their side had some memorable characters. Among the promising young players was a certain David Ginola, while I also recall a promising 20-year-old centre-back called Manu Thetis, who later ended up at Ipswich. My personal favourite was the skilful playmaker, Alim Ben-Mabrouk, a veteran, shaven-headed Moroccan. The crowd idol was Olmeta, who had a particular penchant for kamikaze sorties from his goal area, which he obviously retained: several years later, I saw him produce a typically ill-judged excursion for Lyon in a televised UEFA Cup match against Nottingham Forest, which resulted in the Forest penalty that won the tie.

When I look back now, it isn't just of Racing that I think with affection. The whole year was immensely enjoyable, and indeed the only year I had between the ages of fourteen and twenty-three when I didn't have public exams. I met several friends with whom I'm still in contact. And it wasn't just among the monks or the erratic young football team I'd followed for the year that there were characters who've stayed in the memory.

Students came and went with bewildering frequency, and I was the only one who stayed all year. While the majority of them were British, there was certainly a varied cast list; the nationalities included French, Italian, Norwegian, Swiss and German. And they ranged from eighteen-year-olds fresh out of school to mature students in their forties. My own circle of friends used to meet regularly in the room shared by Linda, a blind Scottish girl studying Russian at Strathclyde, and her auxiliary helper Fiona. We took it in turns to dictate lecture notes for Linda to type up on her Braille machine, against a backdrop of the evenings of card-playing and alcohol consumption to which she and Fiona regularly played host. Meanwhile, the place was a haven of gossip, most of it surrounding who was sleeping with whom; the focus for much of it was John, from Bristol University. I later heard news of him through a friend of a friend; I believe he had a business selling agricultural machinery in southern Russia and went bankrupt in the aftermath of the 1998 financial crisis.

The Russians who taught us were also an interesting bunch. I recall Sergei, a small bearded man who loved playing practical jokes. There was Lev, a thespian before he'd emigrated, who used to make us act out scenes from classic Russian plays to the embarrassment of all concerned. Andrei, who taught us Russian history, fancied his chances of working his way through the girls on the course, while his female equivalent was Aliona. Married to a balding, serious and pious man who edited the monks' religious magazine for them, she was, for reasons possibly not unconnected with that fact, one of the most outrageous flirts I've ever met before or since. Most of the male students, though, preferred Sholpan, who was originally from Kazakhstan and had a slightly oriental appearance. Her strict manner only added to the allure (imagine Anne Robinson only with sex appeal).

Most of all, though, I remember Dyadya Kolya (the name means 'Uncle Nick'). He was eighty-five then and had emigrated from Russia just after the Second World War, prior to which he'd served time in Stalin's labour camps. A small, white-haired man with glasses and a walking stick, he resembled everyone's favourite grandfather, and people used to vie for the honour of bringing him Marmite, which he regarded as a great delicacy, back from our trips home to England. His lessons used to involve him rambling on whatever subject took his fancy, and in truth they weren't especially useful. However, as he had taught Russian literature at university in France, I ended up arranging extra lessons with him on my own. We'd drink tea and discuss my set texts for the following year at university, but as time wore on, we became closer and I would occasionally pop across to his room for an afternoon chat or to drink a glass of beer or two in the evening. I've had plenty of farewells in my life and rarely regard them as a cause to become emotional, but this wasn't the case when the time came for me to return to England at the end of the academic year. Dyadya Kolya thanked me for helping to keep his mind agile but it had been a pleasure; that was one of the saddest goodbyes in my life.

In the run-up to that goodbye, the year at Meudon had ended in an appropriately eccentric manner. At Easter, a strikingly attractive

Italian girl called Maria had arrived. She and I started to study together and always seemed to get on well. She was, however, extremely unpredictable and frequently vanished for two or three days on end. She was also six years older than me and was engaged to Agosto, a man from back home in Milan whom, she said, she had no intention of marrying because he was "weak". Maria and I became much closer as time went on, and I found I didn't really mind her disappearing acts (including one when Agosto turned up and whisked her off to a hotel for a few days) as I viewed our relationship more as a diversion than anything else.

What I remember Maria for most, though, is an incident that happened at the end of the year. A Russian poet called Viktor Nikolayev had arrived at the monastery, and it soon transpired that he liked his vodka. He may well have been imbibing before an incident one afternoon, when he and Maria were both in the library, and I recall entering to find him chasing her round the table. When I came in, he fled, and thereafter, Maria was desperate for me to defend her honour. The means through which she envisaged this being achieved was the infliction on him of extreme physical pain; I, however, was desperate to avoid doing anything which would encourage the Institute to inform my tutors at Cambridge that my conduct had been less than satisfactory, since in theory such a verdict could give the University authorities ammunition to expel me from my degree course. This argument didn't convince Maria, though, and so when Viktor Nikolayev hastened away of his own accord after arguing with the monks, it was a source of much relief to me.

Racing, meanwhile, offered a rollercoaster ride of their own to match mine in the monastery. They stayed in the relegation zone all season. They flattered to deceive, often giving hope that they could pull clear of trouble by producing fluent, progressive football which belied their league position. As tends to be the case with struggling sides, this wasn't matched by the end product. Typically, the final ball was poor. When it wasn't, the finishing was erratic. Add to this an unfortunate habit of leaking bad goals and their plight was scarcely a surprise. However, they did manage an improbable cup run.

It began, for me at least, with the home quarter-final against Bordeaux. In contrast with the previous match between the sides, Bordeaux dominated virtually from the first whistle to the end of extra time. Olmeta had one of his inspired matches and was almost entirely responsible for a 1-1 final score. His heroics continued in the penalty shoot-out and Racing were through. The semi was away to Marseille, then perennially the top team in France, who had just edged out Bordeaux for the title. The game was televised live on the subscription-only Canal Plus, so I spent the evening glued to my radio. Racing fought valiantly, but when they went 2-1 down in the second half, the adventure seemed over. Then two late goals brought a victory as sensational as it was unlikely.

I managed to get a ticket for the final, which, as usual, was played at the Parc des Princes, then the national stadium. Since Racing played their home games at the same venue, and since the opponents were Montpellier (a respectable enough side but not in the same class as Bordeaux or Marseille), hopes were high. In fact, Racing found it was a bridge too far. Second best throughout a dull game, they were finished off in extra time by two Eric Cantona goals - I was probably the first Manchester City supporter whose life was blighted by this man, who later inspired Manchester United to success after success.

The final was Racing's last game at the top level. For financial reasons, they didn't play in the second division the next year. Instead, they dropped straight down into the regionalised third division, which for the most part isn't even professional. As far as I know, they're still there. Somehow, it feels fitting that I witnessed their swan-song as a major club.

I knew as I returned to England that summer that I would be hard pressed to repeat the drama of that year in Paris. It had been similar to Cambridge in that it was cut off from the real world, but it differed in that the characters and the events were so much more out-of-the-ordinary. Over the year, my day-to-day existence had actually mirrored the bizarre world of Manchester City rather than offered a contrast to it - and I'd even found a local team that did the same.

14

The Hand of Fate

YOU NEVER KNOW what's around the corner. Of course, you can plan for the future, you can do everything in your power to ensure that events take a certain course. But if fate has another idea, then sometimes there's nothing you can do, no matter how hard you try. An incident on a football field in Manchester one balmy September evening and a few weeks in one of the most picturesque parts of France brought the lesson home to me with some force.

Having finished at Meudon, I spent the summer of 1990 in the Loire Valley. I'd completed my year's study abroad and, having become focused for the last nine months on the Russian-based life in the monastery rather than the French life outside its walls, was keen to develop my French further. I ended up working in what was called a "centre medico-sociale" just outside Vendome; what this meant was that it was a residential home for people who had lost their mobility either through being in an accident or having contracted some kind of degenerative disease such as muscular dystrophy. The patients were admitted to the Centre when it was certain they'd never recover and when their family lacked either the means or the will to look after them at home. I was on the 'entertainments team', which basically meant organising social events and outings for the patients.

It was an enjoyable summer. It gave me a chance to spend time in an especially beautiful part of the world and as I had access to a car for days off, I was able to explore. There were frustrations - the main one being that I had to share accommodation with an Algerian who was friendly enough but whom I strongly suspected of stealing my money. And the work was hard - in theory, I was supposed to have five eight-hour shifts each week, but the hours were purely nominal. Nevertheless, the work was rewarding, and as no-one else there had even a rudimentary knowledge of English, my paramount objective of continuing to practice my French was certainly met.

Towards the end of my stay there, the English football season started. After City's revival at the end of the previous campaign, and as it would be the first full season for our proven, successful manager Howard Kendall, I awaited the season with more than a little anticipation, and tuned in to listen to the opening match. This was the radio commentary game (mainly because of the glamour of our opponents), and the newly launched Radio 5 was just about audible in the Loire. This was the summer after the 1990 World Cup in Italy, in which the England team had reached the semi-finals. Their progress in the tournament had aroused great national enthusiasm often now cited as the start of football's resurgence in terms of its mass appeal. The most memorable moment for many was when Paul Gascoigne burst into tears having been booked in the semi-final against Germany; England eventually lost the match on penalties, but the decision meant he'd miss the final if England won.

Gary Lineker, the striker whose goals were instrumental in England's progress, joined new national icon Gascoigne in the Spurs side that beat City 3-1. Thereafter, we settled into a run of solid form; although many matches were drawn, and it was a functional rather than an exciting unit, the next league defeat wasn't until mid-November. A week after the Spurs game, I was back home to see a 1-0 win over Everton at Maine Road, and four days later, City hosted Aston Villa for an exciting match described in the highlights shown on regional TV that evening as showcasing the best English football had to offer. I remember this fact because it was a first experience of live football for the girl who accompanied me to the game, and I congratulated myself on having selected such an auspicious occasion. I felt that the team had managed to exhibit what I saw in them, whereas on most occasions when I accord a neutral the dubious pleasure of seeing them in action, they delight in proving my insanity for following them in the way I do.

The game really was as good as the Granada Soccernight presenter had said. These were two of the better teams in England at the time (Villa were the previous season's runners up, while City were on the way to finishing fifth that season) and between them, they produced much high-quality football. Most of it came from the visitors, and, in truth, Villa were hard done by as City won 2-1. However, the outstanding moment of the game did come from a City player. Paul Lake, playing as a central defender, took the ball from deep in his own half to the edge of the Villa penalty area, beating several players in the process. Only a last-ditch tackle by the one remaining defender between him and the goalkeeper prevented what could have been a truly incredible goal. Within a few minutes, he was departing the arena on a stretcher and, apart from a brief abortive comeback two years later, he would never play again.

Any fan who reads the newspapers will learn fairly frequently of players' careers being ended through injury, and any such instance is invariably a desperately sad turn of events for the individual concerned. But what happened to Lake always strikes me as particularly poignant. He was City's third major loss in this manner in a couple of decades (the previous two coming in the early and mid-1970s), and while I don't seek to belittle the trauma endured by the other two men, somehow his loss seems more affecting. At least Glyn Pardoe and Colin Bell, though neither had reached thirty at the time and though both would undoubtedly have continued to make a contribution to the club , each had the opportunity to play more than 300 first-team games and to win several major prizes. Meanwhile, even the brightest youngster who has to give up at eighteen, before his potential has been tested, knows that the odds are stacked against him. Look at an England youth side of the past, supposedly featuring the cream of the crop, and you'll almost certainty find that a majority of the players never made it big.

The point with Lake is that he'd already proved he could reach the top level - he'd already made the England squad of thirty from which the 22-man party for the Italian adventure was chosen - but never had the chance to progress further. Maybe he wouldn't have become a regular England player or won major trophies (and I don't mean with City - if he'd become as good as I expected him to, we wouldn't have held onto him), but plenty of good judges thought him destined for the top. And when one of them includes Sir Alex Ferguson, who regrettably, I have to concede, is something of an authority, it's a proposition that at least has to be taken seriously.

Desperately sad though it was, I wouldn't seek to claim that Lake's story was as heartbreakingly tragic as some of those I witnessed in the Loire; nevertheless, both he and Vendome are now wedded in my mind. It isn't just because of the temporal proximity, for that summer I learnt a lesson that's also exemplified by his story.

I'd done voluntary work before. For example, there was work with the mentally impaired, which basically involved games, singsongs and entertainments, such as dressing up as an ugly sister in a production of Cinderella. I'd also been on holidays with underprivileged kids, where the entertainments were of a different nature. And I'd helped out with the severely mentally impaired, which was more distressing and which primarily seemed to entail attempting to prevent them from harming themselves. The time in the Loire, though, was the first time I'd ever worked with the physically disabled. It was an experience that affected me deeply.

What I found was that I was dealing with people who were often incredibly mentally alert but who were assumed by huge chunks of the general public to be stupid. I'd never before realised the assumptions people made when they clap eyes on a wheelchair. Perhaps it was because these were people who could articulate their concerns and unhappiness, but I became much more aware of how they were thinking and feeling than was the case with any of the voluntary work I'd done previously. I don't think it's useful to become too emotionally involved on these occasions - it's far more beneficial if you relate to people you're supposed to be helping simply in a human way, and by and large sympathy is the last thing they want. But there were occasions on which it was impossible. Watching one woman who had no use of her hands paint using her mouth was incredibly touching, while there was no shortage of stories so poignant they'd make you want to cry.

Of those, the one that stayed with me was Jean-Marc's. He was in his forties, I think, and the light of a bright, vivid intelligence shone from his alert, blue eyes. Everything in his life had been progressing smoothly. He'd graduated from university, and had become a teacher, a profession which is relatively better paid in France than here. He'd done well, exceptionally well, in fact, becoming deputy head of a secondary school at a remarkably young age. He'd married and had two young children, so his personal life was on track too. And then one day, a day like any other, it was all taken away from him. At the time, he was 28 years old.

What happened was this: he was driving home from school, and as he went round a bend, he smashed head on into another car, which was on the wrong side of the road, overtaking recklessly and at speed. The other driver, a drunk, was killed. Jean-Marc once told me he wished he'd been too. In fact, he was in a coma for some weeks, before coming round to discover that he'd sustained severe spinal injuries and would be paralysed from the neck down for the rest of his life. It cost him his dignity - he needed a nurse to bathe him, dress him and take him to the toilet - and his family. Although his wife visited him at first, little by little, she stopped coming, and then she divorced him to marry someone else. His children had also abandoned him. He was an only child and his parents had died, so he had literally no-one at all. He used to put a brave face on it, but I could tell it devastated him. I could understand that after the accident, his wife might want to move on to a new relationship, since he could no longer be a husband to her in any meaningful way. But for her and his children to have forgotten him like this seemed unspeakably cruel.

He was keen to remind me that his life hadn't always been this way. "I used to be a teacher," he'd say sometimes. "I was married, you know," he'd tell me on other occasions. I assumed he didn't want me to think that the bed-ridden figure in front of me was the real him. Somehow he'd been trapped inside this body that wouldn't function, but the true Jean-Marc was still there inside, and hadn't been lost forever on a winding country road one evening twelve years before.

Things never got that bad for Paul Lake the footballer, but all the glories he must have dreamt of were snatched away and he was last seen on a football pitch in Middlesbrough in August 1992. Following his injury a couple of years previously, he'd been expected to be back in action within a week or two. Then we were told he'd return at the start of the next season. When he did finally re-emerge, at the start of the one after that, he broke down after just eight minutes of his second game. We knew it was finished for him then, even though he spent nearly four more years, enduring sixteen painful operations, trying to get back. Without the injury, he'd have probably spent those years as a major star earning a fortune instead of embroiled in an agonising, lonely and ultimately futile battle to rescue the one thing that mattered to him. It must have been a bitter blow to him to see other players, like his City team mate Niall Quinn and Manchester United's Roy Keane, recover from similar injuries in around twelve months.

I've thought about Jean-Marc a lot over the years. He's living proof that even when you have it all, it can be taken from you in an instant by forces totally beyond your control. Although it doesn't happen to most of us, it could happen to anyone. That's true in football as in life, and while the people at the centre medico-sociale got more or less as rough an end of the stick as it's possible to get, fortune didn't smile on Paul Lake either.

15

The View From Afar

HAVING LEFT MEUDON, and having completed my stint in the Loire, I returned for my final year's study at Cambridge. Not surprisingly, it was an uneventful few months compared to what had gone before, and with many of my friends having left twelve months previously after their three-year courses, I was rather pleased finally to graduate.

After four pleasant but rather aimless years, I considered it was time for me to make my mark on the world. I'd selected the law as the arena in which I'd create an impression, mainly because this was an idea I'd had for a long time and nothing better had occurred to me in the interim. And while the choice entailed a couple of years of extra study, I had no doubt that I'd soon secure a sponsorship, that this would be a prelude to a glittering career and that I'd go on to make lots of money. It sounds naïve now, but at the time, it really did seem that simple.

I had a couple of months to kill before I started law school, though, and I chose to spend that time in Russia. As I was still a student, I wasn't exactly cash-rich, so I had to justify the outlay to myself; I told myself that, having prioritised French in my last year of my degree course because I felt it offered me a better chance of a high mark in my finals, I needed to practice my Russian. In fact, I just wanted to go back because I felt it would be interesting. I wasn't wrong.

As ever with my summer travels, the downside to the arrangement was that I'd be away for the early part of the new football season; the big kick-off was in mid-August and it would be early September before I returned home. This was a source of some regret, for it was actually a season I was awaiting with a keen sense of anticipation. Unaccountably, something strange had happened - City had actually become quite good.

After the travails of the first post-promotion season, the next year had, despite the shock resignation of Howard Kendall to return to manage his former club Everton, been remarkably successful. Remarkably successful, that is, by City's standards. The final league position of fifth was the club's best top-flight effort since 1978, and for the first time in several seasons the team included several players who were the envy of rival clubs. For instance, the tall Irish striker Niall Quinn had just bagged over twenty goals in his first full season at Maine Road and showed a deftness of touch to surprise even his admirers. David White, a fast, direct winger who was often also played as an orthodox striker throughout his Maine Road career, was erratic but still had an excellent scoring record and possessed the pace to trouble even the best defences. And shortly before I departed for Leningrad, we paid a British record transfer fee for a defender to land sought-after centre-half Keith Curle. So, as with the many occasions before and since that I have been travelling or living away from Manchester, I was totally determined to do all I could to follow events at Maine Road. It proved to be a more difficult task than I'd expected.

I can hardly claim to be unique in my resolve to keep myself informed from afar. For example, one of my friends from school was an avid City fan, and after graduating he spent three years teaching in provincial China; before that, he lived for six months in Romania. Throughout those periods, I sent him detailed letters to keep him updated, a compliment he's repaid when the boot's been on the other foot. I remember him once asking for a particular piece of information, and adding plaintively, "You are my only source of this information". Fanzines and Internet pages for most clubs are full of letters or messages from exiled fans (I don't mean the long-distance glory hunters who've never been within thousands of miles of the ground). Obviously, each has a personal story but there's one common factor - a passion surviving despite personal circumstances which drastically limit contact with and information about their club.

Nick Hornby writes in Fever Pitch that his career has probably been shaped by a subconscious desire not to do a job which would entail missing Arsenal home games. People like me clearly do not conform to this pattern. By spending most of my life from the age of eighteen studying or working away from Manchester, I've made a fairly unequivocal decision that the pursuit of my career takes precedence over regular visits to Maine Road, though I've made the effort whenever I could and still have a season ticket today despite now living in London. Other exiled fans have, for whatever reasons of their own, made a similar choice.

The Internet has made a huge difference to those of us who've regularly had to follow events at a remove, but I only had Web access from 1997. Before then, it was always a case of making the best of the resources available. Things were better in some places than in others. Some years after my 1991 trip to Russia, I lived for six months in Brussels. There, the same day's English papers are sold from first thing in the morning. English radio stations (most importantly, Radio 5) can be picked up without any problems. I was living in a flat which had cable TV; one of the channels provided was BBC1 so I could watch Match Of The Day when I got in on a Saturday night. I was about as well informed as if I'd been living in London (though as Anderlecht weren't on the fixture list, I had no 'local' away games).

Paris always proved slightly more difficult. Newspapers were as readily available as in Brussels, but I found the radio a bit more problematic. In my Meudon days, I always had trouble getting World Service. I was able to pick up Radio 5, but only when it was dark, so it was no use except for midweek games and for the second half and final scores during the winter months. I later returned there to work for a couple of months and couldn't receive Radio 5 at all; fortunately, I found I could get Talk Radio UK, which at least gave out scores and results as they happened. Again, there was no reception in daylight hours, but as I was there only in winter, it wasn't a problem on that occasion.

Needless to say, Russia was always a different proposition altogether. When I later returned there to work, I bought an expensive short-wave radio so that I could listen to BBC World Service, which should have been all I needed to find out results. It wasn't. Erratic reception meant I lost the transmission when it was dark (I might understand all this if I had any grasp of the laws of physics), and in winter there it's dark quite a lot. Even as the season came to an end in May, I never made it through to hear the end of the classified results. The saving grace compared to my student days was that once I was in a job, I could afford international phone calls. This meant that no sooner had the match ended than I was on the phone home to find out the result.

That situation was luxury compared to the summer I experienced in 1989 and what I again had to endure on the 1991 trip. In those days, international phone calls cost over three pounds a minute, had to be booked in advance and reception was invariably awful. Not even I wanted to know the results that badly - or at least, I didn't when I was travelling on a student budget. As I had no short-wave radio, newspapers were my only way to find out news. In 1989, the Morning Star was still the only English paper sold in Moscow. It printed results together with the odd match report and carried some general football news. (On my way home, I stopped off in Berlin. I got off the train and rang home as soon as I found a phone to hear news of City's characteristic League Cup defeat at Brentford that evening). In 1991 in Leningrad (as St. Petersburg was still called), the only foreign paper I could find was USA Today.

That summer, on the day after my birthday, it was announced that there'd been a coup and Mikhail Gorbachev had been overthrown. Everyone was speculating that it was the start of a civil war. Tanks were supposedly on the point of being ordered into the city (it never happened). Flights to and from the local airport were said to have been suspended (this wasn't true). Once my hangover had cleared, a terrible realisation dawned. I'd found out that USA Today printed European football results. The only place it was on sale was a hotel overlooking the Gulf of Finland. With fifteen minute walks to and from the metro at each end, it would be a round trip of almost an hour and a half, but at least I had a way of finding out the City scores. When I heard about the coup, I knew my chance had gone. If I couldn't find out how the Blues had got on at Highfield Road in the first match of the new season, I really don't know how anyone expected me to be remotely bothered whether Russia was on the brink of civil war. What price witnessing living history compared with twenty-two blokes chasing a ball round a field in Coventry?

Thankfully, the plotters had the decency to give up the ghost in time for me to find out that we'd beaten Liverpool at Maine Road in the next game. That was as good as it got. Despite four more trips to the Gulf of Finland, I had to wait for my plane home to find out the Coventry result and the results of the three other games during my stay. Even then, I had to work them out from a league table.

Fortunately, I discovered that all was well with the world. City were second in the league table with ten points from their five league games and I was relaxed and ready for my new course. I also had a round of job interviews planned (crazily, it seemed to me, law firms expected me to fix myself up for two years' hence). I was keen to get started and to assure myself a successful future. But that Leningrad trip had also planted the seeds of a dangerous compulsion which was to mark the next decade of my life indelibly. And it wasn't just the excitement of the coup or the fine start Peter Reid's City had made to the season that was responsible.

16

Olga Tongue

I HAVE A PLAQUE in French on the wall in my living room, and my parents say it could be my personal motto. "The best way to put a stop to temptation," it translates, "is to give in to it." Or, as the English equivalent has it, when in temptation - yield. It's advice that I've followed all too often over the years. And while much of the drama of that 1991 trip to Leningrad derived from the political circumstances there at the time, it was whole turbulent package of what happened that summer which ensured Russia would remain a dangerous temptation for me in the future.

This was a worrying state of affairs, for I have a hopeless lack of will-power in almost every area of my life. I am simply unable to turn my back on what I know is bad for me. I eat and drink to excess, for instance, and am woefully incapable of forcing myself to follow a healthy lifestyle. I know that crisps, kebabs and beer are unlikely to become part of the BMA's recommended diet anytime soon, for instance, but I just like them too much to give them up, and I dislike exercise enough not to use it sufficiently to compensate to any meaningful degree for my other excesses. At least those things bring me pleasure, though. There are plenty of things which bring me only harm or misery or grief. But when push comes to shove, what I need loses out to what I want - even when I know I'm crazy for wanting what I do.

Being a Manchester City fan joins life in Russia in this latter category. I ought to be able to turn my back on the club, since for most of the quarter of a century I've been following them, they've delivered disappointment. The break-up of the team of the mid-to-late 1970s was my first inkling of this, but there have been plenty of other lows, too many, in fact, to give anything but a very selective list.

The sale of star player Trevor Francis in the summer of 1982 upset me greatly, while relegation in 1983 was a hammer blow given that it was so unexpected. So, after a few short years, I'd already come to understand that City were thoroughly bad for me. In the seven or eight years after my Leningrad trip of 1991, there were simply too many disappointments to relate here yet I've always persevered, sometimes despite solemn vows not to.

Certainly no-one will have been able to hack life as a City fan over the last quarter of a century if they can't cope with disappointments and let-downs. This has been our staple diet. Those who watched us when we had a decent side and who couldn't handle perpetual frustration will have given up the ghost long ago. Those who stuck with it, or who started following us since the end of the days of wine and roses, wouldn't have done so if they didn't have a long-suffering, fatalistic nature. One would suspect that we must derive something from the experience, but it can't be an association with success or joy from regularly watching high-quality football; we have managed it on occasion, but for most of my City-supporting life, such occasions have hardly been plentiful. But it never mattered to me how bad things have got; City have never ceased to exercise a hold over me. Russia had already started to seduce me on previous visits but in the summer of 1991, with the help of alluring women who would cause me nothing but problems, my fatal fascination was sealed.

I'd arranged to make the trip to Leningrad with Anneline, a Norwegian girl with whom I'd studied in Paris on the compulsory year abroad on my Modern Languages course. We each booked through an agency to stay with a separate family, and as soon as we'd received details, the thought had crossed my mind that there could be a matchmaking agenda at the Russian end. Anneline was placed with Igor, an ex-soldier, and his mother while I was to stay with Olga, a 20-year-old architecture student, and her mother. Anneline, who had a serious boyfriend at home in Norway, wasn't the slightest bit interested in Igor but I couldn't say the same about my hostess.

I should explain at this point that, for me at least, Russian women are not, on their own, a reason to visit the country. On the other hand, they undeniably represent a fortuitous bonus, as most men who have spent time in Russia will testify. Exceptionally attractive women exist everywhere but I'm far from alone in believing the supply in Russia is more plentiful than in other countries I've visited. And foreign men enjoy many advantages when playing the dating game over there.

Consider the circumstances. The male population has been depleted by protracted wars in Afghanistan and, latterly, Chechnya. The average salary is pitifully low compared to what most expatriates working there can earn. Alcoholism is rife among Russian men. And as there is a scarcity of young, single, solvent, sober Russian men, a presentable foreigner will not usually be too hard-pressed to find an attractive, willing female partner. A decade ago, things were even better for foreign men than today. The economic imbalance was loaded in my favour even as a non-wage earner and while, even now, a relationship with a foreigner is to some degree considered prestigious by many Russian girls, in those days the prospect had even more allure.

For a visitor looking for a more-than-casual partner, it can be hard to discern when interest from a Russian girl is genuine and when more material considerations come into play - aside from the monetary aspect, there was, and still is, the fact that marriage to a foreigner may be a passport to exit Russia. With all the attendant difficulties of life there, this on its own can be a powerful motive, and I was later to gather experience in spotting when someone was driven by such considerations. But at the age of twenty-one, a protracted or serious relationship certainly wasn't on the agenda for me. I was determined to use my exalted status as a means to obtain all the short-term gratification I could get. And I was optimistic about my prospects.

Olga (whose surname translated as 'Tongue') was sophisticated, intelligent, cultured and artistic. But while I value and appreciate these qualities in a woman, any female readers will no doubt groan inwardly at the predictability of the male romantic ideal when I confess it wasn't these qualities which attracted me most; Olga was also blonde, very attractive and had a body to die for. So on the day she came to meet me at the airport, we sat together in the back of the taxi on the way back home, and as she talked animatedly about how she planned to entertain me during my visit, I looked over at her and began to formulate my own plans of how I might brighten up my stay in Russia's second city.

At the start, things had seemed to be progressing promisingly with Olga Tongue and I'd begun to believe that my most dishonourable intentions might be spectacularly realised. But soon matters began to deteriorate markedly.

In retrospect, it should have been no surprise that money was a bone of contention; I've alluded already to the relative wealth of foreigners, but it's really worth outlining this in more detail. Over the previous couple of years, the rouble had collapsed completely, resulting in any foreigner at all, even an impecunious student like me, seeming impossibly rich to almost any Russian. On my previous visit in September 1989, the official exchange rate was one rouble to the pound although a couple of months later this was slashed to ten roubles to the pound. By August 1991, the official rate had dropped to fifty and far better deals were available on the black market. To put this in context, I'd arrived with £250 to last me for my stay, and Olga's mother, an engineer, earned 350 roubles (or £7) per month. My spending money equated to three times the national yearly average wage.

Our hosts couldn't help but look at us almost with dollar signs in their eyes, but on the other hand, there were parts of the picture they couldn't appreciate. Anneline and I were both students, and money was tight for us both. While we weren't inclined to penny-pinch, each of us wanted to take back home with us any money we could save. We knew that it would be unforgivable to flaunt our relative wealth and scrupulously tried to avoid doing so, but we also were both happy to treat our hosts to luxury goods which were not then widely available, like imported beer, at western prices from foreign-currency shops. It was all to no avail - and looking back, I'm not sure there's anything we could have done to avoid this difference of opinion. It was inevitable given the situation and culture differences between them.

Olga and Igor had mutual friends, a married couple called Alexander (known by the diminutive name 'Sasha') and Julia. Igor and Sasha had given up their jobs to become, effectively, unlicensed taxi drivers, simply driving round the city in their cars and offering lifts, for money, to anyone who flagged them down. They suggested that for a monthly retainer of $200, Anneline and I might like to have the exclusive benefit of their services, and they took our refusal badly, greeting it with disbelief and even anger. We explained that we didn't need a taxi all the time, only when we had certain trips planned, and said we'd pay a much better daily rate on those occasions we did require the car. But this counter-offer was rejected out of hand, and Olga Tongue seemed as unhappy with us as did the two men. "We want to be capitalists too," Igor had said bitterly when we'd rejected the car offer, but he had an oddly Soviet view of capitalism. Instead of presenting Anneline and me with a deal which both benefited him and suited us, he simply proposed what was most advantageous to himself and expected us to agree readily.

Analysing the difficulties caused by Russia's transition from a planned to a market economy isn't really part of my remit here, but I think it's worth pausing to reflect on this episode. The lack of a tradition of capitalism and seventy years of a planned economy has been advanced as a factor in the difficult and turbulent transition to the new system. Certainly, our hosts' attitude showed up the fact that they weren't used to thinking the way we were.

How, I reflected as I argued with Igor, he must have wished he was dealing with the-then City chairman Peter Swales, who oversaw transfer dealings in which the club regularly accepted ludicrous, one-sided demands made by their rivals. There was the time, for instance, in 1979, that we smashed the British transfer record to sign journeyman midfielder Steve Daley, a man who wasn't even close to being good enough for the England squad. And this is only one of a litany of examples of a cavalier and ultimately catastrophic attitude to finances.

There was even a story, apocryphal I'm sure, of the bid for Michael Robinson, the 20-year-old striker who'd appeared in just a handful of games for Third Division Preston. Two months before the Daley madness, we paid a bewildering £750,000 for his services. The tale had manager Malcolm Allison on the phone to his Preston counterpart, Nobby Stiles, discussing the bid. "We'll give you half a million," Allison is reputed to have said. "What?" the shocked Stiles is supposed to have replied, incredulous that City would pay so much for the untried novice. "All right, three quarters of a million, then," Allison is alleged to have countered.

This was exactly how Igor and Sasha expected us to behave, and in later years as I have reflected on the post-perestroika Russian capitalist model, their outlook has struck a chord. And the Russian government's negotiating stance in IMF loan negotiations also seems to mirror their attitude. Indeed, on reading the newspapers when I was in Russia in later years, I always suspected that John Barnwell, the Wolves manager who pushed the Daley fee up from an initial offer of £550,000 to a ludicrous £1.4 million, must have been on the Finance Ministry's payroll as a consultant somewhere along the line.

To be fair to Igor and Sasha, $200 for a month's use of their car was a far better deal than the signings of Daley and Robinson represented for City. But the fact that we didn't find it tempting was a cause of great resentment. And things deteriorated further when Anneline fell ill with salmonella (though in Russia the bizarre original diagnosis was an ovarian cyst).

She and I had gone by train to see the old palace at Pushkin, outside the city, and she collapsed on the way back. I managed to get her home and call an ambulance, but even so was roundly blamed for her health - I had allowed her to eat a bad diet, without which she would, I was told, have been fit and healthy. While I'd concede that few nutritionists would have enthused over our picnic lunch of export lager, crisps and Mars bars, I refuse to believe that this caused her ailment.

Anneline was hospitalised for several days and then went home early - though not before she'd argued with Igor and his family, who'd asked her for money for coming to visit her while she was ill. When she left, I was without moral support, and by this time a genuine hostility had built up. I hardly saw Igor or Sasha again, and while I could scarcely avoid Olga Tongue given that we were living in the same flat, she barely had a civil word for me.

Only with Julia did I have anything remotely resembling a cordial relationship, though it soon became clear that her interest wasn't purely platonic. In retrospect, given that she was married to Sasha, I suppose literally anyone else would have seemed an improvement (and yes, even after nearly a decade, I do still feel petty and vindictive enough to want to bitch about him). But Julia was clearly reluctant to betray her husband, and in any case I was always in Olga's company when I saw her, so the chance of a romantic interlude to brighten the rest of my visit seemed remote. I resigned myself to seeing out the rest of my stay convinced that all the drama was behind me.

It turned out that I was wrong. Events took a completely unexpected turn on my birthday, the day after the football season had started. I was determined to commemorate in suitable fashion reaching the age of twenty-two. Olga and I had called a truce and she insisted on cooking a celebratory meal. Her mother was there, with her boyfriend Dima, and Julia was also invited. It was a pleasant enough occasion, and afterwards all of us except Julia traipsed off to spend the evening with another friend of Olga's. Tanya lived with her parents, but they were out of town at their country home so it was a perfect venue to continue a party. She and I hit it off immediately, and having spent my entire trip pursuing Olga with no success whatsoever, I regretted that we hadn't been introduced earlier. But needless to say, the attentions were far from unwelcome, and I stayed on alone with Tanya when Olga, her mother and Dima left.

Having finally made my way back to Olga's flat at dawn, when Tanya had gone off to work, I went to bed looking forward to the final two weeks of my stay with much more enthusiasm than had been the case just a few short hours previously. But just as quickly as things had appeared to take a turn for the better, the illusion was cruelly dashed. I got up the next morning at eleven suffering from a hangover, and things went downhill from there, as Olga greeted me with news of the coup. At first, I thought she was joking but the radio soon made clear otherwise. Martial law had been declared, and a list of emergency decrees was being read out. All public gatherings of more than three people were banned. Troops were to be deployed to maintain social order. And no newspaper, other than Pravda, was allowed to be sold.

At first, I wasn't worried about my own safety, but that changed in the evening. Several family friends had converged on Olga's flat. They were relaying rumours that the airport was closed and that the city was encircled by tanks ahead of a planned mass demonstration the next day. To general murmurs of agreement, someone opined that we were witnessing the start of the Second Russian Civil War. It had to be admitted that things didn't look particularly good.

I could, then, have done without the next little piece of news I heard - although it had nothing to do with the coup. I'd gone out to the kitchen to get myself a drink, much needed in the circumstances, when the telephone rang in the hallway. Olga left the assembled company to take the call. Something about her agitated manner made me want to eavesdrop, but I immediately wished I hadn't. I only needed to listen to one side of the conversation to understand that the person on the other end of the line clearly perceived himself to be a wronged husband.

Olga, having realised I'd been listening, confirmed as much to me when the conversation ended. "Didn't you know?" she sneered, having first spat out the news with real venom. I genuinely hadn't suspected a thing. When I met her Tanya hadn't been wearing a wedding ring and had mentioned that she lived with her parents. But she'd said nothing about a spouse, and I'd been a little too preoccupied to check the flat for evidence. How he'd found out that my relations with his wife had progressed a considerable distance beyond limits a husband might find acceptable I don't know; I can only assume she must have told him. Musing on this, however, was the least of my concerns. Self-preservation was more of a priority given that for most Russian men, physical violence is mandatory in such a situation.

In fact, I needn't have worried. My fortunes had ebbed and flowed all summer and my troubles soon disappeared. There actually never was any threat that Tanya's husband would inflict severe injury on me, since it transpired that he was in hospital having broken both legs in a work accident. And, of course, the coup had ended in next to no time; frankly it couldn't have been more shambolic had it been organised by Alan Ball, the man many City fans regard as the club's worst-ever manager. On second thoughts ...

The upsurge in my fortunes continued as matters with Olga also took an unexpected turn, too. She showed signs of jealousy at Tanya's having taken away my attentions, and was prepared to use all her feminine qualities to regain first place in my affections, making my last couple of weeks very pleasant. I think she may have hoped that I'd invite her to England, too, though I never did - there was a temptation, obviously, but I was never prepared to guarantee her medical bills as visa regulations would have required. We did stay in contact for a few years, during which she occasionally used to send me photographs of herself in a bikini, but eventually we lost touch, and by the time I returned to St Petersburg (as the city had by then become called) she seemed to have moved from the flat I'd stayed in. But at the time, I went away having convinced myself of the charms of the Russian female population, and that conviction has never wavered since.

In keeping with my expectations, it had been a memorable and eventful summer - in terms both of my personal relationships and the historical context. I was convinced that if I returned to Russia, life would be equally unpredictable and exciting so I left Leningrad knowing I'd certainly be back at some point. In fact, it would be longer than I expected, almost five-and-a-half years, before I went there again. Little did I know that during that period, Manchester City would anticipate the need for additional drama in my life and would excel themselves when it came to providing it.

17

Law and Order

I'D THOUGHT ABOUT becoming a lawyer since that trip to London to stay with Auntie Alice and Robert all those years before, so it was natural that my first instinct was to study law when I applied to go to university. I thought about it again after my first year at Cambridge, when I actually made known my wish to change courses and move into the law faculty for the remainder of my degree. The system at Cambridge was set up to allow this kind of change, but so many people were trying to make the same switch that a quota was imposed by the college. I was fifth in line and in the first-come-first-served system, there were only four places. But when I graduated, I still hadn't had any brighter ideas, so I decided to stick with the only long-term career plan I'd ever had. Thus it was that in 1991, I returned from my dramatic summer in Russia and began law school.

Like many people I know who've embarked on the study of law, I had no great passion for it. It was a means to an end, nothing more or less. And that end was a comfortable life. Not for the first time, it was based on an erroneous premise. I didn't realise that the study would be tough and relentless at the outset and that the working environment when I actually became a solicitor would have little to commend it.

One route into the legal profession is to take law as a degree subject. There's then a supposedly more practical one-year course geared to becoming a solicitor or barrister, followed by a period of on-the-job training. Complete that little lot and you're professionally qualified. But those who have another degree have a chance to make up lost ground by taking a one-year course known as the 'conversion course' before proceeding along with the law graduates onto the solicitors' or barristers' course. It was hard work - on a typical law degree, students cover fourteen papers in three years, whereas we had to do six in a year, so it was a grind. And I was then on the last year of the old-style solicitors' course (I hated public speaking so had no intention of becoming a barrister), which, if not exactly known for being intellectually tough, certainly had a justified reputation for submerging students in a bewildering welter of detail, huge chunks of which had to be regurgitated in an exam.

To do both courses, I returned to Manchester and lived at home for two years. This wasn't so much a matter of choice as of financial necessity - or at least born of a desire to avoid beginning my legal career inconvenienced by a mountain of personal debt. It also meant that I once again became a season-ticket holder at Maine Road rather than just someone who attended on a casual basis. And it seemed, in the summer of 1991, a particularly opportune time to be making the transition. Having prospered the previous campaign under new player/manager Peter Reid, who'd taken over Howard Kendall's side, City were fancied to be once more, if not title-winners, then at least a contender in the higher reaches of the top flight. And early results, while I'd been otherwise occupied on the other side of Europe, seemed to indicate that the optimistic prognostications were not misconceived.

Having supported a desperately unsuccessful team over a long period, it might be thought that the couple of seasons in the early nineties in which we achieved a modicum of success would represent a pinnacle. In fact, this isn't a period of Manchester City's history on which I, or many other fans I know, reflect with particular affection. Reid's team managed a second successive fifth-placed finish in 1991-92, but even though those two years represent the best efforts in almost a quarter of a century, there was little excitement, and that's an ingredient we particularly prize at Maine Road.

Fans simply didn't enjoy watching this team. We're used to failure and self-inflicted catastrophe, but at least things are normally interesting, with the occasional stunning and unexpected success. For instance, in 1961-62, City thrashed the Spurs team which had won the double the previous year; after the 6-2 win, which had happened just after astronaut John Glen had gone on a famous space mission, The Manchester Guardian was moved to comment famously that so enthralling had been City's display, no-one would have noticed Glen if he'd encircled Maine Road on a magic carpet. There was nothing like this from Reid's team, which played fairly depressing long-ball football and despite the improved results, the faithful really had no great enthusiasm for it.

I wasn't greatly enthused by the law, either, although I was glad of one thing - that I'd only spent the one year doing what could, had I chosen it as a degree subject, have dominated my life for three. There were occasional moments of interest - there were a few entertaining criminal law cases on the syllabus, for instance. But most of all, the course was pretty dull. Whether there was really any need, over these two years, to prize rote-learning over any kind of meaningful analysis, I'm not sure, but I really didn't enjoy it much.

Effectively, I can see that I was making the same compromise as I was being asked to make at Maine Road, i.e. the pursuit of success to the detriment of colour. I wasn't expecting to have a wild and tempestuous time studying the Law of Property Act 1925 and its various ramifications (land law was especially tedious) but I believed that I'd be guaranteeing my future if I did so. And that made the monotony at least tolerable. All of a sudden, instead of meandering through a degree in which I had little more than a passing interest, I had a purpose and drive. Even if this course was by and large less interesting than the one I'd been doing the previous year, this one had no pretensions to be fun, and at least it was leading somewhere.

If my life had suddenly acquired a direction, the clubs of the English First Division were also finding themselves looking towards the future. And just as I had one eye on my own financial enrichment, there's no doubt that they had one eye on theirs. For 1992 was the year in which the Premiership was formed, and the change had a colossal impact on football in this country. Even those who care little for football will probably have heard of this institution, and it is credited by many with helping the top clubs to construct impressive and, more importantly, safe stadia. And it has lent glamour to the domestic game by enabling English clubs to have for the first time the wherewithal to compete in the transfer market with top continental clubs.

Essentially, what happened was this: the clubs of the old First Division decided they'd had enough of the system whereby clubs in the lower divisions took a share of television revenues and sponsorship deals sealed as a result of the top division's pulling power. As a result, the top clubs broke away and elected to negotiate their own deals in these areas, leaving the Football League's 72 other clubs to fend for themselves. The result was that English football arguably changed more in the space of the next decade than it had in the 104 years of its existence up to this point.

From its outset, the game in this country had been democratic when it came to the distribution of revenues, and this had ensured that clubs of relatively modest means could compete against the big city clubs. Right up until the early sixties, small-town Lancashire outfits like Burnley, Blackburn, Preston and Blackpool would show themselves capable of out-performing the better-supported teams from the county's big cities of Liverpool and Manchester. In part, that resulted in a system that ensured clubs could treat players like chattels. The imposition of a maximum wage for players, only abolished four decades ago, ensured that a superstar of his era, like Tom Finney, could earn as much by staying at his hometown club Preston as by moving to a richer club. And players didn't have what was known as "freedom of contract" until 1978, the football authorities finding a new system to achieve this aim when the old one was declared illegal in 1963. This meant that even when a player's contract had ended, his club could prevent him from finding a new employer unless their demands as to a transfer fee were met. From 1978, the player could move wherever he wanted, the buying club having to pay a fee fixed by a tribunal comprising footballing luminaries.

It's hard to condone the notion of imposing on footballers restrictions on their ability to earn a living that would horrify the rest of us were we subject to them, but these developments certainly made it harder for less wealthy teams to retain the services of their best players. Then, in the early 1980s, the smaller clubs lost another of the advantages that had helped them compete with the abolition of the rule requiring gate receipts from a league game to be shared between the two clubs; now, the home team kept all the money. Prior to this, the smaller clubs in the old First Division could look forward to big pay days every season at Old Trafford, Anfield, Highbury and the other big grounds. Now they had to survive on their own relatively meagre revenues, and were unable to match the big boys in the transfer market or in terms of player wages. It's no coincidence that, whereas in the 1970s, teams like Derby and Nottingham Forest won the title and Ipswich competed for it more than once, no club with comparable resources to those three has ever seriously threatened to emerge as champions since.

The formation of the Premier League, then, was merely another step down the same path, since it further concentrated an even greater percentage of the money generated by football in the hands of the elite. I know there's an argument that those clubs are responsible for most of football's income anyway, since they're the ones who really interest spectators, television companies and sponsors. But whatever the advantages of the new set-up, I think to most true lovers of football, it's a source of regret that the pinnacle English league structure has become such a closed shop. There was a real romance in the possibility that a Wimbledon could come from non-league to the top flight in nine years, or that Swansea could win a place in Europe five years after competing in the old Fourth Division. Now, those days are gone, and the only way a lower-division club can hope to emulate such feats is to be bankrolled by a fabulously wealthy sugar daddy.

Ironically, in view of the fact that over the next decade Manchester City would spend as many seasons outside the Premiership as in it, we were one of the prime movers behind the formation of the new structure. And when the new television deal resulted in the live transmission of top-flight fixtures on satellite channel Sky Sports, City's home game against QPR became the first match to be screened on a Monday evening. There were fireworks and dancing girls, while at half-time, some insipid, ephemeral pop band performed a poor cover of Gerry Rafferty's 1970s hit Baker Street. The unsatisfactory nature of the entertainment notwithstanding, it was clear that this was a whole new way of presenting football, and as such offered a pointer to the direction in which the game might be heading.

It's foolish and hopelessly idealistic to expect the football industry to be founded on the passions of the supporters; the game's popularity and the unstinting loyalty of fans ensure that in the modern age, opportunities abound for those looking to make money from it. Thus it is that Rupert Murdoch has referred to sport (and football is by some distance the biggest sport of them all) as a "battering ram" for pay television services. And this is scarcely surprising, as Murdoch's Sky empire in the UK was making heavy losses until it paid big money for the exclusive right to screen Premiership football. All of a sudden, the number of subscribers to his service increased exponentially and the company became hugely profitable.

It was the large sums of money Sky poured into the game at the top level that transformed the big clubs. Stadia were improved (in the wake of the Hillsborough disaster there was a legal requirement to go all-seater anyway, but the Sky money facilitated further improvements and expansion of capacity). This, coupled with the game's increased media profile since the 1990 World Cup, in turn attracted people to football who had never previously taken an interest in the game. With clubs desperate for success, most of the additional cash found its way into the pockets of players and agents. And with their income streams bolstered in such spectacular fashion, the clubs themselves increased enormously in value, making the owners of some of the major outfits in the land very wealthy men indeed.

Television cash wasn't divided among Premiership clubs exactly equally, but the mechanism for distributing the funds ensured each team a significant share. And the disparity between these amounts and those available to clubs outside the top division saw a large gap begin to open up between the haves and the have-nots, exacerbated with the onset of new and more lucrative TV deals for the Premiership in 1997 and 2001. Unfortunately, and with typically inept timing, Manchester City chose the period from 1993 onwards to 'enjoy' their worst spell in their history. This wasn't, however, apparent from the start of the 1992-93 season, when everything seemed plain-sailing despite the style of play.

My own progress had been more than satisfactory since my return to Manchester. I came through the conversion course with few problems and also seemed set to do well on the next. It was, needless to say, a grind, but the achievement of my long-term objective was in sight and that kept me going, especially as I'd landed a job to start in the September after the course ended. City, meanwhile, seemed to be set for more of the same after their two sojourns in the rarefied heights of fifth place. They'd been erratic throughout the first half of the season, and the footballing aesthetics as unappealingly one-dimensional as ever, but they were always managing to stay in the top half of the table. And when Reading, in an away replay after a desperate draw at Maine Road, Port Vale and Barnsley were brushed aside in the FA Cup, it even looked like the hunt for a trophy (note for City fans - big silver thing with handles that's awarded when you've won a competition) could be coming to an end. In fact it marked the start of a desperate period for the club.

The Cup quarter-final draw paired City with Tottenham, a game selected for live television coverage. The new Platt Lane stand was in use for the first time, so there was a packed house (one end of the ground had been a building site for the past ten months), and the faithful were in optimistic mood. And Mike Sheron swept City into an early lead, which only served to reinforce the sense of expectation. Of course, we should have known better. Spurs' Moroccan-born midfielder Nayim scored a hat-trick as the Londoners rattled in four without further reply from us, before a run by City full-back Terry Phelan through their defence provided what, given that only a couple of minutes remained, could only be a consolation goal. But it proved also to be the trigger for scenes which would lead to widespread media condemnation of the City support.

There was a sense of overwhelming frustration in the crowd by the time of Phelan's strike and the fact that the team had managed a fine goal when it was patently of no use seemed to be adding insult to injury. Around 150 fans invaded the playing area and the teams had to be led to the dressing rooms while police horses cleared the pitch. The players did then return to play out the last couple of minutes, but even that was enough time for Spurs to win and miss (deliberately, perhaps, in view of the security situation) a penalty. There was an FA investigation and fine, while the disapproval in the press was unanimous ("I feared another Hillsborough," The Sun quoted the match referee as saying, which seemed ludicrously over the top). All in all it was a thoroughly depressing afternoon, after which the season petered out. The two home games in the season's last week summed it all up: after a stultifyingly mediocre goalless draw against a Palace side relegated three days later, we capitulated 5-2 against Everton to round off the campaign on an afternoon when the crowd stayed off the pitch but certainly made its collective disgust abundantly clear.

Many observers of Manchester City in the 1990s attribute great significance to the fact that as all this was going on, Manchester United were winning the league title for the first time in more than a quarter of a century. This, so the argument goes, was a matter of great significance for City fans, who expected their team to compete with their rivals, and who reacted with venom when we failed to do so. At least for me, this was untrue. It was our own failings that concerned me - not the fact they'd remedied theirs. What had happened on the pitch gave me a feeling that things were badly wrong at Maine Road, and the events of the summer proved me right.

I completed the solicitors course in July and prepared to move on and start my first job feeling optimistic that I'd start to make my mark on the world. It seemed an exciting period in terms of my personal life - but City's plight was a disquieting cloud on the horizon. In fact, if I'd known just how bad things would get in the years to come, I'd have felt much more troubled.

18

An Unusual Preference

THE SUMMER OF 1991 didn't just show that Russia was turbulent enough for me to find echoes of the Maine Road rollercoaster. It also demonstrated my talent for wandering into similarly complex and ill-fated romantic encounters. That ability was to be amply demonstrated in 1991-92, and was to be a frequent feature of life thereafter.

I suppose I was never destined to be someone who valued stability above all else in my personal life. I'm not quite sure whether I inherited a bizarre genetic disposition for stormy, self-destructive relationships or whether I developed a fascination for them through observing them at close quarters at a young and tender age. But either way, that was the type of romantic attachment that surrounded me as I grew up, and that's what I've always managed to replicate as an adolescent and an adult.

After one particularly miserable episode, I remember seeking advice from a female friend who offered the view that I really only had myself to blame for my travails, and that I should just look for someone "nice" and "stable". I responded by saying that, given my singular lack of success in this regard, she ought to find someone suitable for me. I had to reconsider, however, when it occurred to me what the concept of suitable would be in her eyes. She'd have picked someone without complications, without problems, who wouldn't have made my life hell. And, of course, I wouldn't have had the slightest interest.

I'm loathe to compare any of the women I've known to Manchester City, in part for fear of a libel suit after publication of this book, and in any case I'm not sure how appropriate it would be to draw the parallel, though given our number of relegations over the years, it might facilitate a few cheap innuendoes centred on the theme of going down. But I've always tended to go for women whom I regarded as interesting and unpredictable. And this was the stage when I first started to equate interest with experience of life.

It isn't uncommon for a young man to have a fixation with older women, usually with the most mercenary of motives. For example, a female friend of mine in her early thirties once told me that the 16-year-old son of a friend of hers was "in love" with her. I had to explain that love was the last thing on his mind. My interpretation was that he simply wanted to learn everything he could from a physical relationship with an experienced woman before trying it out on every sixth-form schoolgirl and then first-year female undergraduate he could get his hands on.

For me, it wasn't quite like that. Of course I'd had those same thoughts when I'd been younger, but by the time I'd reached the age of 22 and become involved for the first time with a woman in her thirties, I was really beyond initiations. I just felt that my older woman was more interesting than girls of my age. She'd done more in her life, had richer experiences but still had her looks. So to me, the prospect of a relationship with her was far more alluring than would have been the thought of becoming involved with one of the students on the course who had gone to university straight from school and had just completed their first degree.

City in the early 1990s, meanwhile, weren't exhibiting too much in the way of interesting behaviour (ostensibly, we were behaving much more like a normal football club), but in fact we were storing up for ourselves problems that would traumatise Maine Road for years to come. After paying a British record fee for a defender to land Wimbledon's Keith Curle in August 1991, the club a year later matched the £2.5 million outlay to bring Irish international full-back Terry Phelan to Maine Road, also from the Dons. Phelan, a native of Salford, had publicly professed his desire to return north, but, even so, Crystal Palace entered the bidding. They were Wimbledon's landlords, and their interest bumped up the fee for the player as surely as if the chairmen of the respective London clubs had connived to wring the maximum money possible out of City through Palace making a spurious big-money offer.

The Phelan deal, and the prior acquisition of Curle, didn't quite herald a return to the transfer insanity of Malcolm Allison's era - despite our having unquestionably paid well over the odds, both men, unlike Steve Daley, at least showed themselves to be more than capable performers during their City careers. But the fact remained that this was cash we could ill afford to spend. At this stage, most major football clubs were concentrating on improving their grounds, the Government having followed the recommendations of the Taylor Report, which examined the issue of spectator safety in the wake of the Hillsborough disaster in 1989 and concluded that all-seater stadia were the answer. As others budgeted for the necessary large-scale construction work and cut back accordingly on other expenditure, City were sadly oblivious to the demands of the legislation.

The Deloitte & Touche Survey of Football Club Accounts shows that between 1992 and 1994, our net transfer expenditure was greater than that of all but one of the other clubs in the top division. That exception was Blackburn Rovers, who were being bankrolled to an unprecedented degree by the millionaire industrialist Jack Walker. City, of course, lacked such lavish financial backing, but pressed on regardless and also undertook ground improvements not relating to the Taylor Report. The new stand at the Platt Lane end of the ground was rebuilt at a cost of £5 million, but in addition to its 48 executive boxes, it provided seating for only 4,000 fans. Neighbours Stockport County, then in the lower divisions and attracting average gates in that order, built a new stand behind one of their goals at the same time; theirs had a bigger capacity.

Even if the old stand had to be replaced because the local authority would no longer issue a safety certificate - and this was advanced in mitigation by some apologists, although I have no evidence as to whether or not the assertion is true - it was clear that there was no coherent stadium development strategy. Meanwhile, the outlay on new players failed to transform the team into an outfit capable of challenging for the English game's major prizes; in fact, in those two years we went from a top-five outfit to relegation strugglers. Normal service had been thoroughly resumed. Indeed, the scene was set for events more turbulent than any in the club's entire history, some achievement given the rollercoaster ride the club has inflicted on its followers over the years. It was to be a period that would leave even the most committed of fans cursing the fact they'd been born as Blues.

In most cases, 'born' into fandom is exactly the right word to use; as with others, I had no choice in the matter at all. And this has meant that we have to witness the never-ending parade of Manchester United trophies and at the same time have to put up with all kinds of disasters. In many ways, I identify with women, who are discriminated against in the job market and who still often don't receive an equal day's pay for the same day's work. They have to bear childbirth, PMT, breast-feeding and periods. Men have to shave.

But although I'm glad I'm not one, I can't help thinking that there's one great thing about women - however trite it may sound, they're not men. Maybe it's through being a man that I can appreciate my gender's true nature, and that allows me to make one observation which is true beyond doubt: if I were a woman, I'd be a lesbian. It's a generalisation, of course, but men are crude and boorish, gauche and inelegant, faithless and trivial and emotionally immature. So just as I don't value effeminacy in a man, I certainly don't have much time for women who seem to prize masculinity above all.

That I like and get on with women is shown by the fact that I have plenty of friends who are men, but more who are women. I am not sure if this is typical - experience among my own male friends tends to indicate not, while I read one lad-lit novel last year in which the narrator considered himself something of a pioneer because he had just one lone platonic female friend. (As an aside, I always feel slightly sorry for Plato, since to have lent his name to this kind of relationship, he must have spent his whole life failing to get laid). At the last count, apart from those who are ex-girlfriends, I'm still in contact with many more women with whom I have this kind of relationship.

Most of these women are intelligent and attractive, but for some reason - and with literally two or three exceptions - I couldn't envisage the blossoming of any romance. And lest that sound too conceited, let me reiterate that in most if not all of those cases, I almost certainly don't have the option anyway. But in any case, most of them are just too ... well, too uncomplicated. This is why I had to refuse my friend's offer of assistance in finding a new mate. Only once have I ever found a kindred spirit; some years later, when I went to work in Russia, an English girl in the office turned out to have exactly the same predilection for a disastrous love life. We used to compare notes regularly, each vying to outdo the other with our latest tales of woe.

And all of this teaches me a lesson. I used to think that somehow I'd been born into following Manchester City, that it had been a remarkable coincidence that my family had moved back to Manchester in time for me to become an avid follower. I know now that this simply isn't true. I'd have found City come what may - and my unshakeable conviction is buoyed by the awareness that, in my personal life, I've constantly managed, like a homing pigeon, to arrow in on the option that will cause me the most grief.

People who don't like football will doubt the truth of this observation, but somehow there's a big similarity between personal relationships and those football fans have with their teams. With City, it's hard to avoid the conclusion that we are like the spouses who stick with nightmare partners no matter what. Despite all the mental torture, all the glaring failings and inadequacies in the relationship which mean we know all too well that we should pack the whole thing in, a compelling force always draws us back.

I remember a friend telling me once how about 5,000 City fans locked in the away end at Nottingham Forest (after a 1-0 defeat to a freak goal in a game crucial to our prospects of avoiding relegation) started singing along to the Madness song 'It Must Be Love' when it was played over the tannoy. I always thought it was a shame this never caught on as a regular chant, as it more or less sums the whole thing up. It's not your idyllic Mills & Boon kind of love of course, but the fact remains that there's something about the club which encourages a deep and irrational loyalty and makes us unable to turn our backs even though it's what the club would deserve (if football fans could sue for divorce, we'd be able to bring a library full of evidence in support of our claims of unreasonable behaviour).

I haven't found much idyllic Mills & Boon love in my personal life over the years, either, but then there's not much I've done that would be consistent with looking for that. Not since 1991-92, when I found an older, divorced mother of three and going through a period of great upheaval in her own personal life. That particular profile isn't one I've sought out since, but I've managed to end up in situations which have been equally problematic. Those kind of complications make life interesting - the same effect is produced by supporting Manchester City.

19

The World of Work

THE SUMMER OF 1993 was a time of change. Finally, I finished in higher education after six years and was to begin work. And it was fairly clear even in pre-season that things were about to change in a major way at Maine Road. Despite City's collapse at the end of the previous campaign, manager Peter Reid was handed a new three-year contract and was keen to strengthen his squad. But it soon became clear that all was not well.

Swales publicly promised Reid an extensive transfer budget, though in truth there were minimal funds available - the club was all but broke. Initially, the manager targeted ex-City player Paul Stewart of Spurs, whom he'd tried to bring back to Maine Road on several previous occasions, and Geoff Thomas of Crystal Palace. Neither man seemed to me to be the answer to our problems, but, as it happened, it didn't much matter whether they'd have been good buys or not: Stewart signed for Liverpool, with City unable to match the level of the fee, and the Manchester-born Thomas, despite commenting that he'd crawl up the M6 over broken glass to join his boyhood favourites, opted to drop a division to join Wolves. Other big-name players were linked with moves to Maine Road, but by the time the new season kicked off, the only new face was the little-known (at least outside his native land) Dutchman Alfons Groenendijk. Reid tried to talk up his new acquisition, but the bizarre claim that the midfielder "could shell peas with his left foot" did little to convince.

The failure to add significantly to the squad added to a sense of unease which was only intensified by news of the pre-season games. A Dutch tour brought a 5-1 defeat against AZ67 Alkmaar together with tabloid allegations arising from the drinking habits of some of the players. And then there was the incomprehensible appointment of a former tabloid journalist as general manager to act as a "buffer" between Reid and the autocratic chairman Peter Swales. The press conference at which John Maddock was paraded was farcical, with the bluff pressman seated next to a visibly bemused Reid.

If events at Maine Road gave little cause for optimism, the same wasn't true in my own life, as I looked forward to starting my first full-time job (I'd worked at an examination board in the summer, but that was just low-level clerical work to supplement my student income). I'd moved to Yorkshire to start a two-year stint as a trainee solicitor with one of the aggressively expansionist Leeds-based firms that helped to change the legal profession in this country. The promise of a stint in Brussels had attracted me to the job, and given that the firm had also opened offices in Manchester and London, there would also be the opportunity to work there. I took a room in a shared house with four other young professionals, one a student on a year's work-based placement, and it was with him that I struck up an especially propitious relationship. It turned out to be a meeting that ensured that the pursuit of my career away from Manchester would never deflect me from my passion for City.

Pete was from Salford, a place often cited as a part of Manchester but in fact a city in its own right and a Manchester United stronghold. He, however, had managed to escape the path of darkness. I'd actually decided to abandon my season ticket at this time because I'd anticipated a cooling in my enthusiasm, but going to matches with Pete made me more passionate than ever. However, when City became embroiled in a takeover struggle, I limited myself to attending away games only.

I'd actually taken up residence in my rented room a couple of weeks before I was due to start my job to get acclimatised to the area, but as soon as I left, all hell had broken loose at City. The season started as badly as the results of the pre-season tour would have led fans to fear. I saw the opening home game of the season, a 1-1 draw against Leeds. Thanks to a combination of inspired goalkeeping from City's Tony Coton, the co-operation of the woodwork, and both profligacy and misfortune on the part of the Leeds strikers, the away side failed to build up the four or five-goal lead that wouldn't have been an injustice given their superiority. City, completely against the run of play, scored a lucky goal with three minutes remaining, but still couldn't hold onto the three points - Leeds equalised with the last kick of the game having been denied seconds earlier when the referee mystifyingly ruled out a perfectly valid goal. The next three games produced equally wretched performances, which actually were reflected in the results - no goals and three defeats - and Maddock acted. He unceremoniously dismissed Reid.

I still remember the Manchester Evening News headline of the next day, when I'd gone home to see a Friday night fixture against Coventry. For that game, the team would be under the stewardship of veteran former manager Tony Book, but the paper explained that a permanent appointee had been secured. "Mr. Right", screamed the headline of a story promising an inspiring appointment, a perception encouraged by Maddock, who was interviewed at regular intervals on his car phone during a mystery journey south for negotiations with the boss of another club. Throughout the day fans had speculated as to who the new manager might be. But if Maddock was showing the ability, no doubt honed in his previous job, to ensure that the club made the headlines, he evidently was unconcerned if that publicity rendered it a laughing stock.

After an improved performance had brought a 1-1 draw with Coventry, a result that did no justice to City's domination of the game, the new man was unveiled. Yet Maddock's folly in inflating expectations was proved by the next morning's press, and by the reaction of supporters after the game. "Brian who?" asked the tabloid headlines the next day as the hitherto low-profile Oxford manager Brian Horton moved into what was a particularly scorching hot seat. Fans, meanwhile, demonstrated their anger outside the ground, news having broken during the match itself.

There'd been no ground-swell of opinion calling on the club to dispense with Reid. That isn't to say that there was universal satisfaction with the Reid regime; the youth policy appeared to be disintegrating, while the first team played a depressingly ugly, monotonous style of route one football. But it was assistant manager Sam Ellis, an enormously unpopular figure, who bore the brunt of crowd frustration. Or rather, it was Ellis and, much more so, chairman Peter Swales. Now the latest sacking, in its manner as much as its effect, enraged the fans. Swales was no stranger to such controversy (and I personally had scorned his abilities for over a decade), but he'd ridden out previous storms because of the lack of a readily identifiable alternative. This time, things were different.

Received wisdom has it that everyone can remember where they were when they discovered that John F. Kennedy had been shot. Even I recognise that the announcement of a takeover bid for Manchester City is, in the overall scheme of things, not quite such a momentous event, but I can nevertheless recall how I found out that former player Francis Lee was hoping to oust Swales. This might make me sound something of an anorak, but to be fair, it was a momentous day on a personal level. I was at Leeds station on the way to my first day of work when I saw the banner headline in someone's copy of that day's Daily Mirror newspaper. I immediately bought my own copy, which I then determinedly hid in my new briefcase all day lest my employer consider my choice of reading material too downmarket.

When I look back now on Francis Lee's takeover saga, I'm struck by the role played in the whole conflict by personality. Maybe if I hadn't been in my first week of my first proper job then maybe I wouldn't have been so surprised. For there I learned that it wasn't just in football clubs where those in charge like to build their own personal little fiefdoms.

I'm not saying that law firms are worse for this than anywhere else - it's simply that law firms are what I know best. But I do suspect that the way they operate makes them more susceptible to being populated by a certain type of individual. The thing is that they operate as partnerships with a large number of partners. A substantial chunk of the legally qualified staff (often called 'fee earners' to denote that they bring in the money and thus make the rest of the employees feel small) will be partners. This means that they own a share of the business and have a correspondingly heightened degree of authority within the organisation. It is the kind of environment in which egos thrive. Given that the career in itself is lucrative, it often attracts ambitious and driven people anyway, and when intoxicated by power to boot they can be fascinating to observe - though many of the incidents there are preferable to look back on rather than to be part of.

I used to have a line I used at interviews. When asked about my impressions of a career in the law, I always said that I didn't expect it to be like LA Law. What I meant was that I felt I knew what was really involved, and wasn't just being seduced by the glamour of the portrayal of law firms in the media. It proved to be just as well that I didn't particularly harbour any illusions, as the slick, American TV series certainly wasn't how it really was. Of course, there were, as in all workplaces, the usual affairs and gossip. I remember at one firm, in which I'd worked in a very small office, becoming aware after I'd left that the (married) senior lawyer in the office had been conducting a sexual relationship with a more junior member of staff for three years. That in itself wasn't such a surprise, but I'd assumed that in such a closely-knit team, there'd be no such hidden indiscretions and this was news to all of us. On another occasion, in a pub after work one night, one of the secretaries pointed at one of the senior lawyers. "I've had him," she told me, "and he's crap." But the recurrence of this type of story - and needless to say, there were many more - wasn't the only revelation to me.

On a completely different tack, there was the relentless nature of the work. I specialised in corporate law, and spent much of my time in mergers and acquisitions (buying and selling companies) because I thought there might be an international element there in which I could find an outlet for my languages and international ambitions. It was a gruelling branch of the profession, because the clients are paying big money and expect things done to their timetable. But what struck me even more about my new job were the personalities and attitudes of some of my colleagues and superiors.

One aspect that surprised me was that some of the lawyers actually seemed to relish the long hours. I knew it was part of the job and put up with the demands when they arose, just as I would now. But I couldn't get my head around the idea of being happy when I had to sacrifice having any kind of life for a couple of weeks to complete a deal? I could scarcely comprehend those who felt this way. "Sad bastards", as Mancunian bloke calls them.

There were, though, plenty who didn't succumb to this kind of madness. However, plenty of them were dysfunctional in other ways, and on many occasions I've thought of populating a sitcom with characters I'd encountered in my professional life. At one firm I was with, the cast boasted such luminaries as 'The Juggler', so called because of his distressing habit of placing his hands in his pocket and rummaging frantically in the front of his trousers during any conversation. There was 'Lurch', a tall, awkward man with no social skills or aptitude for modern technology whose prime means of communication with the outside world was to bellow from his office. There was 'Porter', so named because of his resemblance to British Rail station staff in his bizarre electric blue suit. And there was 'Numpty', whose nickname, the Scottish word for a harmless buffoon, was earned by some comical mannerisms. The reference to the inoffensive wasn't entirely appropriate, though, as his self-esteem seemed to depend on his ability to make life unpleasant for junior members of staff; when he used to boast that he had "panache", I could only assume he was using one of that word's lesser-known alternative meanings. There were several possibilities - an odious, oily little shit, or a parochial, small-minded tosser being just two of them.

I hated having to ingratiate myself with these people, and it was always a difficult task for the Mancunian Bloke inside me; he doesn't exactly suffer fools gladly. Thus it was, for instance, that I failed to hit it off with one smarmy, self-satisfied and irritating boss who ended up giving me a slightly ambivalent appraisal. He was more than content with my work, but he expressed the criticism that I was 'lugubrious'. I had to share an office with him, and he used to complain that I didn't share aspects of my personal life with him. I'd also been told he liked to enjoy 'banter', but I didn't laugh at his jokes - quite reasonably, because they weren't funny. It was just a pity that, given his influence over my career development, I couldn't revert to Mancunian Bloke's slightly more forthright voice in the appraisal. "I'm sorry," he'd have explained calmly, rationally and with absolute justification. "It's just that you're a complete wanker."

His similar earlier verdict on Peter Swales hadn't been revised either. Despite some relative on-field success since I'd paraded round the Maine Road forecourt six years before with a banner advocating his dismissal, the City chairman's stock hadn't risen in my eyes in the intervening period. Swales's behaviour over the summer had been completely irrational. He'd ignored the need to make the stadium all-seater (his anxious appeal to the Government to repeal this legislation was nothing short of pathetic). He'd signed away all the club's merchandising possibilities on ludicrous long-term franchise from which we received an annual flat fee of £60,000 - at this time, Manchester United were turning over £8 million per annum and Newcastle £6 million from the same activity. Despite being one of the better-supported clubs, we were one of only four in the new Premiership to make a trading loss in 1993-94. We were severely in debt, yet still had to find the resources to build a new stand to replace the one accounting for a third of our stadium capacity. There were the ludicrous public statements containing assurances to the fans that would always prove to be unfounded.

For all these reasons, he simply had to go if the club was to have any chance of making progress. The only other route was selling the best players to keep the bank happy, which, with the team struggling anyway, would have meant certain relegation in 1994.

Needless to say, Swales wasn't of the same view. More charitable fans than I claimed that this was because he loved the club. I rather suspected it was his own personal domain and that his own sense of importance was fed by the television appearances that went with being chairman of a Premiership football club. And since the 1970s, he'd enjoyed the trappings of being an FA Counsellor - a position he'd never have held but for his club role and which gave him, in his capacity as chairman of the International Committee, regular trips abroad with the England team.

The battle to oust him was protracted and bitter, lasting almost six months. And in that time, fans put immense pressure on him - pressure that was blamed for the heart attack from which he died just over two years after he stepped down. Certainly, his close friends thought so, and it seems plausible. I have mixed feelings about this. I may have wanted him removed from the City chairmanship, but I'd never have wanted him dead - that would have been terribly vengeful.

There's no doubt that a minority of football fans place figures in the game under intolerable strain; some of the behaviour is disgraceful. And in the battle for Manchester City, I have no doubts that some of the threats to which Swales was subjected were intolerable (though it should also be noted that after the most widely reported incident, when fans were supposed to have broken into the nursing home where his sick mother was staying, the Daily Express quoted the matron as saying she was unaware of the occurrence).

Whatever, the actions of some fans were undoubtedly beyond the pale, as has been the case ever since. However, most fans were sincere in their wishes and restrained in their expressions of dissent. And Swales was lamentably slow to accept the fact that any owner of a football club must understand: it's a different game from simply owning your own company. A football club has ties to its community, not just its shareholders. And it has fans, not customers or consumers, the difference being the emotional bond they feel. That means they'll fight for changes at the club, rather than simply taking their patronage elsewhere. A chairman who has lost the faith of the support and who is unable to turn things round (City were headed for relegation and their financial state was dire so there was no question of buying their way out of trouble) is in a very vulnerable position. He should have accepted the inevitability of his fate.

My own form of protest had been to refrain from attending home matches, the first and only time I'd taken such a course of action. I was attending, for the first time in two or three years, significant numbers of away games (a step that may not have happened had I not met Pete), but was determined that my money wouldn't prop up the Swales regime. If all affronted fans had taken this step, Swales would have been removed much sooner and with much less rancour.

When Francis Lee took the fans' plaudits at his first home game with Ipswich in February 1994, hopes were high. How little we knew - his reign would also turn out to be deeply flawed. That doesn't mean we were wrong about Swales, though, and in any case his legacy was one of the primary influences on what was to follow. Even by City standards, it was a bumpy ride.

20

Real Life

FRANCIS LEE WAS a genuine City hero. As a pugnacious forward signed from Bolton in October 1967, he'd proved the missing piece in the exciting jigsaw being assembled by Joe Mercer and Malcolm Allison. We duly won the league championship that season and then three more trophies in the two years after, while Lee's form in this period made him an England regular. Having served the club for seven years, he was offloaded to Derby, and vowed to make City regret the decision to dispense with his services. Derby duly won the league in his first season with them, Lee's goals instrumental in the triumph - and none more so than a spectacular last-minute winner for his new team at Maine Road. That strike had also been a big blow to City's own ambitions at the top of the table, but there were no regrets for Lee, who celebrated proving his point to his former employer as if he'd just notched the winner in a World Cup final.

After two years at Derby, Lee retired to concentrate on business interests he'd already been developing during his playing career. He'd become a multi-millionaire, and had also become involved in horse racing. The combination of wealth, success in everything he'd done, a football background and an impeccable City pedigree ensured that fans always viewed him as a potential saviour, hoping that he'd buy the club. He'd always insisted that he'd no interest in doing so, but when his attitude changed, there was immediately a huge ground-swell of support behind him. And when he finally ousted Swales, hopes for the future were sky-high. He didn't exactly lack confidence in himself, either, and his bullish and buoyant forecasts only fuelled expectations.

Maybe we should have known. For most people, it's normal to see hopes and expectations dashed in all areas of life - if not constantly, then hardly on an irregular basis either. And this manifests itself in our attitude to entertainment: while some people are drawn to the escapist, many others find such sanitised diversions wholly unsatisfactory. We Manchester City fans fall firmly into the second category.

It may surprise those with a minimal or just a passing interest in football that this state of affairs can exist. Fans of most football teams are genuinely miserable for much, if not most, of the time. Some end up supporting a team that actually wins things. But the rest - well, for them it's let-downs and disappointments on a regular basis. People who support a team merely because it wins have no part in this debate.

Through gritted teeth, I can admit that Manchester United are currently, and have for the past several years, been a marvellous football team. I can understand neutrals admiring the football they play, and on this basis I suppose that I could relate to seeing a trip to Old Trafford as the football equivalent of watching opera at La Scala or ballet at the Bolshoi. But those who extrapolate this into a claim to the football fan's partisanship - the joys of victory and the gloom of defeat - are really missing the point.

The whole essence of being a football fan centres round earning the right to enjoy the good times by enduring the bad. In other words, those who have maintained their faith through the bad times, those who have suffered but persisted when things looked hopeless - they're the ones who have the moral right to enjoy the spoils of victory when it eventually occurs. Off-the-peg fandom just doesn't work; those who affect to be fans because they think it's trendy and then simply pick a successful team so they can bask in glory are impostors despised by the rest of us, including the genuine Mancunian United fans of my acquaintance.

Of course, the nouveaux are unaware of the irony, but they demonstrate nothing so much as that they've missed the point. For those in this category, redemption is possible in only two circumstances. One is where the fan is too young to know any better, and has no football-supporting parent to guide them; forgiveness is theirs if they repent of their sins when they reach an age at which they should be aware how desperately sad they've been. And the other is where the team they've chosen at the height of their powers obligingly turns into a desperately poor outfit, but the fan keeps faith. Believe it or not, there are City fans who fit this profile (yes, we were quite good once).

So if the fan's life is punctuated with bouts of misery, then, as with anyone who suffers, there's a tendency towards self-pity. Each set of fans assumes that they are worse afflicted, betrayed to a greater extent by the object of their affections than followers of other clubs. Now, this is largely melodramatic and untrue - just as in life, there's always someone worse off. But this doesn't stop us from moaning, and nor should it. Just as in real life, the fact that there are people starving in Africa doesn't negate the validity of complaints from someone trying to survive on the basic state pension in Britain.

As Manchester City fans, our complaints were many and varied. No doubt for many, the publicity that accompanied our fall was overdone, and all those references to the quality of the City support were somewhat over-the-top. Now, it's true that the numbers of fans turning up increased as the quality of the team declined, which over a period of two relegations in three years is rare if not unprecedented. But in other respects, any label of "best fans in the country" was unmerited and I knew few, if any, serious City supporters of my acquaintance believed it. There's a section of the support given over to mindless violence, which, though small in number, is significant enough to constitute a problem. There are plenty who are only too ready to moan mindlessly rather than get behind the team. There are many who are unbearably arrogant and boastful when we play what they rather condescendingly like to see as a "smaller" club. We're just a set of fans like any other, really.

We have, however, had plenty of cause to be dissatisfied with our lot. I know there are clubs like Rochdale, who've floundered around in the bottom division for donkeys' years, whose fate makes anything we've gone through seem trifling in the football suffering stakes. But remember that disappointment is engendered by a failure to meet expectations, and the expectations themselves are engendered in football by tradition and by resources.

None of us would have berated those in charge at Maine Road for failing to dominate English football or win trophies every year. But we had a tradition of at least mixing with the game's aristocrats even if our blood, unlike our shirts, wasn't the bluest - we spent around 80% of the twentieth century in the top flight. And in an age where the whole structure of the game is set up to allow teams with the greatest support to maximise their revenue, we consistently had the status of being the tenth or twelfth best-supported team at worst. That should, if we'd capitalised on it, have allowed us to compete among the top twenty clubs in the land (i.e. in the Premiership).

The thing is, it was all meant to be so different under Francis Lee. He arrived in a blaze of glory, and given his status as a playing legend at the club, he was the beneficiary of an enormous amount of goodwill from the fans, but those promises would come back to haunt him. One year, for instance, the annual general meeting of shareholders was held in a conference suite at Manchester Airport. Lee boldly stated that the change of venue (the occasion had previously taken place at Maine Road) would allow fans to see the place from where the team would fly out when they qualified for European competition. The prediction turned out to be laughably optimistic.

At this point, I was in my mid-twenties and I still wasn't used to things not going as I'd hoped. My progression down the path of life beforehand hadn't always been smooth, but I'd always managed to move on more or less on the course I wanted. Now, City were leading the way in showing me that I could no longer rely on that being the case, and the lesson was brought home to me in my other endeavours. I remember feeling that the firm I'd ended up working for wouldn't meet my international ambitions, so I decided to leave at the end of my two-year training contract, when I qualified as a solicitor. I'd worked for a spell in their Brussels office as part of my time there, and decided I'd like to return for a placement with the

European Commission before returning home and looking for a job with a different firm. It was to be a first major disappointment.

I elected to apply to work in the section dealing with External Economic Affairs in respect of the former Soviet states, figuring that my interests, skills and experience would make me well suited to the role. Colleagues who knew how the system worked told me that I'd have to lobby for my place, and this was when I realised that my impressive credentials might not be enough. "You need an influential sponsor," they advised me. "Do you know Sir Leon Brittan?" At the time, Brittan was the UK's senior Commissioner in Brussels. Needless to say, I'd never met him and I could only have labelled my chances of securing his endorsement as minimal had I been aware of the term non-existent.

I did my best. After I'd gone back to work in London, I spent a long weekend in Brussels meeting the people for whom I'd work were my application successful, and obtained what recommend-ations of weight I could (my MEP did write on my behalf). I received a letter from the head of the section I wanted to work for commending me as an "excellent candidate". And of course, in the end, they turned me down. I was led to believe that the daughter of a Swedish cabinet minister had decided she wanted the position, and given her connections the verdict was a formality, something about which I was rather bitter. That wasn't to be my last disappointment as I sought to find an outlet for my own slightly idiosyncratic talents. At least in this case, I wasn't to blame for my failure to fulfil my own ambitions - I'm not sure to what degree Francis Lee can say the same.

In retrospect, maybe it isn't surprising. Whereas at some football clubs, heroes take on an almost superhuman aspect (in the 1990s, for instance, our neighbours seemed really to believe that Eric Cantona really could walk on water), Manchester City idols have often proved to have feet of clay. I should have known, really, on one cold late December evening in 1976, almost exactly a year since I'd first seen a senior game at Maine Road. City were facing Liverpool in a top-of-the-table clash, and led by a single goal as the match ticked into its final minute. Then Dave Watson, an imperious England international defender and the player above all that I worshipped, gave the visitors an undeserved draw by diverting the ball past his own goalkeeper.

On a simplistic analysis at least, Watson's blunder cost City the title. At the end of the season, we were in second place, a point adrift of champions Liverpool - so without that goal, we'd have finished ahead of them. It may not have worked out like that, of course (Liverpool had eased up at the end of the campaign having sealed the title before their last game, but might well have obtained a result from it if they'd needed one). But in the light of what's happened since, it nevertheless seems apt that my first City hero should go down in the club's history as the man who deprived us of a league championship. That aptness seems hard to refute considering what's happened since. The disastrous second coming of Malcolm Allison was another example, while in the 1990s, the presence of the club's most sublimely talented player of my, and possibly any other, era couldn't prevent two relegations in the most miserable period in City history. This was also the time of Francis Lee, and he also left with his reputation sadly diminished.

Lee's inheritance from Peter Swales ensured he had an extremely difficult job on his hands at Maine Road, and his predecessor must take a major portion of the blame for what happened. It's also possible to cite other mitigating factors in Lee's defence. He only acquired a 29.9% stake in the club, which meant he'd always be relying on others to shore up his power base. His position was later eroded further when others subscribed for shares to pump much-needed funds into the club. The club's debts precluded spending major sums on team development beyond an initial splash to help avoid relegation in 1993-94, with available finance directed at the need to rebuild the Kippax Stand. Nevertheless, serious errors were made - ironically, some of them reflecting the failings of the man he deposed.

Raising expectations was a major error. In the takeover campaign, Lee's supporters regularly trumpeted that fantastic sums of money would be available for strengthening the squad, and never do I recall the outlandish claims being denied. Fans hoped for several star players to be brought in, but it never happened, and Lee quite clearly didn't have the personal wealth or the backers for such funds to be available. When things did start to go wrong, he had a fairly dismal grasp of PR. One complaint was that he allegedly interfered in playing matters, an area normally the preserve of the manager. He bitterly denied the claims, but it's hard to see what he expected when positioning himself conspicuously in the middle of the team's pre-season photograph. Then there was the rebuilding of the stadium. Given that money was short, it might have been better to try to produce a cheap design for the new Kippax Stand. Maybe the cost of the expensive new construction was justified, but it did seem that we'd paid much more for it than other clubs had for stands of a similar capacity, and we could ill afford the outlay. And most disappointingly, there was the failure to appoint and retain the services of the right man in charge of team affairs; this had been a failing of Swales, but by the time Lee stepped down, he'd had five managers in only four years.

Like Swales, he arguably hung on too long. As time wore on, the failure on the pitch and the acute financial position off it put him under pressure. Without a majority shareholding, he needed the support of other shareholders, but there were signs that it was slipping away long before the rancour was explosively brought into the public domain. I felt that Lee, a man used to success in all areas of his life, didn't want to admit failure and wanted to cling to power in the hope things would turn round. He was doomed to failure, and eventually became another of City's tragic hero figures.

I suppose that in real life, those on whom we pin colossal hopes and ambitions can rarely live up to them. Somehow, in football, that kind of expectation can sometimes be met. Not at Manchester City though - a point they demonstrated to me just at the point when I was beginning to doubt my own sense of destiny, and which they carried on demonstrating for quite some time.

Lee's stay as chairman was to last four years, and his fallibility became more and more apparent as time wore on. But at first, things had gone reasonably well. After the takeover, funds were released to sign Paul Walsh and Peter Beagrie, while the German striker, Uwe Rösler, arrived on loan before sealing his permanent move in the summer. The result was that Horton's team survived with a little to spare, having for three months looked in serious danger of going down.

The 1994-95 season began promisingly as the previous term's good finish had let us hope it might. Brian Horton, despite being a Swales appointee, stayed in the manager's job, and, unlike Peter Reid, made a priority of building a side that was attractive to watch. With this quality being coupled with generally positive results (at the start of December, City were sixth in the table), everyone was in an upbeat frame of mind. There'd been some marvellous displays, the most memorable witnessing four exquisitely crafted second-half goals to sweep Everton aside and a thrilling 5-2 victory over a cavalier Spurs side managed by Ardiles and boasting Jurgen Klinsmann as the leader of a five-man attack. The latter was featured on that night's Match Of The Day, with Des Lynam greeting viewers with the news that they were about to witness a match as exciting as any screened in the programme's history. But heavy defeats at Arsenal and Chelsea, together with the particularly distressing five-goal capitulation against Manchester United, evidenced a worrying brittleness which came increasingly to the fore as the season progressed.

A run of two league wins in 23 games, during which we also exited both cup competitions, created a severe danger of relegation. A late Klinsmann winner gained Spurs a measure of revenge for their Maine Road beating, leaving City with five games to save themselves - four against high-flying opposition. In fact, survival was assured over Easter weekend through a surprising win over Liverpool and an even more unexpected but totally deserved 3-2 win away to eventual champions Blackburn. Welcome though the escape was, the fact that we'd gone so close to relegation was regarded as unsatisfactory by Lee, and he decided to act to try to prevent a repeat. In fact, things were to get much, much worse for City, and they weren't exactly to be plain sailing for me either.

21

A Fateful Encounter

I DON'T REMEMBER the first time I saw her, though I know my head must have turned. We spoke briefly on a few occasions, I recall. But I knew almost immediately that I could fall in love with her. And that's what I did, totally oblivious to the complications it would cause.

When I met her, I was 26, and was just settling into life as a solicitor, having completed my training in London in the summer of 1995. I returned to Manchester, not a decision I'd been desperately keen to take, but, unable to give my career the direction I would have wanted at my first firm, I elected to move on. I'd have preferred to stay in London, and felt that I'd be bound to return there or head abroad at some point, as Manchester was not really the place to pursue the type of internationally-based career I'd set my heart on. However, Manchester was where a job came up and was probably as good a place as any to build up experience to add to my other skills with a view to finding a more appropriate environment later on. I bought a flat anyway, sure that I could rent it out if, or rather when, I was on my travels again.

The return north enabled me to buy a season ticket again, having spent most of the last couple of years in Leeds, Brussels and London. So having seen City maybe 20 times in the previous two seasons, all of a sudden I was able to see every game at home and some of the away fixtures too. It proved a rather mixed blessing.

In the summer, there'd been another managerial change (observant readers may have noticed something of a recurring theme here), as Francis Lee resolved to make his mark. In truth, I hadn't been too disappointed to see Brian Horton shown the door, even though he seemed like an unequivocally decent bloke and despite City having produced under his stewardship occasional performances of real verve and flair. Ultimately, though, the facts told their own story. Horton had inherited a squad which had finished fifth, fifth and ninth in the previous three seasons; he'd had a net transfer budget of nearly £4 million (and at the time of his appointment, the British transfer record was £3.75 million - by today's reckoning, our outlay then is the equivalent of around £30million); and he delivered successive relegation battles. Having been appointed under a previous, discredited regime, he couldn't blame the new order for wanting to appoint its own man. We fans, however, could blame them when we found out that man's identity.

We could also blame them for the way they handled the change, although the farce was simply typical of much of what was to come. The day after the 1994-95 season ended in defeat at home to QPR (a strange afternoon on which the Maine Road crowd took little interest in proceedings, preferring to indulge an unhealthy obsession with Manchester United's failure to land the Premiership title), morning newspapers reported Horton's dismissal. The reports were emphatically denied by the club. It has since been claimed that the club had already taken the decision, but wanted to delay the announcement for another month until a director spilled the beans when drunk at a sportsmen's dinner. Horton insisted, entirely justifiably, that his position be clarified, whereupon he was summoned to the chairman's house to be informed of his sacking. The news was made public at a press conference described as "shambolic" by the next day's Guardian newspaper, but this was only the start of the farce.

A rather undignified six-week trawl for a new boss was followed by the appointment of Alan Ball, hardly an inspiring choice given his track record of leading several other clubs to relegation. The pre-season friendlies ended with a 5-1 hammering against Scottish club Hearts, and the first eleven league games yielded just two points. The eleventh of them was an ominous 6-0 defeat away to Liverpool, which came just four days after a 4-0 loss to the same opponents in the League Cup. In the second encounter, they looked set for double figures only to declare after slamming home their sixth with over 25 minutes remaining. Astonishingly, in the light of what had gone before, a run of four wins and a draw in five games through November and early December took the team out of the relegation zone, but it proved to be a blip and most of the season was a struggle - as were most aspects of my life around this time.

My new job had quickly turned into a disappointment. I'd felt at the outset that I'd enjoy myself there, even if I was bracing myself to leave a couple of years down the track. But the enthusiasm soon waned, in part because of the close involvement it entailed with one particular partner in the firm, who, let's just say, wasn't someone I especially enjoyed working for. And I knew in any case that this wasn't where I wanted to stay. I wanted to be involved in groundbreaking international transactions; I hadn't studied languages and travelled extensively only to do a job where that experience would be of no use at all. If I needed to hang around there for a while learning my trade, I was prepared to, but not if I was as unhappy as certain things there made me. I felt that I had the leeway to leave one firm quickly without disfiguring my CV, so within six months I was actively looking for a fresh employer.

At my previous firm, I'd worked in five different offices in a two-year period. I expected, and rather hoped, that my new job search would result in another move, possibly abroad. And none of this was conducive to forming lasting personal relationships. Of course, I had friendships which were long-term and which endured. And I had some relatively short-term romantic attachments during this time, too. Some of these were more meaningful than others, but none had any real longevity. At the time I was unwilling to countenance a long-distance relationship, which was to change later but rather put a block on things for the present.

When I met her, then, I positively wouldn't have wanted to feel deeply for her, but it wasn't a matter of choice. I'd admired her from afar, and we must have had the odd snatched conversation, though I recall none of those either. But when we spoke in greater depth, I was smitten. It wasn't just that she was beautiful, although, despite the word being much overused, she unquestionably was (and no doubt still is - tall, blonde and with a figure to die for). It helped that she had a smile for which the only adequate adjective is electrifying. I mention these attributes first because this was the order in which I became aware of them, but in themselves, they'd have been insufficient to make me feel the way I did.

I felt we hit it off well immediately, and it seemed that our senses of humour clicked. What I actually mean by this is that when flirting, I've always found that making a woman laugh is always a big help. Unfortunately, I only have about four jokes, which I have to recycle constantly, and my basic criteria here are that if a woman laughs at them and doesn't seem to notice they're the same ones over and over, I'm doing quite well. And she laughed at all four, in their various incarnations.

Supporting Manchester City has, however, been a lesson in life, and that lesson has been never to take anything for granted, that things are never what they seem. As this narrative regrettably makes all too plain, a player you break the bank for can turn out to be useless. A cup match against lower division opposition can be tossed away recklessly, notwithstanding the gap in status. And a winning position can be turned into an impending defeat within a matter of minutes. So it didn't entirely surprise me that, despite on one or two occasions thinking I might snatch a victory with her, I ended up suffering another defeat.

I'm no stranger to disappointment with women, and I like to think I'm realistic about my chances. I'm particularly conscious of this, as I see it as a failing many men have. Just listen to them at parties talking to their mates. "Look at her over there," they'll say, indicating the girl who's been snogging another bloke non-stop for the last twenty minutes, "I'm in there." With her, my instant reaction would have been that she was out of my class, so when I suggested I might see her alone I expected to be knocked back. But I wasn't, and I did think for a while that things might really happen as I'd like them to. There were, however, regular signs that it might not.

I met her in February 1996, the same month as City took on Newcastle at Maine Road. The visitors, under Kevin Keegan, were clear at the top of the Premiership (although they were to miss out on the title), and were known for their cavalier attacking approach to the game. City's November promise had long since evaporated, but on this afternoon, they matched Keegan's outfit stride for stride in a thrilling encounter. And it struck me much later that the game was an apt metaphor (I say this in the full knowledge that the ability to compare my personal relationships to City fixtures probably explains just why my love life has been such a disaster for the last twelve years).

Three times, City, whom before the game everyone had fancied to lose heavily, took the lead, and for large parts of the game we looked as if we'd hang on for a victory as memorable as it would have been unexpected. Three times we were pegged back, and on each of those occasions, Newcastle's attacking threat made us fear the worst. And so it was with her. There'd be times when we'd meet and everything would seem to be going like a dream. But there'd be other occasions, when she'd left me making firm promises about future meetings only to be incommunicado for what seemed like weeks.

At first, I simply couldn't fathom it at all, and there was more than one anguished plea from my side asking her simply to let me know if my hopes were groundless. But while she never told me that, she didn't become any easier to deal with. As time wore on, I began to suspect there was something she wasn't telling me - and then she told me what it was. Normally, I'm sceptical when people repeat verbatim chunks of conversations conducted long ago, but this one was unusual enough for me to recall it as if it happened yesterday.

We were on the phone one day, arranging to meet, and because of commitments on both sides, we set a date a few days in advance. "I've something important to tell you when we meet up," she suddenly told me. In truth, I'd been expecting something like this, and in fact I was relieved that I'd find out what had been going on. The problem was that I really didn't want the revelation to be deferred. Now, I know that in a soap opera, that kind of thing happens all the time - the credits roll, and viewers are kept on tenterhooks until they tune in for the next episode - but this was real life, and I had a marked preference for not having to wait. I told her so, too, although not quite in exactly those words. After some further prompting, she relented, although she still seemed reluctant, and the cat-and-mouse interchange continued. "I think you've guessed already," she ventured. "I may have done," I replied, as I had indeed given the matter some thought (there were certain circumstances - the fact that she had an evening job which was plainly lucrative enough for her to travel everywhere by taxi, for instance - that seemed to point in a particular direction). But I was reluctant to make a guess which, however educated, might cause offence if wrong, so I explained that I felt it was for her to tell me rather than for me to deduce. "I work for an escort agency," she said almost inaudibly, and I'd actually had it right.

We stayed in touch for a while, though any romantic hopes were basically gone (she made it clear that she viewed such a situation as incompatible with her working status, and I actually felt the same way). I was, in football parlance, "gutted" - not because I think it would otherwise have worked out between the two of us but because I knew I'd never know. Just as City failed, despite one or two near-misses, to take the lead for a fourth time against Newcastle, so I had to recognise that this was one I wasn't going to win.

22

Looking Across Town

THERE'S ONE UNIQUE point about Manchester City that I've neglected to mention thus far: no other football team has seen it's bitterest rivals lionised to the extent ours have been for the last forty-odd years. And so, while I don't want to overplay their influence on me or on City, it's impossible for me to complete this book without reflecting on them at some point. This is probably the right stage, because by the mid-1990s, United were enjoying, and were to continue to have, enormous success, while City were about to slump dramatically to their lowliest ever status.

Manchester United is the richest and almost certainly the most famous football club in the world, and after a couple of relatively unsuccessful decades in the 1970s and 1980s, their recent on-field achievements have begun to reflect their off-field trappings. Meanwhile, in perfect synchronicity, City countered the procession of trophies across town with the most wretched period in their own entire history.

Given that I've been a City fan for a quarter of a century, I have as much antipathy towards our neighbours as my allegiance would lead you to expect. It doesn't, however, stop me from being able to step back and look at them dispassionately. It's impossible to deny United's achievements on the field in the last decade. The number of trophies they've won is a testament to that. Their team is full of quality players. Moreover, their style of play over that period has habitually been one which I'd dearly have loved City to emulate. I recognise that they have an impressive, imposing stadium. They have the biggest crowds in the country and have a huge world-wide fan base.

Needless to say, my admiration is somewhat grudging, for I'm incapable of wishing Manchester United well. This is not a sentiment born of jealousy or bitterness, more a reflection of how things were when I was growing up. When I was at primary school, it was just a part of the deal. We, the handful of City fans in the class, hated United but they, in turn, hated us. I remember in the early weeks of the 1977-78 season being slaughtered by my classmates after City exited the UEFA Cup at the hands of the relatively unknown Polish side Widsew Lodz. A few short weeks later, United's Cup Winners' Cup aspirations were damaged fatally by a 4-0 battering at Porto and we in the small band of Blues exacted due retribution. And this was far from an isolated incident - similar banter occurred on a weekly basis.

In those days, there wasn't such a gaping chasm between the clubs, and while I will never react to Manchester United with warmth, the disparity between the two these days means that they have begun to matter much, much less to me. And it isn't surprising. It's as if a particularly hated neighbour has sailed to the top of his career tree, and as a result enjoys immense wealth together with all the trappings. Bilious envy and bitter resentment (though this is a lesson that many City fans seem not to have absorbed) are rather pointless in such circumstances. You're better off getting on with your own life.

Don't get me wrong. There'll always be a part of me that takes delight in their failings - I suffered too much abuse from their fans at too young an age for there not to be some deep-rooted antipathy now. So I'm never sorry on the depressingly rare occasions when they lose, although that this happens so infrequently is not a source of major disappointment to me. What happens to City matters most, and, for instance, if offered a mythical trade off, I would concede another historic treble to United if it could assure the fulfillment of City's own objectives.

Things, regrettably, don't work like that. The fact that City fans have had to endure a procession of success across the city since United's 1990 FA Cup triumph has meant that we've been accorded only the most minor comforts by the footballing gods. With one isolated but magnificent exception, we haven't even had the pleasure of a win against them in the last two decades. United won the league in 1993 and 1994, when they added the FA Cup for good measure, as the promise of our own early 1990s side faded. In season 1994-95, though again we were threatened with the drop for most of the campaign, while they gunned for another double, the outcome of both teams' efforts was as City fans would have wanted: we stayed up as they won nothing. Admittedly, it's more than a little sad to be reduced to seeking consolation from such pitifully small comforts, but the next season, even they were to be denied us.

Following the classic Newcastle game, City had continued to struggle. Going into April, it was clear that we were in even more trouble than in the previous two campaigns. We badly needed a win in the Manchester derby on Easter Saturday to ease our serious position; in fact, it was United who took the points in an exciting game at Maine Road as City twice clawed back a single-goal deficit only to fail to do so on a third occasion. Subsequent wins over Sheffield Wednesday and Aston Villa couldn't ease the position as our fellow strugglers all won. We were relegated on the final day of the season amid farcical scenes in the match against Liverpool; near the end, the hapless manager Alan Ball believed a crowd rumour that one of our relegation rivals was losing, so instructed midfielder Steve Lomas to play keep-ball in the corner to try to hold out for a 2-2 draw. The supposed scoreline from elsewhere was false and we went down, having clung to our not-so-precious point.

United, meanwhile, went on to claim an unprecedented double in three years. They took the league championship ahead of Kevin Keegan's Newcastle, who'd led by twelve points just before they came to Maine Road, and then beat Liverpool in the FA Cup final (they'd also beaten us earlier in the competition thanks in part to a penalty that outraged not only City fans but sizeable numbers of neutrals too).

When this kind of thing happens, it's bound to spark some kind of envy. However, the fact that United inspire dislike among fans of teams other than City isn't quite so mystifying as they make out, and nor is it merely, as they like to claim, born of jealousy, though in some cases that's a factor. United's boasts of being "the greatest club in the world" go as far back as I can remember. As my experiences in Siberia and other places showed, they certainly had a world-wide fame, though even to boast of being the world's most famous club would have presupposed, erroneously, that fame can be measured objectively. But whether the claims of greatness are true or not (and they trumpeted it regularly throughout the 1970s and 1980s, when in terms of achievement and, in European terms, attendances, it was clearly untrue), the fact they and their supporters have seemed to want to remind everyone of it on a regular basis for as long as I can remember is scarcely appealing.

Of course, since the start of the 1990s, United have attained success more in keeping with their self-proclaimed status. The scale of the accompanying media coverage has simply brought their bad side to the attention of a wider audience. And if they tried to look at themselves as neutrals must see them, I don't think those associated with the Old Trafford club can be altogether surprised that the view isn't always positive. If I was a United fan, I don't think I'd care what others thought - I'd simply smile beatifically and think of the club's on-field successes, but with many of their supporters, at least of my acquaintance, there seems to be a desperate need for acclaim and an unstinting belief in a God-given right to glory. Anyone who criticises is belittled as having an ulterior motive. Any setback is immediately cited as evidence of a conspiracy by embittered rivals.

I remember travelling through Frankfurt airport once having not seen an English paper for a few days. It hardly needed a Sherlock Holmes to work out who was making the allegation behind the Daily Mirror's back page banner headline: "You're all jealous". Alex Ferguson, in his pre-knighthood days, was blaming the rest of English football for his team's fixture pile-up. At the same time, the managers of Second Division Stockport and Conference outfit Stevenage were reacting with much more equanimity despite their sides facing even more gruelling fixture programmes.

There are other examples of negative traits which are likely to add to the negative perception of them in the non-United supporting community. Ferguson's habit of standing ostentatiously on the touchline pointing to his stopwatch trying to influence the referee to add more time at the end of the game is one. Another is the lack of sensible perspective in the United-friendly media and among certain fans over anything connected with the club. Eric Cantona was both a wonderfully charismatic figure and a magnificent player whose contribution was the catalyst for turning United from title nearly-men into perennial champions. Yet I lost count of the number of journalists and supporters who seemed to believe he was also some kind of poet-philosopher-genius. I once read, out of a morbid curiosity, the book La Philosophie de Cantona, a collection of the man's various musings. Let's just say that I can't see Jean-Paul Sartre worrying about his place in the pantheon of great twentieth-century thinkers on Eric's account.

No-one would deny that fans of any team want success and glory for their club. United have the lion's share of both at the moment, so to that extent, they're envied by others. This hardly justifies the persecution complex. When bemoaning the public perception of them, United apologists frequently complain that Liverpool were not hated to the same extent when they were dominating English football. This is true. As Liverpool were achieving what everyone else wanted but didn't inspire hatred, there must be additional reasons why United do, and they're not that hard to find. In other words, the jealousy argument, while not entirely without merit, is grossly over-simplistic.

Even so, whatever gripes I may have against them, and it may not be a popular move among City fans to admit it, there's no doubt whatsoever that Manchester United is a truly great club. They aren't English football's historically most successful of all time, though they've outstripped everyone else put together in the last ten years, and have an aura about them that all other teams in this country lack. Their recent trophy-winning run has been astounding, and in terms of their commercial prospects, they dwarf every other club on the planet. But it is the legend of Manchester United that is arguably the club's biggest asset, sown in the 1950s and 1960s with a brilliant home-grown team several of whose members were killed in a horrific air crash before Sir Matt Busby then went about building a new team which went on to win two league titles in the 1960s and the European Cup in 1968.

It would be difficult for any club to compete, and City have the misfortune to be based three miles up the road from them. But it would be a mistake - even though many have done so - to ascribe City's characteristics to the fact that they face such fearsome local competition. For United haven't always been as feted as they are now, and City's characteristics were, as far as I can make out, exactly the same.

In the 1920s and 1930s, for instance, United were a moribund club flitting between the First and Second Divisions, singularly failing to trouble the clubs in the higher echelons of the game and at one point attracting 4,000 fans to a First Division fixture. They found themselves in a terrible financial crisis, and shortly afterwards barely avoided the humiliation of relegation to the old Third Division North. The balance of power in Manchester football couldn't have been more different.

And yet look at how City continued to behave. We managed to reach the FA Cup final only to be relegated in the same season, and then, later, the year after winning the league championship, were relegated (the only title holders ever to suffer this indignity) despite being the divisional top scorers. City's pattern of behaviour has been the same throughout the club's history, and it really has nothing to do with who's located over the road.

Ultimately, it's as if the two clubs are siblings. They're the one who've made it big, who've made their parents proud and who've exceeded all expectations. City are the profligates, who frustrate and disappoint, who've wasted their opportunities in life and who become embarrassingly drunk at family gatherings. When put like that, how can I consider, even for a minute, that I ended up in the wrong camp?

23

Moving On

IT WASN'T JUST because United won the double and City were relegated in 1996 that I'd started to think of leaving Manchester, probably for good. My earlier suspicions that it wouldn't be the place for me to go on and make my career really seemed to be being proved correct, and my anxiety to go elsewhere was increasing by the day.

I'm allowed to criticise - it's my city. OK, I know I wasn't born there, but that's just an accident (I have a friend who was born in Kampala but whose parents came back to England when she was a toddler and she certainly isn't a Ugandan). So, for example, when it rains in Manchester, I can joke with impunity that it rarely does anything else. But even though I know this to be true, woe betide any non-native coming up with a similar observation. I can remember fragments of my life before we moved north when I was three, but real, conscious memories only begin after that. I left for university at the age of eighteen, and though I have returned since, spending over three years there after graduating, I've by and large elected to make my home elsewhere. Somehow, though, Manchester still feels like home in a way that nowhere else does.

Sometimes I wonder to what extent growing up in Manchester has formed me, to what extent I've been shaped by the backdrop of this, rather than any other city, in my youth. It might well not have been like this - in my infancy, my dad was offered a job in Australia, while I suppose we also could easily have stayed in London. And who knows what the effect would have been on my personality had my parents taken either of those courses of action. I can't say I'd have been a different person (who can tell, and this nature versus nurture debate is far too heavy for me to get into now). I suppose that I might have developed different likes and dislikes through being in another environment - in the Antipodes, I might have developed a passion for surfing, for instance, whereas that never seemed much of an option on the Manchester Ship Canal. And I'd at least have had a decent national cricket team to support over there. I wouldn't have grown up with much top-class football at all, though.

In London, my local team for the first three years of my life was Crystal Palace, so I probably wouldn't have grown up with much top-class football there either, not that after my first two or three seasons I ever really did at Maine Road. In fact, Palace might well have captured my attention had I remained down south. During my lifetime, they've yo-yoed between the top two divisions, once slipped from the top flight to be relegated again the next season, have had an incredible turnover of managers, and both in the dugout and the boardroom have had a series of flamboyant figures of dubious competence. Indeed, Palace might not have been a bad option at all. Not bad - but not the best.

Luckily, as a result of my parents' decision, I was able to witness at first hand the original football eccentrics rather than a bunch of imitators. Palace fans might not think so, of course, but then other supporters rarely do appreciate that their team's instinct for farce and unpredictability is outdone elsewhere. I remember once watching Dinamo Moscow play Skonto Riga in a UEFA Cup tie. After taking a second-minute lead, the Russians proceeded to squander what seemed like more chances than most teams create in a season, before conceding disastrous goals in the last minute of the first half and opening minute of the second. A crestfallen fan in the next seat turned to me. "Only Dinamo could play like this," he said. I didn't have the heart to let him know they were just beginners, albeit novices showing a certain aptitude for the task in hand. I knew because I grew up with the masters.

The longer time has gone on, the more I've come to understand that City's characteristics derive in large measure from the place in which they're located, and, indeed, the same is true of Manchester United. It's all to do with the history.

Manchester is a progressive city, whose impact on the modern world can't be understated. Don't just take my word for it - listen to the unbiased website from the University of St Paul, Minnesota, which refers to Manchester's "historic leadership in the industrial process". And here are just a few firsts associated with the place. The world's first passenger railway went from Manchester to Liverpool in 1830. The world's first major industrial estate was built at Trafford Park in 1905. There have been radical developments in scientific theory, too. John Dalton founded modern Chemistry in Manchester in 1803 with his theory of atoms, while James Joule, whose true occupation, incidentally, was brewing and who gave his name to the international unit of energy, founded the science of thermodynamics in the 1840s. Meanwhile, in physics, Rutherford first split the atom in Manchester. The world's first the world's first stored-program computer was invented at Manchester University in 1948 and the Ferranti Mark I, the world's first commercially available computer, appeared in Manchester shortly afterwards. All of these developments really did help to change the world, and I'm proud of my links with a city that can boast such a record of groundbreaking accomplishment.

Manchester was also the birthplace of the Football League in 1888, though the city didn't have a team among the twelve participants in the inaugural competition. However, when the league was extended four years later, two Manchester-based teams were admitted. Then known as Newton Heath and Ardwick, these clubs were the forerunners of United and City respectively, and both were to enjoy success in the first decade of the new century. City did so first with a team inspired by arguably English football's first iconic star, Billy Meredith, who was what fans of alliteration would call a Welsh wing wizard. There was an FA Cup triumph followed by a couple of near misses in the league before the team broke up. And, in typical City fashion, our demise heralded United's first great era. In 1906, City were found guilty of counts of bribery (in an unsuccessful attempt to ensure what would have been a title-clinching win at Aston Villa in 1905 - we actually lost) and of making under-the-counter payments to players. One of the punishments was being forced to release the players involved in the illegal payments scandal, and the majority headed across town to win another FA Cup and snatch on two occasions the title that had eluded them with City.

In the inter-war years, City were the pre-eminent club, especially in the thirties, when they won both domestic competitions and played before record crowds as United floundered in the Second Division and flirted with bankruptcy. But just before and then at the end of the Second World War came two events which enabled United to seal their place as the dominant partner on what has been, and looks certain to continue, as a permanent basis. First of all, they were promoted in 1938 as City (as league Champions, top scorers in the First Division and with several international defenders) contrived to ensure that when hostilities with Germany broke out - and therefore when league football resumed seven years later - United were in a higher division. And they'd also managed to appoint as manager a former City player who would go down as one of the all-time great soccer bosses. Matt Busby's achievements were to forever tilt the balance of power in Manchester football.

Busby built three great sides at Old Trafford, and without his efforts United would have had none of the world-wide magnetism which formed the basis of the club's later commercial success, itself a base for more on-field achievement. One side, which won the Cup and then league in the first few years after the War, broke up and it was the second of his teams which would turn the club from a big city club with the corresponding level of support into a world-wide phenomenon. The brilliant young team was wiped out in February 1958 in a plane crash at Munich as they returned from a European tie in Belgrade. Without wishing to be cynical, or to belittle the tragedy in any way for the individuals involved, it's difficult to avoid the conclusion that the resultant wave of sympathy did much to help to transform United's horizons, laying the base for the club's worldwide support. The 1960s triumvirate of Law, Charlton and especially the icon that was George Best reinforced this position. They played sparkling attacking football, and won the championship twice plus a European Cup. And even when we could match them on the field, in glamour terms, City couldn't compete.

It wasn't that City were without their successes in this period. A more than decent side at Maine Road, featuring one of English football's greatest ever goalkeepers and, using innovative tactics, reached a couple of FA Cup finals, winning one, in the mid-1950s. And in 1968, as United finally won the European Cup, City were winning the league with a side that would out-perform their rivals for the next six or seven years. In head-to-head confrontations around this period, the blue side of the city ended on the losing side only twice in fifteen league encounters against the old enemy. After a period of relative parity in the late 1970s, United's on-field dominance has gone virtually unchallenged for over two decades to a point where it is now, at least by City, practically unchallengeable. And for much of the 1990s, as United enjoyed European and unprecedented domestic success, City floundered desperately. That last game before my grandad died in 1989 remains an isolated success.

The thing is that supporters of both clubs, with their different qualities and divergent recent fortunes, are both clearly characteristic of the city whose name they share. With United, whose fans have boasted of being the "biggest club in the world" for as long as I can remember, it's the mouthy, self-aggrandising, confident, self-believing aspect. With City, it's the wilful contrariness, the willingness to continue to support a team which, all logic dictates, should be abandoned forthwith. At no time was this more apparent than when City were relegated from the Premier League in 1995 and after suffering two relegations in the next three seasons were playing to bigger crowds in the Second Division than in the top flight.

I'm not trying to come out with the 'best fans in the country' line that lazy commentators trot out when it comes to City, or that some of our supporters latch on to with unjustified alacrity. There are many respects in which the tag is richly undeserved. For one thing, like everyone else, we have our share of morons who think a trip to the football is an excuse for violence directed at opposition followers. For another, there are those who are unable to 'support' the team in any way at all, preferring instead to bellow incoherent abuse at their own team's players the moment they do something wrong. Plenty seem to take an inordinate interest in the affairs of our neighbours, and jibes about the Munich air disaster do no-one any credit. And while similar misgivings could be voiced of most if not all groups of fans, it probably makes 'best' supporters a somewhat meaningless tag. Nevertheless, the way we stuck with it in years where we regarded ourselves as lucky if the team served up mediocrity rather than failure was a cause for considerable pride, and was an oddly Mancunian response to events on the pitch. (In the interests of even-handedness, United's crowds held up excellently, too, in the early and mid-1970s when Matt Busby's last team broke up and the team's fortunes declined to such an extent that they were relegated).

I always felt that Manchester had a big influence on me outside the football context, too. In strict population terms, it's not the biggest provincial city in the UK, but it likes to think of itself as the most important. It has the biggest concentration of media outlets outside London and the UK's major non-London airport. It's geographically convenient (Birmingham may be closer to London but around fifteen million people live within an hour's drive of Manchester). But most of all, the invention and pioneering spirit that inspired the city to influence the world in the way it did are the qualities which make me proud to consider myself a Mancunian.

There's a dichotomy here. Despite my pride in the place, I'd be reluctant to go back to Manchester to live. Somehow, when I was there, I just felt that it was too familiar. I'd grown up in the city, been shaped by it and I just felt that I understood pretty well all there was to understand about it. There was another place that was dear to me about which I certainly couldn't say the same, and I decided that it was time to head back there.

24

Back in the Motherland

IT WAS THE AUTUMN OF 1996 when I left Manchester behind - or at least abandoned it, probably for the last time, as a permanent place of residence (I have retained sufficient family and friends there to be a frequent visitor, while I still have my season ticket). I had lots of choice in terms of a new location for a new job. I could have gone to Paris, and had lots of interest from firms in London. I chose, however, to go to Russia. In terms of enjoying an easy life, at least, it wasn't the logical option, and I knew times would be tough on my arrival. But somehow I felt that I'd regret failing to take up the opportunity. And so take it up I did.

If life in Russia promised to be an exciting new adventure, then, just as I left, affairs at Maine Road were also becoming compelling viewing for someone watching from outside. After relegation in the spring, City began the new season as strong favourites with the bookmakers to win an instant promotion. A couple of the better players were allowed to leave, with Quinn and Curle, who'd both been mainstays of a City side finishing in the upper reaches of the top division, allowed to move to Sunderland and Wolves respectively. However, with our star man Kinkladze staying, the bookie's faith didn't waver. This continued a process started over the previous year. Players like Coton, Phelan, Flitcroft and Walsh, all among our better performers, had also gone. The replacements had been lower division players (such as the drastically overweight striker Creaney, bought from Portsmouth), foreigners of dubious provenance (the worst being abysmal German full-back Frontzeck) and other people's cast-offs (the creative but pedestrian Nigel Clough was signed from Liverpool when in fact we were lacking pace and width). It wasn't a promising mixture.

Unfortunately, City decided to prove that the odds-layers weren't infallible. Manager Alan Ball soon left, unlamented, after two defeats in the first three games, and things quickly went from bad to worse. There was quite clearly no money to spend on new players, and those who were already there were having great difficulty adapting to life in the First Division. Chairman Francis Lee, having promised big successes upon his arrival at the club less than three years previously, was evidently finding delivering the anticipated success much harder than he'd expected. And it became evident that there was no credible candidate who was willing to replace Ball, George Graham and Dave Bassett rejecting the job with almost indecent haste. The club was quite simply a laughing stock.

Then things went from bad to worse. Astonishingly, it had taken almost six weeks to appoint a new manager, in which time the team floundered, and reaching a nadir with home and away defeats against Third Division Lincoln in the League Cup. Fans were so relieved when a new man was appointed that his Manchester United playing pedigree was overlooked. But then, after presiding over a mere six games, the ex-England winger and former Crystal Palace manager Steve Coppell walked out, citing ill health as the reason for his shock resignation. This sparked another period of uncertainty; it was the best part of two months before a fresh face was installed, by which time I'd left the country and City had suffered many fresh humiliations. Under the temporary management, we picked up a distressing tally of seven points from ten games.

The first game after Coppell had left (and his departure still ranks as the single most astonishing event in all my time following the club) was the last before I headed abroad. City turned in a performance of what at the time was almost unprecedented ineptitude to lose 3-2 to a mediocre Oxford side. As I rushed from the ground that night, I looked back to see a crowd gathering on the forecourt in front of the Main Stand to give vent to disappointment, dismay and disgust.

I understood what was happening. The players were thoughtfully doing their best to ensure that I'd be more than happy to head a couple of thousand miles across to the other side of Europe. Indeed, so wretched had been that last display that I really rather regretted that I'd only managed to put the breadth of the continent between us. And though I arrived in St Petersburg at the onset of the bitterly cold Russian winter, though I found it hard to settle in, though I seemed to have forgotten all the Russian I ever knew so was finding life difficult at work - none of this mattered. I escaped from having to watch City flounder desperately against Portsmouth, Tranmere, Oldham and others. Indeed, when I made the brief trip home for Christmas, they managed to lose 1-0 at home to Port Vale, playing even worse than they had a few weeks earlier against Oxford. I reflected that this game, and the entire miserable sequence that preceded it, were merely designed to ensure that there was no prospect of me being homesick enough to want to come back to England.

In fact, City weren't the only reason I was relieved to find myself at a distance from Manchester. I also felt it would be a benefit for me to be at a remove from the escort. Once I'd understood that my hopes of a relationship with her were no more promising than were City's aspirations of promotion (and we were in the bottom four at Christmas), I'd worried that I'd be hard pushed to find someone who'd mean the same to me. But after my experiences in 1991, I had a feeling that Russia might turn out to be a happy hunting ground for, at the very least, someone to provide an entertaining distraction. Thus it proved.

I hadn't been in St Petersburg long when I met Natasha, and while the relationship turned out not to be particularly long lasting, it was certainly eventful. For once, I was involved with someone younger than myself, but she certainly fulfilled my basic criterion: she complicated my life horribly. Natasha was twenty, bright, very attractive, sweet, attentive and funny. She was certainly keen to put herself out on my behalf (I remember her coming round one Sunday morning when I was under the weather and bringing me cooked marrow so that I'd be well fed during my convalescence). And though I don't think that, despite her admirable qualities, she ever quite aroused in me the same passions as I'd had for the escort, she genuinely made me happy and I had at least put the previous episode behind me. For a while, everything seemed to be going uncharacteristically well, but appearances were deceptive and actually it was a case of out of the proverbial frying pan, into the metaphorical fire.

If Natasha was flattering to deceive in those early months of 1997, then so were City. And just as she failed to deliver on the promise of smoothing a path which had certainly not run smoothly, so did the new City manager. The financial crisis at the club had been eased by a new share issue which raised over £10 million. This meant that there were now funds available for incoming transfers, which in turn meant that the gap between managers could be curtailed with the appointment of a credible candidate to take charge of team affairs. Just as in my personal life, things were looking up.

On the face of it, Frank Clark - a fifty-odd-year-old Geordie bloke with a drooping moustache and a permanently mournful expression - had little in common with a leggy young Russian babe, but in fact there was a distinct parallel. My misguided assumption that things couldn't go wrong with either was based on the fact that neither ostensibly possessed the faults of those who had gone before them. Clark quickly bettered his immediate predecessor by remaining in the post beyond his first month in charge, while he could hardly have seemed any less competent than the ginger-haired, squeaky-voiced, flat-cap-wearing failure who came before that. And, at least as far as I knew, Natasha wasn't a professional escort, so at least I wouldn't have with her the same problems as those that had been at the root of my previous romantic disaster. As it happened, both of them were extraordinarily inventive when it came to finding new ways to make me suffer - but there was no sign of this at the outset.

Clark took over immediately after a Christmas programme that had yielded no points and no goals in two games (the first of which was the Port Vale debacle). He immediately inspired a revival and his down-to-earth, even dour, demeanour was just what was needed after years of highly dubious publicity. He appeared instantly to identify the team's failings, and he sought to remedy them with judicious signings. He made an astute tactical switch which ensured that the brilliant but mercurial Kinkladze was used to the optimum effect. He immediately inspired a sequence of eight games unbeaten, including at one point five successive wins, to transform the team from serious relegation contenders to an outfit with hopes of a play-off place. He couldn't quite turn those aspirations into reality, but the way the campaign ended gave grounds for optimism next time out.

I should have known that it wouldn't be so - the way things went with Natasha should have warned me. After the early stages of the relationship, little by little things seemed to deteriorate, as she started to behave rather erratically. First, there was a day when she was supposed to be taking me out to meet her parents, who lived in a country house outside St Petersburg. She didn't turn up to collect me as arranged and wasn't at the flat in the city she shared with her brother. All this was in spite of her having borrowed money to pay for food and drink when I visited the family (her parents, she'd explained, would be far too proud to accept the money from me, so we agreed to pretend it had come from her). There were various other no-shows, and when I did catch up with her eventually, there were bizarre conversations of which she later had no recollection. There was also an occasion when I had friends over to visit and she called, begging me to meet her on the street outside the block where I lived. Sobbing uncontrollably and barely comprehensible, she didn't articulate what was wrong but refused either to come upstairs or allow me to walk her home. Eventually, I put her in a taxi to go out of town to her parents. Finally, there was the evening when it all came to a head.

It was a Thursday, and I was due to have someone round at 8 p.m. to install a satellite TV system. Normally, I'd have had no problem getting home in time (I only lived fifteen minutes' walk from the office), but as it happened, I made it with only five minutes to spare after a rush job came in that afternoon. Almost immediately the doorbell rang, and I assumed it must be my workman, but he followed ten minutes later. In fact, the first caller was Natasha. She was already visibly somewhat the worse for wear, but still attacked with alacrity the half-empty bottle of whisky I'd bought in duty free on my last trip away a few weeks before. Swigging the liquid as if it were water, she focused her attention on the unassuming, middle-aged man who by this point was standing in the hallway, pondering how best to take the cable out of my flat and onto the roof of the building. "Do you know him?" she slurred, not bothering to keep her voice down and thus ensuring he heard everything. "You can't trust him, you know. He'll come back and burgle the flat."

My embarrassment continued as she made further strident observations almost until he left, by which point she was in the toilet, her imprudent whisky consumption having made her violently ill. Finally, she emerged and I found out what the problem was. She was drinking because she'd been thrown out of university for failing to sit her exams, and was terrified of telling her parents because of the shame they'd feel - they both worked at the same institution, and her father was quite eminent. She asked me for money so she could bribe one of her teachers to let her continue her studies, and that for me was the end of the line. She did leave me one legacy that survived our last, surreal evening together, though - she managed to put two whole rolls of toilet paper down the toilet after being sick in it. It remained blocked for five days because I couldn't get a plumber round on the Bank Holiday weekend.

Great girl though she basically was, I could see that to continue with her would bring a string of similar problems (I'd suspected for a while that she had a drug habit) and I simply didn't have the stomach for more of the same. I had enough difficulties with City, who, despite handing Frank Clark the largest net transfer budget in Division One in the summer of 1997, went straight into the relegation zone and stayed there.

There's a sad footnote to this story. I later heard from her brother that within a year of that nightmarish evening, Natasha had died. He didn't really explain - "She just fell ill, and that was that," he said -

but given what I saw of her lifestyle, I can't say I was terribly surprised. I still think of her sometimes, though, and always with genuine affection, so the way things turned out makes me sad. She had so many good qualities and such potential that her demise was a tragic waste. The football context is slightly trivial set against something like that, but for what it's worth, Frank Clark didn't last long either. And while, unlike Natasha, he didn't die after his experiences at City, his reputation as a football manager was effectively killed by his time at Maine Road. Meanwhile, I thought that after Natasha and after Frank Clark, City and I would be set for a more stable period. Not for the first time, I was proved wrong.

25

The Real Deal

ANYONE WHO FOLLOWED Manchester City through the mid-to-late 1990s, and who's followed this narrative thus far, will feel that recent chapters contain a serious flaw: I've said nothing at all - bar a couple of passing references - about a figure who was arguably the most naturally gifted player in the club's recent history. Georgi Kinkladze was a Georgian international midfielder signed at the age of twenty-one from Dinamo Tblisi. He arrived in the summer of 1995, and stayed for three years. He suffered relegation in his first season, then played in the City side which earned what at the time was the club's worst ever league position a year later, and was in the team that was even worse, managing to be relegated again, twelve months after that. Yet for fans he was a beacon, lighting what was otherwise total darkness.

I wouldn't say that my first few months of my stint in Russia could be seen, metaphorically, as total darkness, and nor was the whole of my time there - I wouldn't have missed it for the world. But just as Kinkladze was a huge presence at Maine Road during his time there, there's one person I always think of when I reflect on the period I spent in Russia in the late 1990s. There was another link between them, too, and even though it might have seemed spurious to some, it certainly struck a chord with me. After all, the most striking part of Kinkladze's game had always been his jinking slalom-style runs, and his supreme balance had been honed, so it was said, by taking ballet lessons as a child. And Nadia was a former ballerina, whose poise, elegance and grace could, I always felt, be attributed in large measure to the elite classical training she'd received.

I went more or less straight from the short-lived attachment with Natasha into a relationship with Nadia, but it was more intense from the off. Maybe when I think back, I was desperately seeking something like this: things hadn't worked out with the escort, after all, and they'd turned rather sour with Natasha after the initial promise, so perhaps I was keen to fall for anyone who'd contemplate having me. But time lends perspective, and I still like to think that Nadia and I had something special, even though it's now ended. Still, nor am I blind to her faults, just as I'm fully aware of Kinkladze's shortcomings.

I met Nadia at a propitious time: the 'White Nights' season, which normally runs from June 11 to July 2, was about to start. This is the time when it doesn't get dark properly, as, owing to the city's northerly location, the sun doesn't go under the horizon deep enough for the sky to darken fully. As a result, the dusk meets the dawn. St Petersburg, though parts of it are decaying and though some of the infrastructure is not so much crumbling as disintegrating, is a strikingly beautiful city, and this season showcases it to its best effect. The phenomenon, of course, isn't unique to St Petersburg, but as it is the world's most northerly major city (defining major as meaning with a population of over a million - in fact, its inhabitants number almost five times as many), then it receives most acclaim there. And there's a romantic, almost poetic quality to all this. I've come across few settings more appropriate for lovers than walking along the banks of the rivers and canals in the midnight twilight against a backdrop of such classical beauty. This was the setting for the opening weeks of this relationship.

Kinkladze's arrival at Maine Road a couple of years previously had been in much less ideal circumstances. He'd come to a club which had struggled for the previous two years and which, under the stewardship of the man who was probably the least popular manager ever to be at the club, was destined to perform even worse. The policy laid down from the boardroom was that the higher wage earners (who, not entirely coincidentally, tend usually to be the better players) had to be sold. The season turned out to be one of unremitting struggle and the next two were worse. But it soon became clear that Kinkladze was a player we could take to our hearts. Most of what was on offer at Maine Road was thoroughly depressing, but stellar pieces of individual magic from the Georgian were often, as the cliché goes, worth the price of admission on their own.

Having looked a forlorn figure in the side which made a cataclysmic start to the 1995-6 season, he began to find his feet. He made the decisive pass in a sweeping move which led to the only goal against Bolton - the team's first win of the campaign. He scored a late winner against Aston Villa a couple of weeks later, a quality strike. There were sensational solo goals at Middlesbrough, where even in defeat his performance outshone that of the home side's much-vaunted Brazilian Juninho, and in a Cup-tie against Leicester. And viewers of BBC TV's Match Of The Day programme were treated to a spectacular show against Newcastle and a stunning effort against Southampton where he skipped past five men before lifting the ball impudently over goalkeeper, Dave Beasant. The rest of the team may frequently have been hopeless, but at least we had one major star whose moments of magic really were, as the cliché has it, worth the admission money on their own.

A couple of weeks before I met Nadia, the 1996-7 season, Kinkladze's second at Maine Road, had ended. We'd continued in to struggle for half the campaign after relegation the previous season, before Frank Clark had arrived briefly to arrest the decline. Thereafter, as things improved, it began to look as if Kinkladze could be the fulcrum of a side which could storm back to the top flight the next year. There was, however, a problem: we didn't know if he'd stay, or whether the lure of a bigger stage elsewhere might tempt him away. The season ended at home to Reading in a game irrelevant in terms of league position, and the injured Kinkladze wasn't even playing. Despite witnessing a seesaw game which ended in a 3-2 win, the crowd had only one agenda all afternoon: pleading with their idol to stay, a task pursued with even more fervour when he joined the rest of the team in a lap of honour after the game.

Supporters' efforts were rewarded - a couple of weeks later, he signed a new contract.

So once I met Nadia, I felt that everything would be in order in my world as well as City's. She quickly made a huge impression on me, and I was smitten. Not surprisingly given her background in ballet, she was petite and svelte, graceful and stylish. She was strikingly attractive and highly intelligent. She was cultured but passionate, fun-loving yet determined. It was a highly potent combination, and it would have taken a particularly demanding man to ask for more. I wasn't such a man, and at the time I regarded her as the love of my life.

As time wore on, however, it became clear that there was a down side to Nadia. She was wilful and capricious, what might be termed decidedly high-maintenance, or, as Mancunian Bloke would have put it, bloody hard work, even by the standards I was used to. I must confess that I noticed less at the outset, when we enjoyed a high-octane start to the relationship, than later on. I assumed that in the beginning she was unsure as to where the relationship was going, so felt she should make the most of it while it lasted. From various comments she made, she certainly seemed to be assuming it would be a short-lived affair, and, after all, I suppose the portents weren't particularly good. She was 36 when we met, while I was 27; while that to me was no barrier at all, as my personal history shows, it isn't really a conventional pattern (and I suppose at this point there was no reason for her to conclude that I'd take a somewhat non-conformist approach in these matters). She had, it transpired, a 13-year-old daughter, a fact she wanted to hide from me until she thought we might be together long-term, expecting that my reaction would be negative. In the early stages, she made much of the running, but when things were obviously getting serious, she evidently decided it was time to lay down some rules, and she had plenty in mind.

As time marched on, the one thing above all I was to find about Nadia was that she liked things her own way, and she had very fixed ideas as to how that way should be. She viewed the man's role as being that of provider, and this isn't untypical for a Russian woman; they still hold to a fairly traditional view of gender politics. I was fairly sympathetic to this, given our differing earning potential. Nadia, however, took it further. "If I was a millionaire and you were down to your last five dollars," she once said, "I wouldn't give you anything." She felt that a woman should be treated like a lady, which meant that I was expected to hold her coat, open doors for her and the works. Again, it was something I could live with (if it mattered to her, I was happy to accommodate it) but once more she took it to extremes; I recall being berated by her once with real fury for stepping ahead of her as we were walking down the pavement. And while she expected me to make my decisions based on what was right for us as a couple, she seemed to think that if she wanted to do something herself, I should adjust. Never was this more plainly demonstrated than when, with my firm asking me to return to London, I elected to stay working in Russia so that we could be together. A few months later, she emigrated on a few days' notice without prior discussion.

I loved Nadia, genuinely, sincerely, unconditionally and passionately, and even at that stage I wasn't ready to call it a day. She did reciprocate my feelings (whatever else I say about her, I wouldn't impugn her qualities as a mother and I couldn't ever have imagined her letting me build up a relationship of real warmth with her daughter were that not the case). But she reciprocated in her own way, and that wasn't really compatible with my way. At times, I was as happy with her as I could have asked to be with a woman, but those times were counterbalanced with just as many down periods. Ultimately, she was a woman who, having seen the ballet The Taming of the Shrew, would say proudly, "That's exactly how I am!" Being in a relationship with such a person simply requires too much of an adjustment.

Kinkladze was exactly the same: he could produce for us moments when we were as happy as fans can be made by a footballer, but to get the best from him, everything had to revolve around him. He couldn't play in an orthodox central midfield role or an orthodox striking role, so the formation had to be changed completely to suit him. We tried all kinds of different ways of accommodating him, but none was altogether satisfactory. At times, we dispensed with one of the usual two strikers and consequently reduced our attacking potency. At one point, we were fielding a chronically unbalanced team with no-one on the left side of midfield. And we ended up with a wingback system - such a formation is appropriate for some players, but unfortunately not for most of ours at the time - we had wing-backs who couldn't cross the ball properly, for instance, a serious obstacle to success using that formation. While he rewarded us with flashes of brilliance, he didn't deliver consistently enough to make it worth our while (his return of four league goals, one a penalty, in 30 matches in his last season tells its own story). In that campaign, City slid to the club's lowest ever status, despite Kinkladze's presence. I always felt that if we'd sold him the previous August, retained wingers Nicky Summerbee and Peter Beagrie, and thus played in a manner appropriate for the rest of the squad, we'd never have suffered the indignities we did.

So, on reflection, how could I do anything other than see them as a pair. Kinkladze was capable of brilliance, but maybe it's a revealing fact that he bombed at Dutch giants Ajax when surrounded by considerably better players than we could field alongside him. In recent years, after a move back to England with Derby (one of the poorer relations in the Premiership in this period), he's been able to make himself something more than a peripheral figure there. Meanwhile Nadia, who had all the fine qualities I'd have looked for in a woman, was also, at the end of the day, just too difficult. With both of them, the good times weren't enough to leave me contented with the overall package.

I'm grateful for the wonderful experiences they both gave me, and I would never want to airbrush either from my own personal history; both were truly special in their own way. But as for the idea of taking either of them back? Not a chance.

26

Beyond Belief

THE FACT THAT I'D met Nadia was one of the reasons why, in the summer of 1997, things looked good. After several months in Russia, I'd adjusted to my new surroundings and new job. I felt things were going well at work, and I was spending most of my time in the office on an interesting, large-scale project for a multinational company client; I'd made good progress, and all signs were that I was highly regarded in the firm. I'd met Nadia and the relationship, especially in its early stages, seemed idyllic. I experienced the enchantment of the White Nights' midnight twilight for the first time. I was more than enjoying my new location, and was reflecting that during the next year, things could surely only go from strength to strength.

All also appeared rosy in the Manchester City garden, at least to the bookmakers and to me. The recovery in the last four months of the previous season under a new manager, coupled with the availability of funds for squad strengthening, appeared to indicate that the misery of the first half of the previous season wouldn't be repeated this time round. Lee Bradbury, a £3.5 million buy from Portsmouth, had scored prolifically during the previous season for his club and was expected to grab the goals we needed in the push for promotion. He made his debut in the last pre-season friendly and scored twice as City notched a commanding win at Burnley to end an encouraging warm-up programme unbeaten.

In fact, despite the promising outlook, 1997-98 was not to be a happy season for the club, and neither was it to be a time I look on with great affection. I can pinpoint the exact date when things began to go wrong on a personal level as Saturday, 23 August, since I recall that the previous evening, City had managed an unconvincing draw at home to Tranmere in a televised game. That Friday, Nadia and I had gone out for a meal to mark the three-month anniversary of our acquaintance (we were a day late, but felt that Friday was a better day to celebrate) and the next day, she decided to introduce me to her daughter, Anna. We met at a sauna, and were having an enjoyable time until I slipped and fell on a wet tile floor. I landed on my left arm and knew immediately that something was badly wrong. I'd smashed my upper arm so that pieces of bone were displaced (I believe medics call it a spiral fracture) and was in excruciating pain. I suppose at least I must have made an impression on Anna.

The recovery was far from simple. I was in plaster for two months, but for the first week, I was in what I understand is known as an aeroplane cast. My entire torso was encased in plaster from the waist up, as was my left arm, which was held out in front of me, supported by a wooden pole which was embedded in the plaster at my waist and my elbow. Aside from making me look ludicrous, this meant I couldn't fit any clothing over my upper body, so I wasn't able to leave the flat. Needless to say, I insisted on the bizarre contraption being removed to make way for a different type of cast (it took two agonising hours to cut away) only for it to replaced by one that left me in extreme pain again because it didn't actually stabilise the break. The only solution was for me to be evacuated out to Finland to be operated on there.

My fortunes, as ever, were just mirroring City's. Before my accident, they'd managed two draws and a defeat in the first three league games, and had lost at Blackpool in the first leg of a first round League Cup tie. The second leg took place four days after my mishap. My unconventional plaster cast meant that I had to sleep in an armchair, a task I found nigh on impossible, so I waited up into the early hours to phone home for the result. I discovered that the tie had gone to extra time (and we'd needed an undeserved late goal even to achieve that), so called back half an hour later. I should have known better than to have expected us to have asserted our supposed superiority in the additional half hour; in fact, it had gone to penalties and we'd lost, which was just about the crowning glory.

It was similarly depressing for most of the season. There was the odd welcome surprise, such as a win away to promotion contenders Nottingham Forest, but for the most part it was a story of unremitting gloom. Ringing my parents on midweek nights in October and early November to find out fortress Maine Road had been breached by poor sides like Stoke, Port Vale and Huddersfield, all relegation contenders that season, was bitterly disappointing, and made me think that my summer promotion aspirations had been hopelessly unrealistic. Making a brief five-day visit home for Christmas and listening to the Boxing Day commentary from Gresty Road as City stumbled to a defeat against Crewe was another black day. Despite the odd result which brought hope, things got no better.

In the New Year, I twice (against Charlton and Ipswich) slightly underestimated the time the match would finish, so called home when injury time was still being played. Twice during the course of my phone calls, City conceded crucial goals costing vital points. After the Ipswich game, I decided these late night calls (Russia is three hours ahead of the UK, so it was almost 1 a.m. by the time the match was ending) must be some kind of jinx, so the following Tuesday forced myself to go to bed without knowing the score of the fixture at Reading. My early morning teletext fumblings (for some reason, it was impossible to access text via the remote control so I had to crouch in front of the decoder box manually scrolling through 125 teletext pages one by one to get news from the satellite channel BBC Prime) showed the total lack of effectiveness of this decision. We were beaten 3-0 by the side destined to finish bottom of the division.

I was, and still am, obsessive enough to take this kind of thing to heart, and for Nadia, it was all a complete mystery. Rather than employing the normal word for a football fan, she used the Russian word fanat to describe me. This means "fanatic", and in Russian carries overtones of dangerously unbalanced or extreme behaviour - it's also the word she'd have used to describe a fundamentalist suicide bomber, for example.

When I think of how it must have looked to her eyes, it probably wasn't altogether surprising that she thought in these terms. She'd been there when I insisted on staying up until the early hours for my late-night telephone depressions. She'd seen my teletext woes. She'd seen me go at a stroke from contentment to utter despondency because of miserable tidings either from Maine Road or whichever godforsaken away ground had witnessed the latest catastrophe.

And as City struggled, so did I. I was off work for only a week, but for some time after wasn't functioning at 100%. I had particular difficulty sleeping, as for weeks, I woke up in pain every time I turned over in the night. As a result I saw the world through a kind of exhausted haze. But even when I was fully recovered, things didn't return to the way they'd been in the summer. The major client project I'd been working on came to an end, and there was little work to replace it. Ironically, I was now settled in Petersburg on a personal level, but my firm started to make noises about sending me back to London to gain further experience there before returning to Russia.

That was the last thing I wanted. I'd experienced all the difficulties associated with settling in, and I didn't want to have to come back to go through all the same problems again, so I had no qualms over looking for a new job in Russia instead. That almost inevitably meant a move to Moscow (few of the major foreign law firms had Petersburg offices), but I felt that was a preferable option to having to begin all over again. I eventually was offered two good jobs and had the strong possibility of other offers when I accepted one in principle, but for various reasons the process dragged on; it was mid-June before I finally agreed personal terms and completed the deal.

As a result, I was still jumpy and unhappy around the time when City's own future was up for grabs. There was a change of manager (Joe Royle, who'd been City's centre-forward for three years in the 1970s, returned to Maine Road to replace Clark, who found out about his dismissal over the radio). There was a change of chairman (Lee finally stepped down in favour of his lower-profile deputy David Bernstein, an accountant by training and a respected figure in the City of London). We deployed a bewildering array of players (we had a staggering 54 professionals on the books at one point), and new boss Royle sparked controversy by risking the wrath of the fans, omitting crowd idol Kinkladze. In fact, I could see where he was coming from. Royle arrived in mid-February, by which point we were second bottom in the table after 32 games. The Georgian had played in all but five of those, and had managed two goals in open play despite being almost entirely relieved of defensive responsibilities. Maybe he would have produced a piece of magic to save us in one of the games in which Royle left him out, but the experience of the first six months of the season seems to suggest that his apologists were wrong to suggest that he inevitably would have done.

Nothing could rescue the season. I'd thought that things would never get worse than in the autumn and winter of 1996-97, whereas, in fact, the series of inept displays, the defeats by mediocre opposition, the spectre of an almost unthinkable relegation, the managerial uncertainty and the takeover speculation of those days turned out to be merely an appetiser for a whole season punctuated by these features. The revival of the previous spring had been just another false dawn. We went into the final game at Stoke needing a win to stand any chance of avoiding the drop; even then, we needed other results to go our way.

Nadia and Anna spent the day of the game elsewhere, as I knew that my own thoughts would have only one focus. All afternoon, I was in my office, resplendent in our Kappa laser blue home kit (a meaningless gesture, of course, but I had to feel I was lending support in some way), trying to follow over the Internet events 2,000 miles away. There was a spell in the first half when we were winning and Portsmouth drawing when it looked like we might complete a great escape. As it was, Portsmouth (who, to add insult to injury, were managed by the unpopular Alan Ball) earned a comfortable victory at Bradford and with Port Vale claiming an easy three points at Huddersfield, we were down despite a 5-2 win. I originally thought that, if the worst came to the worst, I would hit St. Petersburg's bars and find solace in alcohol. In fact, I was glad to have my flat to myself; I felt inclined simply to indulge a private grief by having a couple of quiet beers and sitting in tranquil contemplation.

We deserved to go down - over the season, we were awful - but there's no denying our relegation represented a scandalous waste of resources. On this theme, the writer and broadcaster Danny Kelly, a Spurs fan, wrote in the Internet daily Football 365 that ours was the "most astonishing demotion of all time". I was devastated. But as my job search ended in success, I began to take a more optimistic view. It represented a chance to rebuild; if we'd stayed up, those in charge might have been tempted to duck some difficult choices, whereas surely now they couldn't delude themselves that the season of struggle was just a blip. Though I didn't pretend it would be easy, I considered we had the resources to win promotion back at the first attempt, and if in the process we could begin the radical restructuring that was quite plainly necessary, we'd return stronger.

So as the summer rolled on and as I moved on to Moscow, via a training week in New York with the new firm, I felt that both City and I were set for a revival. In fact, things were destined to get worse for both of us before they got better.

27

An Uncanny Resemblance

IT WAS IN JULY 1998 that I finally made my career move. Between leaving St Petersburg and arriving in Moscow, I had to undertake a week's induction in my new firm's New York office, while on the way back I stopped off in London for the wedding of two of my old university friends. It was late July by the time I actually made it to the Russian capital, and three weeks later, all hell broke loose.

I remember the date - it was Friday, 14 August. Nadia had come down from St Petersburg to visit, arriving the previous evening, and I had the day off work. We slept in late, then had breakfast, and I absentmindedly turned on the television to see the news. I didn't expect much cheer - it had been obvious for a while that the Russian economy wasn't in the healthiest of states, and the rouble was coming under pressure. But the Central Bank intervened to prop up the currency, and the Russians were assured that there was no need to fear a collapse of its value. This was a blip, they were told, and the long-term prognosis was bright, so no-one was unduly worried.

That morning, though, such promises were shown up for the vapid, empty platitudes they really were. No sooner had I hit the remote control than Boris Yeltsin appeared. Some of his erratic public appearances were gloriously entertaining - long, rambling and nonsensical toasts at state banquets were a particular speciality of his, while I still chuckle at the memory of him manhandling a visibly bemused Bulgarian President into the path of a television camera to inform the world that, "This man is my friend - my very, very good friend," before walking off again. I settled back hoping for more classic Yeltsin, but it didn't come. Unusually sombre, he stated that the Central Bank would stop supporting the rouble. At the start of the day, the exchange rate was six roubles to one US dollar, but by the close of the day's trading on the Moscow currency exchange, the rate had dropped to fourteen.

That evening, as I wondered what the crash would mean for me personally (and it made the decision to stay in Russia rather than go back to London look foolish in the extreme), my thoughts turned to City. Early signs were that we'd justify the bookmakers' optimism of an imperious sweep to an instant promotion: the previous Saturday, we'd beaten Blackpool 3-0 in our opening league fixture, while we'd seen off Notts County in the away leg of a League Cup tie on the Tuesday. On the Friday, we had a live televised game at Fulham. With Kevin Keegan having arrived as manager and with Mohamed Al-Fayed's millions bankrolling an extravagant transfer policy, the Londoners were the only side in the division rated by the bookies as having a chance of getting close to us, so the meeting with them was already being billed as a title showdown. Nadia seethed as I insisted on waiting up so that I could phone for the score, but I was confident of a good result and really wanted some positive news to offset the dismay caused by the nascent Russian crisis. As it happened, we lost 3-0, and when the video of the game finally reached me I could see that, in the words of the football cliché, we were lucky to get nil.

Over the next couple of weeks, things went from bad to worse. Though we hit Notts County for seven in the second leg of the League Cup tie, only a scrappy injury-time equaliser saved us from defeat to the same opponents in a Second Division clash shortly afterwards. That escape followed on the heels of a goalless draw at home to Wrexham, leaving us in fourteenth place in the early league table. Russia's woes continued, too. When Nadia returned for another visit a fortnight later, the rouble/dollar rate had dropped to 25. Boris Yeltsin had sacked his cabinet, but was having problems finding a Prime Minister to head a new administration; bewilderingly, just as the country needed vision and leadership, it didn't even have a government for a period of three weeks or so. More or less anyone who'd held public office was touted at some point as being the person the stricken country should turn to, but all the potential candidates couldn't dissociate themselves from the speculation quickly enough. No-one, it seemed, wanted the job. "I'm sure I've seen all this somewhere before," I thought, ruefully.

Despite the economic crisis and political uncertainty, there was no sign of any public disorder on the streets of Moscow. However, I was worried - memories were fresh of TV pictures following the collapse of the Indonesian economy a few short months beforehand, which had sparked serious rioting and cases of violence against foreign nationals. This rather disturbingly led the firm I worked for to advise me to book a ticket home so that if things were to turn nasty, I could leave. At exactly this time, my friend Pete, with whom I'd shared the trials and tribulations of City's last four horrific years both in person and in lengthy and anguished phone calls or e-mails, was due to arrive to stay with me for a week. Not surprisingly, I was rather worried about welcoming a visitor from England in the prevailing circumstances. Then I realised that this was a bloke who'd been watching City for the best part of twenty years, so I had no qualms whatsoever about his arrival - for him, this kind of chaos would be like water off a duck's back. And that was when it dawned on me: if the Russian Federation weren't a country at all but an English football club, it would be Manchester City.

There's that sign which is sometimes seen at various workplaces: "You don't have to be mad to work here but it helps". On most occasions, it's a rather lame exaggeration, but occasionally it has a genuine resonance. And I can see an analogy with my life, for I've come to recognise that my enthusiasm for City and my willingness to spend three years of my life in Russia were actually manifestations of this same character trait.

At the first firm I was with over there, I worked with an English girl, Tania, who became a great friend. The two of us used to joke that our whole lives in Russia were being staged for that television programme where Jeremy Beadle sets people up in ludicrous situations and plays the footage back to about ten million viewers.

At times, you can almost hear his voice-overs. When, as often happened, I was met by unbelievably woeful customer service, he'd be chortling in that peculiarly irritating way of his: "This is me dressed as the world's most unhelpful waiter. I'm going to tell Peter and his girlfriend that they can't eat here tonight even though there are only four people in the entire restaurant." On those frequent occasions when I encountered stultifying bureaucratic intransigence, he'd be there too: "This is me disguised as a ticket seller at the railway station. I'm going to tell Peter after he's queued for an hour to buy his ticket that he actually needs to be in a different queue because he's a foreigner." And when Russian acquaintances came up with ideas based on surreal flights of fancy, he'd be saying: "This is me pretending to be a Russian with a great money-making scheme. I'm going to say I'll blackmail an English ballerina performing in St. Petersburg by threatening to cause her untold shame when I show disapproval in the traditional Russian way by throwing birch twigs on the stage during her performance unless she pays me five thousand dollars."

In this alone there's an absolute parallel with City, as the involvement of Jeremy Beadle is in fact the most rational explanation for some of the events I've witnessed at Maine Road. A good case in point was Frank Clark's decision to spend a club-record transfer fee on forward Lee Bradbury. The high hopes we'd had for the hapless striker had long since disappeared, and I could imagine the transfer negotiations: "This is me posing as the manager of Portsmouth Football Club. I'm going to tell Manchester City that we want three and a half million pounds for Bradbury."

The similarity between City and Russia, however, goes far beyond the fact that both have often seemed crazy enough to have been invented for the benefit of a spoof TV show. There are all kinds of other striking allegories, too, and these are not just limited to the fact that both have regularly demonstrated an unerring ability to get themselves into disastrous, largely self-inflicted messes.

City have always had a propensity for crisis. In the club's original incarnation as Ardwick in the 1890s, it managed to go bust within two years of joining the Football League. After its reformation as Manchester City, it managed within little more than a decade to be involved in a bribery and illegal payments scandal as a result of which the club had to sell all its best players for a pittance. Most ended up with our local rivals, who duly won the league twice with the nucleus of our team. Since then, we've had relegations, cup humiliations, boardroom battles and managerial upheaval on a fairly regular basis.

Russia has likewise always been prone to disorder and chaos. There's a period of Russian history in the seventeenth century known as the "Time of Troubles" - there were problems over succession to the throne, leading to infighting and disorder. But it's always surprised me that this title has been conferred on one particular era, as it applies to most of the country's last thousand years. They've had regular invasions (by the likes of Genghis Khan, Napoleon and Hitler), bitter struggles for power, civil war, famine, revolutions and economic crisis.

All the disasters are made much worse by the knowledge that things really shouldn't be that way. City have a fan base which, had the club managed to harness it properly, should have . . . well, let's say with all due respect that it should have seen us not equal in terms of league status with Chesterfield or Northampton, as we were in 1998-99. Russia has absolutely staggering deposits of natural resources, and had it been able to exploit them properly, it wouldn't . . . well, let's just say it wouldn't ever have been in the state it reached in 1998-99.

Life is never dull, though. Both City and Russia seem to have been led for long periods by larger-than-life figures. In the chairman's office at Maine Road, we had Peter Swales, with his Cuban heels and ludicrous haircut, in charge for twenty years, followed by the ill-fated triumphalism of former player Francis Lee's reign. The manager's chair has been occupied by flamboyant extroverts like rent-a-quote, cigar-puffing, fedora-wearing Cockney Malcolm Allison and the outspoken John Bond, with his sheepskin coats and Princess Di hairstyle.

But the Russians actually outdo us in this regard, with rulers like Peter the Great making our club's autocratic, colourful personalities appear positively grey. Indeed, while most of our failed chairmen or managers have simply been guilty of poor judgement, the sanity of some of Russia's rulers really has to be questioned. Questionable tactics and odd team selections may have earned Frank Clark the entirely deserved sobriquet "Mad Frank" towards the end of his tenure, but if Ivan the Terrible had taken charge of the City team, it's doubtful whether he'd have confined himself to buying overpriced dross or selecting players in positions to which they were patently unsuited. And with Josef Stalin in the Maine Road hot seat, players who lost form would have had rather more to worry about than just being dropped or transfer-listed.

In the modern era, it always struck me that Boris Yeltsin's arbitrary style could also have made him a suitable candidate for the City chairmanship. This was demonstrated at the height of the failed August 1998 attempt to reinstate as Prime Minister Viktor Chernomyrdin (which translates as "Victor Black Face"). Chernomyrdin had been sacked five months previously and his stint in the post was of slightly dubious merit, though he did at least seem to want to take the job on. Unfortunately, the State Duma (the Russian parliament) had other ideas. The reappointment saga came in the middle of a period of a little more than a year when the PM's office had five incumbents - reminiscent of the game of managerial musical chairs at Maine Road in the last few months of 1996, when five men took charge of the team.

The similarity continues in the respective recent histories. The period under Leonid Brezhnev's rule is known to Russians as the time of "stagnation" and the failure to undertake any kind of reform of the Soviet Union's creaking economic edifice had serious repercussions. Admittedly, Peter Swales, our chairman for twenty years, wasn't trying to build a huge stockpile of nuclear weapons in Moss Side and didn't go round buying himself huge fleets of luxury cars or awarding himself more medals than he could pin on his coat. He is, nevertheless, City's Brezhnev. He was blithely oblivious to off-the-field developments in football in the 1990s, and ignored for far too long the consequences of the Taylor Report, following which clubs were required to undertake the expense of making their stadia all-seater. Swales instead signed away on long-term contracts virtually all of the club's commercial possibilities and carelessly spent far more money than we could afford.

Mikhail Gorbachev in Russia and Francis Lee at Maine Road began brave new eras but neither proved equal to the modernising task facing them. Both fell on their swords largely, though perhaps harshly, discredited in the eyes of those whose hopes they'd once guarded. In Russia, the constant disasters have bred an attitude of hardy resilience amongst the people, just as City fans, I think, became almost immune to each fresh setback.

This was largely why I didn't have to use my ticket home. Of course, we had a general strike day which saw tens of thousands gathered in protest in the centre of Moscow, but this is the Russian equivalent of a few hundred on the Maine Road forecourt chanting "sack the board". I would never have refrained from attending City matches because demonstrations outside the Main Stand made me fear for my personal safety, and I wasn't surprised that no manifestation of public anger in Russia had me rushing in panic to board a BA flight to London.

When, in the autumn of 1996, I turned down offers to work in London and Paris to go to Russia instead it defied all logic. I did so because, whatever its imperfections (and they are many), life in Russia is interesting. The same is true of life at Maine Road - where's the adventure in making a nine-hour round trip to somewhere like Cardiff on a cold, wet, miserable January Saturday and spending two hours on the way back freezing on a platform at Crewe station if you can rely on your team to do a professional job and win?

For me, Russia was best summed up by Black Face. He's well known for unfortunate malapropisms, but he once came out with a statement which has entered the Russian lexicon because it summed up perfectly how things there almost seem fated to go wrong, no matter what anyone does. "I wanted everything to turn out for the best," he lamented wearily, "but it's turned out like it always does in Russia." Adapt the phrase for City and it could serve as an epitaph for countless ex-chairmen and ex-managers. We, too, have often seemed fated to lurch into fresh failures whatever steps we try to take against them. To someone with the experience I've had of life in Russia and at Maine Road, the analogy is irresistible and compelling.

28

The Red Arrow

AS DMITRI VASILIEV, Chairman of the Russian Federal Securities Commission, wrote in his introduction to the Commission's annual report for 1998: "The acute economic crisis and political turbulence seriously hurt the Russian securities market, and resulted in decreased trading volumes, substantially lower capitalization, and most importantly, in weakened investor confidence in the Russian market." What that meant for my firm was no work. And although there were no wholesale layoffs within our office as there were at some others in the city, there were serious implications for my career.

I had no prior experience of the type of law I was to practice; I'd moved to work in banking and finance, rather than the commercial contracts I'd specialised in before. I'd been wanted by the firm because of my Russian language capability and because I was actually unhinged enough to commit to live there; because these were both rare qualities, they assumed I'd gain the new experience I needed through being busy on lots of demanding transactions. I'd felt excited by the challenge, but when there weren't any demanding transactions coming through the door, there was no experience for me, and the little work we had was, quite understandably, going to those of our number who actually knew how to do it. So for the next few months, I had to make do with editing a newsletter for the Moscow office's clients, updating their manual on Russian law and organising a new filing system for the office. The latter was the killer, and whilst prior to this time, I'd have thought being paid to do no proper work was ideal, I found it utterly soul-destroying.

I'd lost all desire to stay with the firm the moment organising the filing system became my big responsibility. I regarded it as an insult, so there was a healthy tinge of bitterness mixed into my emotions as well. I had talents which could have been useful to the firm in the longer run, and had demonstrated some of them while I was there. I'd have thought an appropriate course of action might be to send me back to the London office where there might actually be some work I could cut my teeth on. But the one time I raised the idea it was dismissed out of hand.

It wasn't just the work that was going wrong, either. After a couple of months, there came the departure of some American computer trainers with whom I'd spent lots of time outside work, which had a major effect on my social life. And in these circumstances, the last thing I'd really needed was for Nadia to emigrate; she wasn't the sole reason I'd elected not to return to England with my previous firm, but she'd undeniably been an important factor. I'd known for over a year that she'd applied for entry clearance to go to Canada, but in truth I'd disregarded the possibility (I'd looked at the rules and it appeared to me that the odds were against her). Now her clearance came through and she left, with my blessing (in the state her country was in, it represented an opportunity she'd have been mad not to take). Though we resolved to try to keep the relationship going at a distance, and though we managed it for the rest of my time in Russia and beyond, it didn't make me any happier about the turn of events since I'd moved from St Petersburg in July.

I was unhappier than I've ever been in my life; winters in Moscow can be bleak at the best of times, but with my career going down the tubes, my social life having departed and Nadia five thousand miles away, it was a particularly miserable time. I succumbed to dangerous self-pity and used to like to wallow in the depths of my own depression. I stopped having any desire to socialise - I'd decided early on that I'd have to move on so I figured that the more money I could save by not going out the better. And separate incidents in which my flat was broken into and in which I was robbed at knife-point with a large amount of cash in my wallet (I was on my way to give my landlord three months' rent - luckily my assailant didn't discover the money, though I almost had a heart attack) didn't lighten my mood much.

I know that I'm dangerously obsessive, but not even I'm dysfunctional enough for all of the above woes to have been swept away by some positive football news; nevertheless, it would have been nice if City could have at least come up with something to cheer me during this black time. It would just have shown that there was at least one area of my life where everything wasn't disintegrating horribly before my eyes. In fact, for four months, City caught the mood and decided that their similarity to Russia should extend to now doing their best to make my life as wretched as they could.

Things got worse than we ever could have imagined. First of all, we stopped winning; there was a draw at home to Chesterfield in which we missed a late penalty, but then we started to need last-gasp equalisers to avert ignominious defeats. Northampton, Millwall and Burnley were all thus denied before we suddenly lost the ability to perform rescue acts. We managed, I think, 18 points in fifteen games in the run-up to Christmas, and there were some really desperate performances mixed in. Those who were there seem divided as to whether it was the loss at Lincoln or at Wycombe which represented the nadir. By this time, the power of the Internet enabled me to gauge the sentiments of my fellow fans; not surprisingly, I can never remember the mood more fractious or discontented. Things continued to get worse; December saw a goalless draw at home to Bristol Rovers and a desperate FA Cup tie against Darlington, won in extra time in the replay, the only goal coming after 108 minutes of mind-numbing tedium. Fulham were running away with the title, but it already looked as if we could give up on our hopes of the second-placed finish that would assure automatic promotion. Even a top-six place to give us a shot at promotion via the play-off lottery looked like a fairly remote prospect.

When I think of this period, both for me and for City, I invariably reflect on a train journey from St Petersburg back to Moscow, which was also a nightmare. It mirrored my own situation and City's in that every time I thought I'd reached the point at which nothing further could possibly happen to make matters any worse, something happened to show me I was hopelessly and desperately wrong. I actually e-mailed an account to various friends who'd travelled on Russian trains, and so I can guarantee things really did happen as they're presented below. The events took place towards the end of September 1998, the day after a late scrappy goal from Shaun Goater rescued a point at Northampton, a result insufficient to keep the team from a disappointing mid-table position, and to keep me from a black mood when I phoned on my mobile from a restaurant to hear the result.

I'd been in St. Petersburg for the weekend visiting Nadia, who was due to emigrate to Canada the following Wednesday. The two days we'd spent together had exceeded even my already high expectations, and on the Sunday evening, we'd had a farewell dinner at our favourite restaurant together with Anna and Nadia's best friend Marina before we headed to the station, where we said our goodbyes. I boarded the 11.55 p.m. train back to Moscow knowing that when I arrived the following morning, I'd be going straight into work.

I was the first passenger into the four-berth compartment, but it soon became apparent that I didn't have the space to myself. Two noisy Russian men who looked as if they were in their mid-to-late twenties came in, and as soon as they entered, the smell of alcohol was palpable. The several bottles of Baltika beer they were carrying hinted that the liquor already ingested wouldn't be the last of which they'd partake before they finally retired. My first task was to attempt, painfully, to side-step entreaties to join the two Russians, who introduced themselves as Vasilii and Sergei, for a drink. My chosen method was a feigned, comprehensive ignorance of the Russian language. Vasilii in particular seemed reluctant to see this as a barrier to continued communication even though the smattering of English words known to him and his friend appeared to be of a quantity only marginally greater than the number of major trophies Manchester City have won since 1976. The conversation was far from sparkling - I recall it following along the lines of "Drink?" "No", repeated over and over for several minutes.

At this point an ally arrived. The final passenger in compartment 8 of carriage 13 was a grey-haired man in his forties. Vasilii and Sergei attempted to engage him in a conversation of slightly more depth, but other than telling them that he was called Felix and was travelling to Moscow on business, he was largely, and understandably, reticent to join the conversation. Vasilii and Sergei talked among themselves while seeing off their first bottle of Baltika. Felix and I were occupying the bottom two beds, but Sergei sat on Felix's bunk, while Vasilii decided to ignore the fact that I'd been in a reclining position throughout and had thus made it impossible for him to sit on the bed and face Sergei. He simply seated himself on my legs instead. It became clear from their conversation that they were employees of the railway company and were on their way to Moscow for a work-related reason.

Felix tried to do a deal. Saying that he was going to the restaurant car for half an hour, he suggested that Vasilii and Sergei have a drink, and that when he returned it would be time for bed. Of course, I already knew that the railwaymen wouldn't want to stop drinking in half an hour but rather naively hoped that they might continue their alcohol consumption elsewhere. I wasn't enjoying being alone in their company, but Sergei convinced Vasilii that further entreaties to Felix or me to join the fun were pointless - I heard them regretfully observe that as I was foreign and Felix was old, the two of us couldn't be expected to behave like real Russian men. Putting down my copy of the St. Petersburg Times, I turned my back and attempted to fall asleep, though I knew that, with the light still on and the conversation continuing with its volume unmoderated, the task was likely to be a forlorn one. I caught one last glimpse of Sergei taking from his bag a bottle containing a luminous yellow liquid which, according to the label, should have been lemonade. While this may have been true, their rapid further intoxication gave rise to the suspicion that another substance may have been added. But when Felix came back to the compartment and got into bed, the railwaymen left and things briefly looked slightly more promising.

For the next two hours, the light remained switched on. The railwaymen came and went, regularly failing to close the door when they left, and managing to increase the volume of their conversation the longer time went on so that any rest was fitful at best. Sergei's watch sounded at one o'clock and would do so again, every hour on the hour, throughout the night. However, the biggest inconvenience came when Sergei attempted to pour the luminous yellow liquid into two cups, but his aim was somewhat lacking; he managed to direct liberal quantities directly onto my bed below.

At this point Felix intervened. Turning the light off, he told the railwaymen that if they wanted to drink and talk, they should do so outside the compartment. Sergei wondered whether he and his friend had been disturbing their fellow passengers, to which Felix replied emphatically in the affirmative. Sergei's apologies were, needless to say, noisy and lengthy, and thus completely counter-productive. Sergei and Vasilii then abided by requests to continue their merriment outside the compartment, but unfortunately their location of choice was directly outside the door. They awakened passengers from other compartments and, entirely predictably, the recriminations were loud and prolonged. At this point the two men admitted defeat, and went to bed. It was twenty to three, and I looked forward at least to five and a half hours of rest before the train arrived the next morning.

In fact, I woke less than an hour later. The railwaymen had apparently found it impossible to sleep and were talking in what they probably assumed, mistakenly, to be whispers. It wasn't the voices, however, which had roused me. It was the fact that Sergei had dropped a (mercifully unopened) bottle of Bailey's Irish Cream, which landed on my legs. Felix woke up, and, after he had remonstrated with them, the railwaymen elected to continue drinking outside the compartment. I don't know where they went, but thankfully it wasn't immediately outside, so I managed to doze off for around an hour.

At 5 a.m., the railwaymen noisily re-entered the cabin, and, almost on cue, Sergei's digital watch beeped to signal the new hour; it was to be the worst hour of the night. Vasilii and Sergei managed to reach their bunks, not without difficulty, though Sergei in particular looked to be perched slightly precariously, his legs dangling over the edge of the bed but, within a few minutes, I was asleep once more. After a further quarter of an hour, this was no longer the case; Sergei had fallen out of his bunk, landing on my legs before rolling onto the floor. Having with some difficulty managed to stand, he made concerted but unsuccessful efforts to reach his bunk before eventually giving up and lying on the floor once more. Sergei next began to mutter incomprehensibly to himself, prompting Felix to rouse himself angrily and demand that Sergei got into his own bunk. Sergei was incapable of understanding the request, and eventually Vasilii got up to assist him in complying. He failed.

This had all taken more than half an hour, and I managed to get back to sleep just before six o' clock. Then came the crowning glory; I was woken by Sergei's watch, which instead of beeping to signal the new hour, played "The Yellow Rose of Texas" for a whole twenty seconds. Sergei was still lying on the floor (as he would be when I left), so I had to forcibly restrain myself from getting up and kicking him repeatedly and with considerable force.

I managed to nod off again, until an hour later the radio was turned on throughout the carriage, rendering further sleep impossible save for the alcohol-facilitated slumbers of Vasilii and Sergei. And then I went to work, where I was tired and bored and miserable and full of self-pity. It had been a nightmare.

Now, though, I understand it for what it was - a metaphor. When I think about that journey, it doesn't seem half as bad as at the time. First of all, it was just like events at Manchester City in the same period. Each new low made it seem as if the worst had now happened, yet each time things did deteriorate; in quick succession we had home defeats by Preston and at the hands of Reading, and then the disasters at Lincoln and Wycombe before the miserable three weeks at the start of December. Yet that journey now almost takes on a rosy glow when I contemplate it; it's just the kind of crazy, wacky thing that used to happen to me in Russia and I kind of miss it. In fact, I frequently think I'd like to go back.

That's what supporting Manchester City is like, too. I've lost count of the number of games they've put me through that have been the footballing equivalent of an evening with Sergei and Vasilii, but my loyalty has never seriously been tested. I think it's because no matter how awful things become (and we went into Christmas 1998 with things more spectacularly wretched than ever before, a defeat at York leaving us forlornly in mid-table ahead of the festive fixtures), life at Maine Road is full of surprises. That train journey in fact mirrored the club's fortunes over several years in that every time I thought the worst was over, things deteriorated further. But the thing about City is this: we stick with it through the bad times because occasionally, just occasionally, they're capable of making up for it all. They were about to do it again.

29

Wembley

WHEN IT CAME TO Manchester City, I thought I'd seen it all. I'd seen us smash the British transfer record to sign a mediocre, journeyman midfielder and I'd seen us play keep-ball in the corner with an eye on preserving a result which would seal relegation. I'd seen us throw away a three-goal lead in the last twenty minutes at home to Bournemouth when a win would have clinched promotion and I'd seen us rescue the situation the following week with a desperately late goal in the season's last match. In short, I thought I'd experienced more or less everything City could throw at me. On May 30th, 1999 I learned that I was wrong.

Given the character of the club, it was hardly surprising that in a quarter of a century following Manchester City, I'd witnessed many dramatic and improbable moments. I was no stranger to the club's seemingly insatiable appetite for self-destruction and was well acquainted with its remarkable flair for failing to do things the easy way. But on one incredible Sunday afternoon, they were to showcase both traits more dramatically than they ever had before.

As I was preparing to end my period of exile in Russia, City had reached the Division Two play-off final against Gillingham, a match which was to be played at Wembley on the Bank Holiday weekend at the end of May. It was a startling transformation, of which I'd been home to witness the start: I braved torrential rain and a howling gale on Boxing Day to travel to North Wales for the fortuitous win at Wrexham, while two days later at home to Stoke, we produced a compelling display marked by a rousing second-half fight-back in front of a passionate Maine Road full house. In the end, only two of the 24 league games since Christmas were lost, and we rose nine places in the table, just missing out on the second place berth that would have conferred automatic promotion. Instead, it was the play-offs, and we managed a 2-1 aggregate win over Wigan Athletic in the semi-final, recovering from conceding a ludicrous comedy goal in the opening minute of the first game and edging through in an electric atmosphere at Maine Road with a Shaun Goater goal disputed by the visitors, who claimed the striker used an arm rather than his chest to bundle the ball home.

In the build-up to the Wembley final, I was yet again unable to resist drawing what I felt was a fitting parallel with my own personal circumstances. At the beginning of September 1998, I'd told my visiting City-supporting friend Pete that I felt the onset of the economic crisis would result in my leaving Russia. In November, I was miserable enough to consider returning to England and taking a 75% pay cut to take a six-month contract in a legal publishing job to enable me to look more easily for work in London. In February, I arranged to come home for a couple of interviews which came to nothing, though it did allow me take the train up to Manchester to see probably the least prestigious opposition ever to visit Maine Road in a league fixture - Macclesfield Town. Finally, in April, the decision I'd been putting off was taken and I returned home for good in May, armed with two months' severance pay and primed to devote myself fully to looking for a new job. The experience of the previous few months had indicated that conducting the search and attempting to make myself available for interviews from a couple of thousand miles away wasn't the most efficient method of securing the position I wanted.

Leaving one job without another to go to is a rather unnerving experience and in my position things were worse. The turn of events in Russia ensured that the experience I'd gained in the previous three, crucially formative years of my career wasn't directly relevant for the type of role I was forced to seek. While I felt that I could bridge the gap fairly easily, I was competing against other candidates with no gap to close. I hoped that someone might be attracted by my international experience and language skills, and would tolerate a learning curve in order to benefit later from these attributes.

However, I also knew that such a long-term view is rarely encountered in the legal recruitment market. By and large, if firms anticipate a future need for international experience and language skills, they will defer recruiting until the need actually arises.

The potential for disappointment was, in truth, considerable so I was looking for omens, for portents which could reassure me that events would unfold satisfactorily. When I look in the cold light of day, and from the perspective of now being in a job which I enjoy and which makes use of my talents, it seems quite spectacularly unwise, but, as usual, what I seized on was Manchester City's progress. I felt that if City were to ease past Gillingham and put the club's darkest days behind them, my own rehabilitation would inevitably ensue. If City could win promotion, I expected to follow suit by marching into a new job and putting the misery of my last year in Russia behind me. So, despite being old enough to know much, much better, I convinced myself that little Gillingham would be vanquished with an appropriate flourish, and a new era would begin both for me and for my team.

Needless to say, given my all-too-painful awareness of City's perversity and contrariness, I was keen to bolster this rather flimsy pretext with evidence of more substance. It came with Manchester United's success in winning an unprecedented treble of the Premiership title, FA Cup and UEFA Champions' League. Again it's clear, with the benefit of hindsight, that this was also not a particularly sound basis for my conviction. However, at the time I thought that the timing of United's treble, that it should arrive in this of all weeks, could mean only one thing. It was the price exacted by those malevolent football deities for allowing City's progress away from our darkest hour to proceed unimpeded. And though it was an unreasonably steep price to ask, I decided I could live with the terms of the deal. The footballing gods had been cruel to City, and therefore to me too, many, many times over the years but surely they couldn't be so sneeringly, vindictively cruel as to allow our neighbours to bask in the glory of three trophies in a season and to deny us a mere win over Gillingham.

On the morning of the big match, the slate-grey sky and intermittent drizzle lent an authentic Mancunian air to proceedings, helping to ensure that my faith never wavered. I'd come down to London for the weekend to stay with an old school-friend and his wife. I already had a ticket for myself and had managed to procure one for him, too, and we made the journey from the south-west to the north west of the capital together before going our separate ways after a couple of beers inside the ground. "Two-nil, no problem," I predicted authoritatively as we parted for our respective seats. I was sitting with my Moscow visitor Pete and his dad, Eddie, and just before kick-off I experienced my first slight misgivings. It occurred to me that of the several matches Pete and I had attended together, I couldn't recall a single City victory - and the thought was discomforting. An unconvincing start by the team tested my belief further, although the game eventually settled into a tense contest, looking for all the world like a single goal for either side would be sufficient to earn victory.

There was a close shave as City's Goater struck a post on 74 minutes, but the strike I always felt would be decisive came with nine minutes of the match remaining. It didn't come the way I expected, and I was submerged in a sea of panic as Gillingham striker Carl Asaba rushed through on the City goal, making no mistake with the finish. I watched in disbelief as the ball hit the net, sparking delighted celebrations from Gillingham's players and fans. It wasn't supposed to be like this. I told myself that there was still time, that City had scored several late goals during the season, and that it would be typical of City to make us all sweat before going on to claim the prize destiny was reserving for us. But I wasn't sure if I believed these platitudes, for it would have been equally - probably more - typical of City to throw all our best hopes back in our faces, to build up our aspirations only to deliver crushing disappointment when it mattered most.

It was a really pulsating match now, with City fighting for the equaliser, taking risks as they did so, and my emotions see-sawed for the next four or five minutes. Either side could have scored -

Gillingham goalkeeper Vince Bartram saved with his legs when a goal looked certain, then City's Nicky Weaver fingertipped the ball onto the post from striker Robert Taylor. And then it was all over. Taylor drove the ball emphatically past Weaver and into the bottom corner for a second Gillingham goal. As I watched their players cavorting on the Wembley turf and heard the almost disbelieving glee of their fans' chants, I knew that the contest was over. There were maybe three minutes left, plus injury time. It might have been long enough for one goal, but to ask for two was requesting a miracle, and miracles are not in the Manchester City repertoire.

So when City midfielder Kevin Horlock reduced the arrears with only twelve seconds of the match plus injury time remaining, I wasn't suffused with renewed optimism. I knew for sure that my earlier hopes had been unfounded, my faith had been misplaced and the malevolent, United-supporting deities had reneged on our deal. I knew that by allowing us to score when it no longer mattered, they were just mocking us. City throwing away a two-goal lead in the final minute at Wembley could have had a ring of truth - such comic farces have become our trademark over the years - but the reverse could happen only in the most outlandish of fantasies.

I didn't see the fourth official signal how much injury time was to be played, so I spent the whole of the next five minutes thinking that the final whistle was imminent. But play continued, and with the clock ticking past 94 minutes the ball arrived at the feet of City striker Paul Dickov in the Gillingham penalty area. So comprehensively had my faith now been punctured, I expected to see the ball fly wide of the post or over the crossbar. I could only reflect that as we travelled to Scunthorpe the following season, this would be the moment we'd look back to when it could all have been so different. But then the net bulged, Dickov wheeled away in jubilation pursued by team-mates, the Gillingham defenders sank to their knees in utter dejection and all around me there was absolute pandemonium. It was probably the loudest noise I've ever heard in my life from any concentrated group of people. Pete's dad later told me that in the aftermath of our life-saving equaliser, I was hugging him and Pete and behaving like a "big, daft sod". It was that kind of moment.

After a resurrection like that, City simply couldn't lose. The deities, it was now clear, were benevolent and had merely wanted to remind us of how catastrophic things could have been before allowing us to triumph. This made me serene throughout the penalty shoot-out which followed an inconclusive period of extra time. If I'd been told that at the outset I'd be so relaxed and sanguine, I'd have been disbelieving, but when the penalties were taken at our end and the confident Weaver started milking the crowd's applause, I knew we'd win. The Gillingham players seemed visibly to suffer from stepping forward to be met by a vocal barrage described as "deafening" in the TV commentary, and they missed three of the four kicks they took. When Weaver made his second save to ensure victory was ours, he set off on a madcap charge of joy and 40,000 City fans exploded into riotous celebration.

Of course, I soon found that City's ascension into Division One didn't mean my task was going to be easy, and my misgivings over potential employers' attitude to my idiosyncratic CV proved justified. Over the next month, I spoke to a range of firms, only a handful of which held a greater interest for me than offering a monthly replenishment of my bank account, and was just starting to become a little disillusioned. Then I was unexpectedly called for interview at a niche firm in London whose profile fitted my experience admirably and I quickly had an offer I was happy to accept.

As I went away for a holiday before I started my new job, I understood that my break had come because I'd worked hard to ensure my CV lent itself exactly to this kind of job, and because I'd had a crucial piece of luck in the vacancy arriving at precisely the opportune moment. From a perspective of contentment rather than anxiety, I was able to reflect that Paul Dickov's right boot didn't really have very much to do with the whole process after all.

When I understood that, I also realised that we were going to win all along, and I realised why we'd made such heavy weather of it. The reason? Well, it came down again to Manchester United. It doesn't really bother me any more to be compared unfavourably to them in terms of criteria like on-field achievement, stadium capacity or world-wide fan base; those are areas in which we've hardly been able claim to be their equals for a long time. But I always felt that in terms of a propensity to create drama, we were indisputably Manchester's top dogs, and even that title seemed to be under threat as the 1998-99 season drew to a close.

In their European final against Bayern Munich, United had trailed for almost the entire match, and were still a goal down as the game entered stoppage time. The Germans had hit the post a couple of times, but their failure to land the killer second didn't seem to have cost them. Then two United goals in quick succession landed them the trophy. I had to take my hat off to them, or, at least, I would have done if I wore one - it was a nice touch.

That wasn't their only dramatic triumph as they closed in on the three trophies. In the semi-final, they came from two down away at Juventus in the second leg to win both on the night and on aggregate. They clinched the league title on the closing day of the season by a single point; needing to beat Spurs, they trailed before duly registering the victory they required. In the FA Cup, the final had been a stroll against Newcastle, but the semi was a thriller. It went to a replay in which their title rivals Arsenal seemed to have the upper hand. United were down to ten men, and at 1-1 the Gunners had a penalty. Peter Schmeichel saved Dennis Bergkamp's spot kick, and United went on to win through an exhilarating Ryan Giggs goal.

I'd never really rated United much before this as providers of real, edge-of-the-seat, nerve-jangling tension, but I had to concede grudgingly that I was quite impressed. I even began to worry that they might start to eclipse us in the one area where we'd always been their masters. City's Wembley performance, I came to realise, was merely our way of upping the ante to demonstrate that we still held sway.

One thing is that our game was far more important. When I say that, I don't mean it was a bigger footballing occasion; in that regard, comparing our game and theirs is a bit like measuring a royal wedding against the opening of a new Tesco's in Crumpsall. I know that United's pursuit of another European Cup after 31 years was something of a holy grail, and I don't want to belittle that - to equate it to City, we haven't won a proper trophy for 26 years, and when we do, no-one will be happier than me. And no-one should forget that the win was in itself a magnificent achievement that crowned a bigger, stunning and historic accomplishment. But the difference is this: United's win made no difference to them in terms of qualifying for any competition the next season, the financial consequences of failure were minimal in the club's overall context, and if they hadn't won the tournament then, they'd have done so at some other time anyway. We, on the other hand, would have suffered enormously by staying down; the club could afford to absorb the monetary losses we did for one season in the Second Division, but the fiscal repercussions of another year at that level would have been catastrophic. In other words, we actually had the bottle to play brinkmanship when we were staring into the abyss.

And then there was the way we did it. After all, winning after being a goal down isn't that dramatic after all. As legendary ex-Forest manager Brian Clough used to say, "It only takes a second to score a goal." So if you're losing, there's always a chance to pull it back right until the final whistle blows. OK, it was a nice touch to bag the winner without the need for extra time, but we really showed them how to do it. You go two down, an apparently insurmountable deficit, when defeat would have been disastrous for the club's future. You draw back improbably from the brink, but instead of going on to win in extra time and calm everyone's nerves by doing so, you decide to put your fans through the agony of a penalty shoot-out instead. Just for a laugh.

City were to provide more evidence of their ability to dispense gut-wrenching spectacles over the next few years. Meanwhile, chastened by the lesson they'd been taught, United went on and won the Premiership by miles in each of the next two seasons. They'd learned that when it comes to this kind of thing, it's really better to leave it to the experts.

30

Behind the Scenes

WHEN I FINALLY found a job five weeks after Paul Dickov's rescue act against Gillingham, it was something of a dream move. I'd been on generous ex-pat packages in Russia, so had to take a pay cut, which is never good. But it did give me a further benefit, which to my eyes couldn't be underestimated. It allowed me to gain a fascinating insight into the world of professional football.

I can't paint myself as a mover and shaker in British sport by any means. On the other hand, I believe I have a greater insight into the administrative and commercial side of sport than most fans. My professional experience has included advising both sports clubs and governing bodies. At the outset of my career, I spent considerable time researching the relationships between governing bodies, member clubs or associations and contracted players; this was in the context of the impending relaxation of rules prohibiting professionalism in rugby union. Later, I did work advising certain football clubs on the Bosman ruling and other matters. So when I got back to England, I funded myself through a part-time course on sports law (the only such postgraduate course in Europe) at King's College, London. And the firm I ended up working for acted for Arsenal Football Club.

Again, I don't want to misrepresent myself; I'm scarcely claiming that people at Highbury were hanging on my every word. The senior partner at the firm was, as he had been for thirty years, the main contact and I assisted sporadically when required. On the other hand, I saw plenty that was of interest. I went to meetings there and fielded phone calls from directors and senior staff on the commercial side. I was involved, for instance, in international transfer dealings and player contract negotiations, major commercial and licensing deals and arrangements with feeder clubs. And while often the kind of advice needed is no different from that required by clients in other sectors, the football context gave the work another dimension in terms of catching my interest.

I used to think that my ideal would be to have a professional connection with Manchester City, but I'm no longer sure that this is so. The truth is this: I care too much. For a time in Manchester, I was with a firm that didn't actually represent City but acted for a couple of individuals involved with the club. Occasionally work would come in that shed light on matters behind the scenes at Maine Road: of course, I also had access to files containing information on previous deals and to individuals with knowledge of past events. And given that Manchester City has not historically been a well-run club (indeed, this is an understatement akin to saying that Adolf Hitler did one or two bad things), what I discovered sometimes troubled me greatly.

With Arsenal it was a different story. I actually respected the club, its traditions and achievements and they enjoyed my wholehearted and sincere backing as the English club most likely to put in any kind of significant challenge against Manchester United's dominance. However, at the end of the day, I used to feel that if the Arsenal directors decided to take a course of action that was patently unwise, that would lead to ruin and misery, it was entirely a matter for them. I must emphasise that this never happened - the running of the club was unquestionably and, for someone with the Manchester City background I have, rather unaccustomedly competent - but if it had, I wouldn't have lost a moment's sleep.

In fact, I wouldn't just have been indifferent. I must apologise to Arsenal fans here because I have nothing against them personally or their club, but I'm afraid that I would actively have enjoyed it. This is because we Manchester City fans feel that no other well-supported club has put its followers through such misery over the years as ours has, and so I derive a certain schadenfreude when I see it happening to someone else.

It's a characteristic of mine that I like to outdo other people's tales of woe with stories of my own misfortune, and having spent time in Russia certainly gives me plenty of scope. If someone moans to me that the price of milk has just gone up by 2p, I'll inform them that I used to live in a place where the price of milk could quite conceivably double overnight. If anyone whinges about the length of time they've had to stand in a queue, I'll recall the time I twice stood in line to register my visa in St Petersburg; on both occasions, I was turned away after four long and tedious hours because the office was closed. And complain to me about the cold and you'll be met with stories of how it was minus 38 one night when I was in St Petersburg, or how I had to walk from my office to Paveletskaya metro in Moscow when it was minus 25 - disregarding the wind chill factor.

Thus, in a footballing context, I can have little sympathy with fans of some of the big teams when they complain about the actions of their clubs. Spurs fans, for instance: do you think you're hard done by when you're mid-table in the top division? Try being mid-table two divisions further down and see how you like that. Everton supporters: are you angry at grubbing around in the lower reaches of the Premiership? Lose some of your relegation battles for a change, see how it feels then. And what would you think, Aston Villa fans, if you went down and then dropped through the next division like a stone? What do you mean, you once did? OK, so maybe we're not the only ones then, but you take the point - which is that supporters of some teams don't know they're born. And in that category are fans of Arsenal, with their uninterrupted top-flight football since 1919 and where it's a bad season if they only finish second in the Premier League and reach the UEFA Cup final, as they did in 2000.

These, obviously, are feelings I have to suppress in my professional life. A solicitor shouldn't, I feel, actively wish his clients ill. This, I think, illustrates the problem people like me face in this kind of situation and the kind of schizophrenic mental facility we have to espouse to survive in such a setting. For there are aspects of being a football fan which I enjoy immensely, yet which are totally at odds with the kind of professionalism required when people are paying your firm a sum well into three figures for each hour of your work.

In fact, I had no opportunity actually to act on these feelings, and would have been professional enough not to do so anyway. Even so, I think I did subconsciously and unintentionally bring a negative influence to bear on Arsenal Football Club. City had stopped winning trophies as soon as I'd become a fan, and my reverse Midas touch worked with the Gunners as well. In the two seasons immediately before my arrival, Arsenal had first finished ahead of United in the Premiership and then only a point behind, whereas after I'd started having anything to do with them in the next two seasons they were still in second place, but miles back. And oddly enough, having rescued themselves from the depths of the Second Division, City, with my malign tendency suddenly focused on north London, suddenly began to prosper further.

Winning promotion a year before had been nothing more or less than we'd expected given the resources at our disposal compared to those of almost every other club in the section, even if, typically, we'd made much harder work of everything than we should have. But despite fairly bullish pre-season comments from the management, I think most of us expected a season of consolidation to follow. Yet City were in the top four at the end of August and were never out of contention for an automatic promotion spot thereafter. There was a blip in February and March, when we took five points from seven games, none of which were won, but we snapped out of it just in time, and as the season drew to a close, second place (which guaranteed an ascent to the Premiership without recourse to the lottery of the play-offs) was there for the taking.

This was all a welcome break from my Arsenal involvement. In truth, I didn't find being involved in professional football all it was cracked up to be. Perhaps I'm just too much of a fan, because I don't really share the vision of many in the game. For me, football is a passion, and I don't like to think of it as a business; but act as a legal adviser to a major sporting institution, and that's exactly how you have to think, because as it's fashionable to observe, top-level football is now big business. Somehow, and I recognise that this is a wholly romantic view that doesn't square with prevailing views in professional sport, football is on another plane. I can square with my conscience the fact that ordinary considerations of profit and loss, income streams and expanding brand awareness apply in almost any other sphere of commercial activity. It doesn't seem right in football, though; as a fan, it means too much to me, I have so many emotions vested in it, and the game forms such a big part of my life that I almost feel it should be sacrosanct from those kinds of considerations. But I'm also realistic enough to know that things won't change. Football today reflects the modern world and there's no prospect of a return to a more innocent bygone age.

So while I was from time to time performing bits of legal work for Arsenal, I probably derived more pleasure from things I was doing on a voluntary basis relating to Manchester City. And it's not that somehow City are less commercialised or more ethically pure than a club like Arsenal; I know this not to be true. City's travails of the 1990s, when this side of football really took off, meant that Arsenal and the other top clubs had a head start and were thus more sophisticated. But City aspired to the same, and took steps to try to make those considerations a reality - a necessity for any club with ambitions to return to anywhere even approaching the top of English football.

But taking the role I did with City, I could ignore all this. I provided regular news summaries for an e-mail newsletter which went out twice-weekly to several thousand City fans (primarily exiled Mancunians) around the world. And though I eventually gave it up - it became too time-consuming to combine with a full-time job - I enjoyed the fact that it brought me into contact with fans throughout the world. I knew I was providing them with a service that many of them valued, and it gave me a thrill to be quoted extensively in one acclaimed book on the club and on the cover of another tome. I also got a kick from being one of a group of fans who approached Manchester City with an idea to form an International Supporters Club. We felt we were benefiting fans, but using my professional experience I helped to persuade the football club that our plans could have a commercial benefit to it too.

The thing is, these endeavours made me feel that I was benefiting supporters; there was an altruism and a passion for the game involved in what I was doing. And though I don't kid myself that I have been a groundbreaking crusader for fans' rights, I do genuinely feel I've done some good for supporters. Being involved in the way I'd been with Arsenal certainly never engendered that emotion. When I'd arrived at the firm, I'd thought that the football connection alone could always keep me there, but later I realised it wouldn't. I've always felt I'd known in life when to move on, and after a few months, I saw that Arsenal wouldn't hold me back when that time came. As City's promotion destiny came closer to being decided in the spring of 2000, I started to get the idea that it might actually come quite quickly.

31

A Turn for the Worse

CITY REACHED THE FINAL day of season 1999-2000 destined to reach the Premiership, even if it wasn't clear before the fateful afternoon. On paper, the trip to Blackburn was no formality, given that the home side, who'd underachieved horribly for much of the campaign, nevertheless boasted what was probably the division's most accomplished collection of players, a squad that duly won promotion the following campaign. And a televised, high-profile game, I feared, might just offer them the platform to show their fans that better times were round the corner. So though City only needed a draw from the game to be sure of promotion, this was not a simple task. To make matters worse, Ipswich, just two points behind City, faced relegation probables Walsall at home, so were in an excellent position to take advantage of any slip.

Ipswich were probably quite hopeful as the big day approached, but, as it turned out, they needn't have bothered; the fates were quite definitely on our side. There were signs throughout the season that it would be City's year, and in my lifetime, we've always gone up when a promotion battle goes to the last day of the season (we've always lost our last-ditch relegation battles as well). And thus it proved, despite Blackburn's efforts - and our own - to ensure the contrary outcome. City played poorly, and their hosts scored just before half-time. This, it's fair to say, caused more than a slight measure of concern. But in the first fifteen minutes of the second half, it became clear we'd been right all along, and a couple of minutes just around the hour mark showed the futility of all Blackburn's hopes of winning the game - destiny just wasn't going to let them.

First, they hit the woodwork for the third time in the match, a shot from striker Ashley Ward rebounding into the arms of City goalkeeper Weaver as he turned to watch the ball hit the net. Then, almost immediately, an effort from their other striker Matt Jansen cannoned off the foot of the post. Play suddenly switched to the other end, when City strung together almost their first meaningful move of the entire afternoon and Shaun Goater converted a Kevin Horlock cross. Blackburn duly collapsed, handing us an own goal seven minutes later. We then scored two more - the entire four-goal burst took only twenty-one minutes - allowing the team to play out time in a beatific last ten minutes.

It really seemed to me that, since the times we were suffering together in Moscow, City and I had both landed on our feet. I'd managed to get a decent job, one that seemed to be a good outlet for my skills and interests. And City had not only managed - albeit by the skin of their teeth - to escape the clutches of the Second Division, they'd then gone and stormed through the First Division, too. But unfortunately that was as good as it got for either of us.

At the end of May, three weeks after the Blackburn game, I finally split with Nadia. And though it was my decision, it didn't mean I was happy. I felt that the break was preferable to carrying on the way we were, but what I really wanted was for her to understand my feelings and be a little less selfishly uncompromising. Having made the emotional investment I had in the relationship, I was bitterly disappointed that it should end, so though I knew that this outcome was for the best, it was nevertheless not one that I could embrace with any real enthusiasm. I did actually weaken later and try to contact her again, though looking back now, I'm glad she reacted coldly.

Work had also taken a turn for the worse, and I'd totally ceased to enjoy the job I was in. I'd never really been overly enthusiastic about being a lawyer in private practice, but it wasn't just that. I came to realise that my travails in Russia had set me back much further than I'd realised at the time, and I knew it was time for me to look to do something different. English law firms have a very rigid idea of career structure, and given that I'd spent three years out of the loop doing something very different, which would have been fine had I continued down the Russian track. As it was, I felt I'd lost crucial ground. I wasn't sure if I had the motivation any longer to try and reclaim the territory I'd lost.

By the time the new football season began in August, I was pretty down about it all, and things soon got worse. As the summer changed to autumn, I felt under more pressure at work than ever I had done previously. This was mainly because, I think, I was in the unhappy position of being a person to whom five of my colleagues could delegate work, and there was little or no subsequent opportunity for me to delegate it myself. Bits of Arsenal-related interest aside, I could find little to be happy with.

I don't think there's any point in being bitter about this. It's just the way things go in life; I've been unlucky more than once in my career, but I think my ability to withstand setbacks has improved over the years. At one point, it used to be with weary resignation, but now it's with if not exactly a grin, then with recognition that it's all, as the cliché goes, part of the rich tapestry of life and must be borne with good humour. And there's no doubt that I learned this through being a Manchester City fan. City have always delighted in promising their fans much and then failing to deliver. And they were at it again in 2000-2001.

It's hard to overstate how remarkable the 18 months from December 1998 to the summer of 2000 were for City fans. Our club had never been a dominant force in English football over a prolonged period, but for most of our history we'd been capable of producing a decent side every now and again. And these sporadic successes tended to provide at least a measure of compensation for what went on the rest of the time. From 1976 onwards, though, there'd been no trophy (and not even a hint of one) - comfortably the longest barren period for decades. This we could learn to live with, but in 1997, the club had its worst season for over a century. We thought we'd hit the bottom, that the only way would be up. The following season, we finished eight league places worse off than we had twelve months previously. As a result, we were condemned to play in a division in which our participation was almost inconceivable to us.

City fans have sometimes being criticised for being arrogant for saying that things shouldn't be this way. But they shouldn't be this way, not really. I recognise that no-one has a divine right to a certain status, and I know that we were in that position because that's what the quality of our play deserved. However, the point is that when we were trying to avoid going down to Division Two, our average crowd outstripped most of those clubs in whose company we were battling relegation by almost 20,000 - more in one or two cases. This equated to a disparity in revenue of around £6 million per season from gate receipts alone. Our net transfer expenditure since the end of 1996-97 had been the highest in our division, and some of our rivals bettered us with entire squads costing a fraction of one of our signings. Credit, of course, is due to them for making the best of their resources, but it can't be denied that for us to have been in the position we ended up in, there must have been wide-scale under-performance from the playing staff or incompetence from the managerial and coaching staff or a combination of the two. We were entitled to be upset about this and to voice our feelings accordingly.

Halfway through the next campaign, we looked for all the world like we'd no chance of being promoted. Things had become so desperately, miserably bad that we looked as though we'd never stand a chance of returning to the top flight again. And for a club which had spent over eighty of the previous hundred years in that division, that was a bitter blow. So the natural conclusion to the story, the perfect ending after we had clawed our way back, would have been for us to stay in the Premiership and to live happily ever after.

We were favoured by many of the experts to be the strongest of the promoted teams, too. We were perceived to have greater resources at our disposal with which to recruit reinforcements for the potentially difficult task ahead, and we'd also raised hopes by signing the superstar former World Player of the Year George Weah, the most notable of five new faces to arrive by the start of the season. The optimistic mood wasn't to last.

Weah, whose arrival was so joyously greeted by the fans, left two months into the season after a row with manager Joe Royle, having managed a solitary league goal in City colours. And though, after a particularly horrible display on the opening day to lose 4-0 against a Charlton side who'd come up with us, we'd made a decent enough start, soon it began to become clear that we were set for a long, hard winter. Six successive Premiership games were lost, including all four in an especially dismal November, and that set the tone. We only won two games altogether between the end of October and mid-April. Seven points from three games at that stage meant that hopes of an unlikely escape flickered briefly, but it was never going to be enough.

So much for the idea of a happy ending. Maybe fate had meant for us to go up, but that didn't mean anything in the long run. It was savagely ironic that the coup de grace should be delivered, a year to the day after the win at Blackburn, by the Ipswich side we'd condemned to the play-offs that joyous sunlit afternoon. And how poignant, too, that the Blackburn side we beat were celebrating promotion just a few short days before we were condemned to go back whence we came.

So how can I not see the symmetry? Just as City were finding their recovery wasn't as complete as it might have been, that we would be sent back to go and try again, so it was in my life. The relationship on which I'd staked so much had gone, the career in which I'd invested so much effort had fallen apart, and I could barely remember my post-Russia optimism that things would soon be back on track. It would have to be another fresh start for both of us.

32

New Beginnings

I LOOKED AT THE unsatisfactory state of my career and the wreckage of my previous romance, and decided that I needed a week away before returning to make a serious effort to get my life in order. There was really only one place I was ever going to go, and so it was that in October 2000, I headed back to Russia for the first time in well over a year. It turned out to be a fateful journey.

At the time of my departure, there wasn't really any sign of how wrong things were to go for City. The team lay in the top half of the Premier League after ten games, with a respectable fourteen points; not even Weah's departure seemed too much of a setback. We beat Southampton 2-0 away in the next match to encourage belief that we'd cope well enough without him. Though consolidation wouldn't have seemed particularly City-like after the previous few turbulent seasons we'd had, that's what, without the benefit of hindsight, appeared to be on the cards as I headed out to St Petersburg to stay with my friend and former colleague Tania.

Knowing that I was no longer in a relationship and that I was about to stay with her for a week, Tania had told me that she had a friend she'd like to introduce me to, though initially I was a little reluctant. In part, this is because other people's concept of the type of woman likely to appeal to me and my own ideas on this matter rarely coincide - just as if someone who knew me fairly superficially were picking a football team for me, they probably wouldn't select Manchester City. Tania, however, had witnessed at close quarters my misery at City's fortunes over the 18-month period we worked together, which turned out to be the most disastrous even in our club's history.

She also knew all about the Natasha and Nadia episodes; the two of us had supported one another throughout many bouts of romantic misery, and so she knew that I didn't particularly go in for simplicity in my personal life. When I knew that Tania was trying her hand at matchmaking, I should have been delighted. This was someone who wouldn't bother trying to find me someone appropriate, thus killing off any chance of interest from me right from the outset. I think that was what worried me at first; I can only presume I was trying to be sensible. Needless to say, I didn't get very far.

On the Friday evening during my stay, we were due to go out for a meal. Tania's office was hosting the firm's New York-based marketing executive, an Englishman whom we referred to as "Parky", abbreviating his surname. He was in Petersburg but due to head back to Moscow on the Saturday. She invited him out with us, and to make up a foursome we invited Tania's friend, Marta. I knew full well at this point, even before the two of us met, that taking things further was something of a dubious proposition. Marta, I already knew, was married (although the union was on its last legs) with a thirteen-year-old child. With her living in Russia, our chances for getting properly acquainted were minimal, and her complex domestic situation was scarcely ideal either.

I approached the evening with some trepidation, since this was my first date since splitting with Nadia; until a couple of weeks before, I hadn't thought of finding anyone new since meeting with her four years previously. Following the break-up of that relationship, I'd thought for a while that I'd never want to be in another one again, so I was bound to be experiencing anxiety. I felt like I'd guess a footballer must feel when coming back from a serious injury, wondering if the previous experience would affect me. I knew that Colin Bell hadn't been the same player after he returned, while Paul Lake's several comeback attempts resulted in a sum total of less than ninety minutes' first-team action, so I wasn't quite sure about being back in the fray.

Before the start of the evening, Tania and I had discussed what I regarded as the nightmare scenario - that Parky and Marta would really hit it off. Given that neither of them spoke the other's language, it would have been a severe dent to my confidence if my intended date had spurned me in favour of someone she couldn't even converse with. When I saw Marta for the first time, my heart raced, which made for a good start. When we spoke, conversation flowed easily, which was even better, and our senses of humour seemed compatible. Had Parky not been there, I'm not sure I'd even have asked Tania to invite Marta, yet, having done so, I knew quickly that I wanted to take things further. We saw each other twice more during the remainder of my visit and resolved to stay in touch; I promised her that I'd come back to visit.

I went home feeling that maybe City's fortunes would mirror my own and that we'd survive in the Premiership, but after this trip to Russia, things on the City front got dismally worse. The first game after I'd returned from Petersburg was a 5-0 defeat at Arsenal, and, thinking it might be an omen, I wondered if pursuing things with Marta would be wise given the problems it would entail. I feared I'd returned to the familiar pattern - a complex personal life and a disastrous footballing one. The sentiment was only transitory.

It wasn't just my personal life that was looking up - there was also my search for a new job. I'd decided that my career had stalled in private law firms, so I was going to look to find a different type of outlet for my legal skills. I entered a competition for jobs with the Government Legal Service, and was successful, and I had the pleasant experience of being warmly commended by the head of the legal section of my government department for my performance in the tests. It wasn't a decision made on financial grounds, though as I found myself still able to pay my mortgage, run my car, pay for my season ticket and fund trips to Russia, I found the salary acceptable. But I found the working environment congenial and the quality of work exceptional, something I couldn't always say of the places I'd been in my career before this point. Unfortunately, City were slow to catch the mood, and remained the one area of my life where matters were less than satisfactory.

The game before I'd arrived back from Russia in October had been that win at Southampton. Immediately before I started my new government job, I returned to visit Marta in early March, and the last game before I went was a home defeat by the same opposition. Somehow, it was symptomatic of how things had all gone wrong for the club in the intervening four months. In retrospect, it was always going to be a tough season. The team that played in the Premiership in 2000-01 featured several players who had featured in Division Two in 1998-99; we'd got into Division One, then prospered there without extensive team rebuilding. And though it was great credit to the management that we completed the ascent to the Premiership so quickly, we did so without time to devote ourselves properly to the process of building a unit capable of prospering in the top flight. Though we were certainly active in the transfer market in the nine months following promotion, spending over £12 million net on reinforcements, it still wasn't enough.

Joe Royle paid the price. In a ruthless act, the board fired him within 48 hours of the end of the relegation season. But although I thought him unlucky, I could see a case for the action that had been taken. I suspected that, while the directors would have viewed Royle as having a decent chance of taking us back into the Premiership, they didn't see him as the man to stabilise our position there. His top-flight record at Oldham and Everton actually seemed pretty good; he kept the former up for three years against the odds, while he took the latter to an FA Cup triumph and a place in Europe after rescuing them from the drop. However, things at the top of the English game had moved on enormously, even in the few short years since those successes, and the suspicion was that Royle hadn't.

In particular, he looked to have a couple of failings that supporters, and presumably the board, identified as being likely barriers to his building a team capable of performing any better should he lead us back to the Premiership. The first was a doubt over his ability to handle temperamental players. Top-quality international footballers of the type a club aspiring to survive in the Premiership may well want to sign can sometimes be capricious, wilful individuals who are difficult for a manager to handle. Royle's bust-ups with Weah and then leading scorer Paulo Wanchope were seen as indicative of a difficulty in this area. A second cause of misgivings was the tactical approach of the team in the relegation season. He seemed happy to field a midfield woefully bereft of creativity, trusting in a one-dimensional style of direct football that, frankly, looked dated. Football, I'm afraid, is a notoriously unsentimental business, so despite our gratitude for the two promotion successes, they now counted for little.

Three days after Royle's dismissal, the club unveiled as his successor Kevin Keegan, the man who just over six months previously had walked out on the England manager's job. It always seemed like a good fit, even from the start. One sunny May evening last year, I met a friend for a couple of drinks after work. The conversation, as it always does, turned to football, and even he - a lifelong United fan - agreed. We both felt that Keegan and City were ideally suited.

In making the new appointment, City were following my lead. By this point, I'd been out to see Marta on a second occasion. Before the visit, I'd worried that somehow things would seem different after the first time (we'd been speaking over the phone regularly but that isn't necessarily a reliable guide), but I needn't have worried. Again I spent a week there, during which we were together almost constantly and things went better than I could have anticipated. When I'd left Russia, I'd thought that my relationship with Nadia would survive and I 'd expected to put my career on track. In fact, I had to jettison both and, in my personal as in my professional life, start again. I'd managed it, and in the summer of 2001, the task ahead for City was effectively to emulate me.

33

Looking Up

I KNOW IT'S NOT a romantic view, but I say this as a lawyer, and one experienced in contract law: if a client came to me with the usual marriage vows and asked me if it was a deal he or she should agree to, I wouldn't let them sign. Indeed, there's a good case for saying that it would be professionally negligent of me to do so. If you don't believe me, then just think about it for a minute. I know there's the statutory long-stop of divorce, but that's often expensive and messy, and from a legal point of view it's hardly satisfactory. Why not get the contract right in the first place? And it certainly isn't right as it stands.

I mean, for a start, there's the duration - "'til death us do part", with no reduction, remission, or time off for good behaviour. I really think I'd have to take my red pen to that. "'Til death us do part or until earlier termination of this agreement in accordance with the provisions of clause 4.2," I'd revise, making the original line clause 4.1. And then I'd have to dream up a whole new clause 4.2 setting out exactly in what circumstances the agreement could be terminated earlier. Maybe there should be a get out clause allowing either party to terminate the marriage, by serving one month's notice, on the fifth anniversary of this agreement and on any fifth anniversary thereafter, or if the other party has failed to respond constructively to some kind of prior written notice served by their partner of dissatisfaction with the marriage. And, of course, there'd need to be some kind of right to call an immediate halt should your partner do something really serious, like commit an act of infidelity, or cancelling your subscription to your chosen satellite sports channel.

Of course, the infidelity point would only be a reason to terminate if you're happy to go with the "forsaking all other, keep yourself only unto him/her for as long as you both shall live" obligation. But statistics show that's actually quite a tough one, so any lawyer worth his salt would urge you to give some consideration to whether there are any circumstances in which they might want to relax the requirement. However, you'd be advised to guard against embracing the concept too enthusiastically - your prospective spouse's lawyer probably won't concede the point without a reciprocal arrangement for any get-out you might secure.

When I think about what may or may not be fair in such a common life situation, I realise that I haven't always accepted reasonable terms in all areas of my life. And there is, of course, one sphere in particular which has been especially irrational. While I never actually signed a contract to support Manchester City, there's definitely been a commitment to which I've adhered as strictly as if I'd signed in blood. And with this one, there isn't even the possibility of divorce - just living the rest of my life in estrangement.

Somehow, when I look at the terms we've both abided by over the years, I don't think I got the best of the deal. After all, my side of the bargain involved sacrificing my Saturday afternoons, plus weekday evenings and now, with the advent of television ensuring that kick-offs are regularly moved to suit broadcasters, all kinds of other bizarre times. I've trekked up and down the country to all kinds of far-flung destinations spending large quantities of time and money that really could have been more productively used. Add to that the general way in which my life has been consumed by the club, and … well, let's just say I wouldn't have been unreasonable had I expected a little more.

I can see now that I really should have had everything legally documented. I mean, it would have been so much simpler if I'd had a contract and been able to enforce it. I mean, I could have had all kinds of provisions that would have protected my interests. For instance, I'd never have had to endure all those terrible signings if I'd been able to invoke something that in legal language would read like this:

"If Club shall, in any single period of 1 (one) calendar year, acquire, engage or otherwise procure the services of two or more players whose playing capabilities and/or general attitude are, in the reasonable opinion of Supporter, having regard to Club's current status, the player's previous career record and the transfer fee (if any) paid by Club to secure the player's services, manifestly incompatible with the goal of Club's successful performance, Supporter may serve notice in writing upon Club suspending this agreement forthwith until each such player is no longer employed in a playing capacity by Club."

This formulation, not untypical of my profession in its grotesque inelegance, is lawyer-speak for, "Any more Steve Daleys or Lee Bradburys and you can stick it."

And that isn't all the protection I'd have asked for. There are occasional stories about clubs refunding the expenses of travelling supporters but they're very much one-offs; I'd have wanted that as a matter of course. And of course, most importantly, we'd need a right to terminate the agreement in the event of even the most minor inadequacy in stadium catering. This last stipulation is important because, given most clubs' efforts in my time as a fan, it would have provided supporters with a back-door get-out pretty much whenever they wanted.

Despite the fact that I ploughed on without any of these assurances, I was often highly ambivalent about the situation I'd landed myself in. I'm not alone in this; the committed football fan often curses his or her lot, and I knew that the deal I'd accepted as a youngster was bitterly unfair. The difference between that contract with the marriage vows was that I hadn't been seduced into signing up for matrimony at the age of six, but I realised both arrangements to be equally demanding. Then, in 2001-2, everything changed.

After the second successful trip to see Marta, things continued to go from strength to strength. In the summer of 2001, she came over to England for a couple of weeks, which was, I suppose, a major test for the relationship. It was a test we passed with flying colours, and although we obviously weren't going to have things easy, it became clear to me that Marta wasn't going to be a transitory feature in my life. I might say that after a trial and a loan spell, I decided to pursue the permanent deal.

And it took me an equally short time to take Kevin Keegan to my heart. In the early weeks of his first season, the team performed erratically - brilliant one week, wretched the next. Goals rained in at either end, and by the time the season was eleven games old, we'd chalked up one win by 6-2, one by 5-2, two by 4-2 and three by 3-0. At the same time we registered two defeats by 4-0, one by 4-3 and one by a rather prosaic 2-0 margin. In the modern era, the average number of goals per game in the English professional leagues tends to be around 2.5 or slightly less. Our games were featuring an average of five, and spectators never knew how, when or at which end they'd arrive. It was quite bewildering stuff.

By the turn of the year, things had gone forward. City moved to the top of the First Division table on New Year's Day after suddenly and uncharacteristically becoming much more consistent. But for once, I had other things on my mind. After witnessing a 5-1 thrashing of previous leaders Burnley on 29 December, I'd headed off to Russia, and I went with definite intentions in mind.

It's difficult to relate, without sounding mawkish or embarrassingly slushy, how much Marta had come to mean to me in the previous fourteen months. Obviously, on the first trip, there was enough between us to make me want to take things further; I knew I'd have wondered what might have been had we not seen each other again. For the next four months, we kept in touch by phone, and sent each other the odd card or letter. She also sent me a tape, in which she talked about herself and about us, illustrating different points with her favourite poems and songs. It was the most romantic thing anyone's ever done for me. Before the second trip out to Russia to see her, I'd wondered whether the excitement and mutual attraction of our first meeting would survive when we faced the test of being together for longer. It did, and despite the inevitable difficulties caused by the distance factor, we seemed to be developing even stronger bonds. I'd known straight away there was something special about her, and for the first time in my life, I found myself seriously contemplating, despite my inherent scepticism, the prospect of marriage.

I'd decided I just didn't want to let Marta go from my life. She's kind, sweet, genuine and caring but also beautiful and sensual, fun loving and romantic. She also understands the give and take involved in any relationship, let alone a complex long-distance one. Finding someone with this attitude, coupled with all of her other qualities, made me feel I'd found someone to whom I actually wanted to make a lifelong commitment. She accepted my proposal in January 2002, and I was thrilled at the impending union - even though I knew the perils from a lawyer's perspective of the commitment I was about to enter.

The new man at Maine Road also continued to make a huge impression on me. Of course, I still recognise what Joe Royle did for City in his three years in charge. He restored the pride of a moribund club, and allowed it to sample life in the top flight of English football within two years of looking as if such status may never be regained in my lifetime. But would we have him back now instead of Keegan? Harsh though it may sound, I wouldn't and neither would any other fan I know - football fans aren't like that. Arsenal qualified for Europe in their one season under Bruce Rioch, who probably felt hard done by to be ditched before the new campaign began. Yet as they celebrate a second double under Arsene Wenger, I doubt many Gooners now harbour misgivings about the decision to hire the Frenchman.

Thinking back to Keegan's appointment, it's funny now to remember the frantic online message boards that sunny May morning when the news broke. On the various Internet sites, there were more positive reactions than negative, but plenty of doubts were being expressed. I like to think that I was a little more perceptive. "I welcome the appointment," I wrote. "If nothing else, he'll do two things. Firstly, we'll play exciting football (even in the successive promotions under Royle, we'd been more of a functional rather than a stylish team). And secondly, he'll bring in quality players."

He more than lived up to those expectations. The majestic 3-0 win over Watford on the opening day of the season showed the heights that could be reached, and the maddening inconsistency of the first few months was gradually ironed out. As the season wore on, some of the football played was as thrilling as any played at Maine Road in my time as a fan (and probably for a lot longer than that). As we rattled in a club record-equalling 108 goals on our way to the First Division championship (and by a ten-point margin, too, not through the traditional nail-biting last-day drama), we even started to attract the admiration of neutrals for our football, which as any City fan will tell you is unaccustomed indeed. But displays such as the second-half demolition of Premiership side Ipswich on their own ground to win 4-1 in the FA Cup, the scare we gave Newcastle with ten men before bowing out of the same competition and the beatings of eventual play-off qualifiers Norwich and Millwall despite being a man down for virtually the whole of each game following an early sending off, certainly merited such warm praise.

It wasn't only in a football sense that I was happier than I'd been for a long, long time. Genuinely enjoying work for the first time in a long time, I was also looking forward to marrying a woman who means more to me than I can really express. More than one friend told me that I seemed more contented than they could remember. So after all these years, City and I are still in sync, and after plenty of downs, it's an up phase for both of us. It's been long overdue.

POSTSCRIPT

A Match Made in Heaven

IT'S OFTEN SAID that dogs grow to resemble their owners. My dog is very loveable yet completely insane. This isn't necessarily how I'd choose to think of myself, but there are worse qualities to have. A more alarming prospect for Manchester City fans would be that football fans grow to resemble their chosen teams. If it's true, it condemns us to miserable, unfulfilling lives. Unable to realise our potential, we'll fail in our careers. Everyone we form relationships with will be perpetually let down and will spend most of their time wondering what on earth they see in us. We'll lurch from one financial crisis to the next, never managing to remove the spectre of debt. And we'll end up living in a bizarre home which randomly combines several architectural styles, mimicking the jumbled assortment of stands at Maine Road.

In fact, it doesn't follow, and I like to think of myself as evidence for the proposition. On the other hand, our steadfast support of this singular club over the years must say something, and the conclusion that City attract masochistic fans is a tempting one. We're hardly what could be termed discerning consumers - the type who'll turn their back if the product is of insufficient quality. When we found ourselves in the lower reaches of the First Division, our football was of a standard meriting crowds of a similar order to the other teams down there - six or seven thousand. Instead we were pulling in four times as many, and more than in the Premier League a season or two earlier. If it's true that suffering produces great art, Maine Road on match-day must be packed with modern-day Rembrandts, Shakespeares or Mozarts.

But though the masochist theory superficially has much to commend it, I don't think it's actually true. I regard having supported

City for all these years as having been an immensely enriching experience, and say this as someone who's seen dismal cup defeats by the likes of Cardiff and Lincoln, numerous painful humiliations at the hands of Manchester United, three relegations and a host of pitiful struggles against mediocre Nationwide League sides. Sure, it's brought frustrations and misery, but it's also brought unexpected successes and lots of laughs with fellow fans (one thing that following this club certainly does for you is develop your ability to accept the absurd with amused equanimity). I know that they and I are an ideal fit, and had I grown up supporting another team, I doubt I'd have retained a comparable passion so far into adulthood. Life at Maine Road has almost always been interesting, and that's why I regard City and myself as footballing partners who are ideally suited.

The story I've told in these pages makes clear is that this last quality is what I've looked for in other aspects of my life. Why else would I have retained a fascination with Russia? It's because I never know what's going to happen there. The time I've spent in the country has brought me into contact with a superpower confrontation, an abortive coup, economic chaos and political crisis. I love the surreal experiences I've enjoyed there on a regular basis. And, though I'm marrying Marta simply because I love her and I'd commit to her with the same alacrity were she from Peterborough rather than Petersburg, a fortunate by-product of wedding a Russian is that it also gives me a substantive and lasting link with the country.

Just like Russia, my personal life also mirrors City in the absolute suitability of the term "rollercoaster" as a description, and I hardly think that's an accident either. For a long time, I regarded myself as being an expert in seeking out complex and troublesome personal attachments, and, looking at my track record, I still don't think I was wrong in that view.

The funny thing was that, as I compiled this book, as I had to recall quite how dramatic, surreal and chaotic it's all been for City and for me over the years, things really seemed to change. I'd met Marta and the relationship blossomed. Things with her aren't like they've been in any other romantic attachment I've had, and I no longer find myself illogically craving the madcap twists I became used to. I started a new job, adapted quickly and began to feel more settled professionally than ever before. Even Russia's fortunes took a turn for the better, with the country seeming increasingly stable and prosperous with every visit I made there to spend time with Marta as our relationship developed. And, of course, there was City's thrilling and highly successful 2001-2 season, too.

As a football fan, it's hard sometimes not to get carried away. At club level, Kevin Keegan, with his passion, enthusiasm and undoubted charisma, can do one thing above all - and that's allow a club's fans to dream. While we may not reach the stars, suddenly they seem a lot nearer than they did a year ago. Now we're bringing in players of a quality we could only fantasise about before. The most expensive of several high-profile summer signings was the former Arsenal and Real Madrid striker Nicolas Anelka, who arrived from Paris Saint-Germain for £13 million. He may be a controversial figure who's had his share of problems in his relatively brief career, but his ability is unquestioned, and for it to be on show as a City player is a more than exciting prospect. Of course, the deal represents something of a gamble, so there's a possibility that he may crash and burn, but this is Manchester City, and it was ever thus.

Needless to say, Keegan hasn't changed us completely - defeat by a dismal and already relegated Stockport side in the promotion run-in showed that the old unpredictability is still there. But he's supplied the most intoxicating football seen at Maine Road in a generation, and by doing so, even at First Division level, he's earned the gratitude of legions of City fans. If he can inspire something similar in the Premiership, heaven knows how we'll feel. Funnily enough we don't express our adulation that well; sure, there's been the odd chorus of 'Walking in a Keegan Wonderland' but for the most part we're like a guy who's in love with a beautiful and captivating woman and yet who, for fear that the emotion isn't reciprocated, can't quite bring himself to tell her. Let that fool no-one - the man would be an absolute City legend even if he left the club tomorrow.

We aren't unrealistic. We know better than most that in football, it isn't always a matter of happy endings. We're fully aware that both City and Keegan encourage drama, and it's a safe bet that the combination of us and him will bring plenty more, but we appreciate that it can lead to downs as well as ups. We recognise that it's a different game now from the time all those years ago when Keegan's Newcastle finished third in their first tilt at the Premiership after sweeping to the First Division title with real flair. After what we've been through since 1996, if we're able this time next year, as we leave Maine Road after eight years for the new Commonwealth Games stadium at Eastlands, to look forward to another Premiership season, it will be a welcome change.

Keegan has said that he wants to change the mentality of City fans, to make us expect success rather than live in constant fear of failure. I can see where he's coming from, but old habits die hard. I want him to succeed, and he's certainly earned our trust, but I know Manchester City better than he does, so it's hard not to fear the worst. I'm excited by the way things seem to be going, of course I am, but it's still too soon for there not to be a part of me fearing the worst, waiting to see what disasters lurk around the corner.

Indeed, one of the reasons for publishing this book at the start of the 2002-03 season is that we don't know what City will do in the first three months of the campaign. We might end up with one point from the first fifteen games, creating an inauspicious climate for publication. I mean, on paper we look like a reasonable side, but with us, nothing would be a surprise. That warning voice is getting quieter and quieter, though; with City, just as in the rest of my life, I'm more upbeat than I have been for a long time. It may be unfamiliar territory, but for the first time after years spent largely in pessimistic shadows, I'm emerging, blinking, into a sunlight of optimism.

The future won't be plain sailing, of course, for City or for me (when is it ever for either of us?). I'll still be apart from Marta even after we're married, because her daughter needs to finish her schooling before they come to England. And Keegan and the team still have a way to go before they can even approach the best teams the English game has to offer, let alone challenge them meaningfully. But for the first time in a long time, it looks like City and I both have a chance of getting to where we want to be, and I think we can both be grateful for that. Who knows? Everything may even start to make sense. I wouldn't bet on it, though.